Kojo Koram is a lecturer at the ~~~~~~~~~~~~~~~~~~~~~~~~~~~e,
University of London. He is ~~~~~~~~~~~~~~~~~~~~~~~~~~~d
the Global Colour Line. Prior to ~~~~~~~~~~~~~~~~~cial
welfare law, youth work and teaching. He has written for the
Guardian, *Washington Post*, *Nation*, *Dissent*, *New Statesman* and
Critical Legal Thinking.

live. A fascinating history, Koram's unique perspective sheds new light on an old problem'   Robert Verkaik

'A superb and vivid account of the ideas, laws and economic instruments that bind contemporary Britain to its long colonial history'   Will Davies

'Fantastic. Koram clearly and informatively details the links between the economic dependency imposed on Britain's former colonies after decolonisation and the crisis that "Global Britain" now finds itself facing'   Quinn Slobodian

'A tour de force by one of the most brilliant young thinkers writing in Britain today . . . Urgent and relevant'
Oscar Guardiola-Rivera

'A bold and brazen account of the economic afterlives of the British Empire'   Imaobong Umoren

'A superb account of how Britain's present crisis is intimately intertwined with its imperial past . . . Empire shapes all our lives – whether we acknowledge it or not'   Katrina Forrester

'A clear-eyed assessment of some of the British Empire's least acknowledged legacies . . . which are now reverberating back on Britain and shredding the social fabric of British life. In the Covid era, this is essential reading'   Christienna Fryar

'*Uncommon Wealth* makes a very powerful argument that today's privatization, outsourcing, and offshoring of finance to tax havens is a boomeranging back to the United Kingdom of policies first imposed on post-colonial nations'   David Edgerton

'Rigorous, urgent and brilliantly written. This book lays bare the human cost – then and now – of Britain's colonial economic history and demands that we never forget it'   Vicky Spratt

Uncommon Wealth

Britain and the Aftermath of Empire

KOJO KORAM

JOHN MURRAY

First published in Great Britain in 2022 by John Murray (Publishers)
An Hachette UK company

This paperback edition published in 2023

3

Copyright © Kojo Koram 2022

The right of Kojo Koram to be identified as the Author of the Work has been asserted
by him in accordance with the Copyright, Designs and Patents Act 1988.

A CIP catalogue record for this title is available from the British Library

Paperback ISBN 9781529338645
eBook ISBN 9781529338652

Typeset in Bembo by Palimpsest Book Production Ltd, Falkirk, Stirlingshire

Printed and bound in Great Britain by Clays Ltd, Elcograf S.p.A.

John Murray policy is to use papers that are natural, renewable and recyclable
products and made from wood grown in sustainable forests. The logging and
manufacturing processes are expected to conform to the environmental
regulations of the country of origin.

John Murray (Publishers)
Carmelite House
50 Victoria Embankment
London EC4Y 0DZ

www.johnmurraypress.co.uk

Contents

For Albert Nyadu Obeng and Edmund Manteaw Koram

Introduction: Seeing the Boomerang

As a child, I moved homes in a way that took me through not only space but time. I was born in Ghana before moving to the UK as an infant. In the eyes of many, to relocate from West Africa to Great Britain was to move through multiple stages of history. The distance between my two homes was measured not in air miles but in centuries. Britain was celebrated as the cradle of civilisation; on the other hand, African states like Ghana were seen as being barely out of the dark ages. This framework for understanding the world was presented as being as natural as the seasons.

By the time I was ten years old, long summer trips back to Ghana were a staple of our family calendar. It was the 1990s, the height of globalisation, and each year that we returned to Accra, the city seemed to have spread further and further. Areas that were undisturbed coastlines one year would be home to bustling hotels the next. My ever-present companion during explorations across the city was my grandfather, the person I was named after, who was simultaneously a proud Ghanaian and a classic English gentleman. Having travelled to London as part of the 'Windrush' generation of Commonwealth subjects, to work for Royal Mail while he trained as an optician, he retained many habits from his time in post-war Britain, even decades after he had returned to Ghana. He owned a Mini Cooper, began his day with a full English breakfast and a cup of tea, and God help me or my cousins if we disturbed him while listening to the morning report from the BBC World Service.

On one of our many drives across the city, the car filling up with the heat of another Accra traffic jam, I decided to try and pass the time by asking 'the question': 'Grandpa, why is Ghana so poor?' 'What do mean?' came the reply. 'Well, wasn't Ghana once called the Gold Coast?' 'Indeed,' he said. 'And gold makes you rich, doesn't it?' 'Yes, it does.' 'So why is Britain so much richer than Ghana?' After a pause, my grandfather answered me with a simple story. 'Ghana only got its independence a few decades ago, so it has some catching up to do.' That seemed like a plausible explanation at the time. Ghana was a young country; Britain was an old one. Perhaps the relationship between these two places where I lived was similar to the relationship between myself and my grandfather.

I returned to Britain in time for the new school year, and began to recognise versions of this same story explaining the inequality in the world being repeated at every turn. But in the UK it came with an added dose of British exceptionalism. In the education system and wider culture, I would learn about how Britain, as the birthplace of industrialised capitalism and parliamentary democracy, had organically created the ideal political, economic and legal systems for wealth and stability. This is what had made the country rich while others were poor, civilised where others were barbarous. If the empire was ever mentioned, it was only through vague references to how it had helped Britain benevolently spread its political, economic and legal system to all the corners of the world. The story I learned in school to explain the disparities of the world was built upon older, uglier ideas of human classification. Latent within it was a picture of people of different colours belonging to different stages of history, of race as a marker of difference in the evolution of humankind. But this was the 1990s and by this time it was impolite to talk about those old ideas openly. This was the age of the 'end of history', after all; the Cold War was over and all the big battles between nations, races and models of society were supposed to have been settled.[1] We didn't need to talk about racism, sexism, class politics and especially colonisation anymore, the free market had made us all individuals and social mobility was freely available to anyone who wanted it. The rise of the internet and the growth of global travel promised us that, over time, it would make all the old inequalities and divisions that disfigured our world into a thing of the past. This was the age of meritocracy, where inherited privilege and huge gaps between the rich and poor would soon be confined to history. Instead of talking about racial or civilisational hierarchies, ideas of human difference had been rechristened by lawyers and economists as a bloodless and bureaucratic process called 'development'. And the core belief of development was that it was a one-way road.

The Boomerang

This story of linear development is still widely accepted by many across the political spectrum. From doctrinal Marxism to libertarian capitalism, most theories of modern political or economic development begin with the tale of British exceptionalism.[2] When we tell the story of how modern capitalism emerged, it is through the enclosure of medieval English villages and the growth of the 'dark satanic mills' of the industrial revolution. When we speak of the rise of democracy, it is through the nobles holding King John to the Magna Carta or Cromwell cementing the power of Parliament. With this story, the striking inequalities that even a child couldn't miss when travelling from Britain to Ghana (or anywhere else in what was then called the 'Third World') could be easily dismissed as just the necessary growing pains of new nation states. If a developing country was being torn apart by huge disparities between the wealthy and poor, spiralling sovereign debt or divisions between ethnic communities, this wasn't a question of economics, history, the global legal structure or the legacy of empire. It was just a question of time. Such crises were part of the maturing process that these developing countries would have to pass through. We could rest assured that, across the world, progress was moving in an orderly queue. And if Britain had long stood at the front of this queue, there was no real need to pay much attention to what was happening behind it.

And yet, writing from the vantage point of twenty-first-century Britain, we have to ask if this picture of history as an orderly line still holds. It is now the United Kingdom of Great Britain and Northern Ireland that is going through a national crisis and being carved up by internal divisions. England is against Scotland, towns are against cities, the young are at war with their own grandparents. The country's wealth is being scurried away offshore while multinational corporations gorge themselves on public resources. The rich getting richer was supposed to be a rising tide that lifted all boats. Instead, a tsunami has crashed through the country, leaving many families drowning in a wreckage of insecurity, inequality and in-work poverty. What is worse, everyone is losing faith in the ability of the old institutions of democracy – Parliament, elections, the media – to save them. Development's promise to flatten the world has failed to materialise. Globally, we are now in a new age of great divergence, with wealth inequality accelerating not only between countries but within them as well. These trends are not exclusive to Britain, of course, but they have hit this island particularly hard.

In the era of globalisation, Britain has consistently stood out as the most unequal of the 'advanced' European countries. The levels of income inequality across the country have been measured as being not only larger than in its neighbours, such as France, Germany or the Netherlands, but also larger than the levels found in supposedly 'less developed' Mediterranean countries like Italy, Greece and Portugal.[3] Politicians keen to downplay the inequality crisis often argue that while the rate of income inequality is high, it has remained steady since its steep rise in the 1980s. However, a 2020 study by the Resolution Foundation showed that when the definition of income is expanded to include not just salaries received but also the profits made each year from selling assets (capital gains), then a continued rise in the country's already high levels of income inequality over recent years becomes clear.[4] The problem is even worse when one looks not only at income – how much money you bring in – but also at wealth – the value of all the assets that you own. Wealth inequality in the UK has been measured as being twice as high as the inequality we already see in terms of income.[5] Credit Suisse's *Global Wealth Report 2014* highlighted the UK as being the only 'developed' Western country to record a rise in levels of wealth inequality over the entire period of 2000–14.[6]

And this disparity isn't going anywhere on its own. After the financial crisis in 2008, everyone thought that the good times had come to an end for the country's top 1 per cent. Instead, the decade that followed the crash saw the share of wealth held by Britain's richest families increase further, while the middle 50 per cent of the country witnessed their share of the pie collapse.[7] With wealth and opportunities being hoarded by an ever-smaller percentage of the population, the Institute for Fiscal Studies has had to conclude that now 'the UK is unequal by international standards'.[8] Home to some of Europe's poorest areas, as well as to its richest financial centre, life in the UK is becoming determined by luck of birth once again.[9] All the statistics above only tell part of the story. The truth of how inequality has become concrete over recent decades is to be found on the night bus packed with workers travelling to their first shift of the day; at the job centre where benefit applicants are left to navigate a complex, digital system alone; or in the city's tower blocks of once secure council flats providing homes for families that are now owned by giant commercial property companies overcharging overworked, precarious renters. Beneath the triumphalist headlines of a resurgent 'Global Britain' seizing the initiative in the twenty-first century, across the country millions of people in unaffordable cities, deindustrialised towns and neglected rural villages are struggling to make ends meet. It wasn't supposed to be this way when we imagined what Britain would look like in the new millennium. An unbalanced economy has also left the country wrestling with some of the problems of social polarisation it once saw as a mark of primitive nations still trying to find their place in the world. Instead of simply accepting the image we are sold of history moving in a line, perhaps a better metaphor for history would be that of the boomerang.

The idea of history as a boomerang is one that I borrow from Aimé Césaire, one of the twentieth century's most influential thinkers on the subject of empire. A surrealist poet turned politician, as comfortable translating Shakespeare as he was holding high office in his native Martinique, Césaire described how colonial relations are subject to 'the boomerang effect' – meaning that experiments carried out in the peripheries of the empire eventually come flying back to its very heartland.[10] Writing in the middle of the twentieth century, during the era of decolonisation, Césaire's words were a warning to Europe to remember that it did not exist in a different ecosystem to the colonial world and that the policies tried out in laboratories across Africa, Asia and the Caribbean would have consequences for its own future.

The image of history moving like a boomerang provides a new frame through which to examine the legacy of the British Empire, a topic which has recaptured the public imagination over the past few years. For decades, we were told that the empire was something that was long behind us, a remnant of a quaint but now largely irrelevant past. But what if empire's aftermath isn't just something we need to debate when thinking about the place of a particular cultural artefact or whether or not a particular building's name is offensive? What if it stretches to our legal and economic systems, which produce vast wealth disparities, both at home and abroad? What if the dynamics causing inequality and insecurity that I witnessed in Ghana as a child were not further evidence of primitiveness, but expressions of the post-imperial economic changes that were shaping the world to come?[11] From the outsourcing, privatisation and marketisation of health, transport and education; from the weakening of labour protections and welfare support to trends of mega urbanisation; when we examine the evolution of global economic and political trends today, we find many of them are actually at their most advanced stages in the so-called backward parts of the world, the former colonial world.[12] The megacities that now dominate our planet, where frequent-flying glitterati live alongside millions struggling for survival, are largest not in Europe or North America but in Africa and Asia.[13] Cairo or Karachi sit at the frontiers of globalisation. China, still officially classified as a 'developing' country by the World Trade Organisation, is becoming the world's dominant economic power. Yet the experiences of these countries remain largely outside the purview of political conversation in Britain, despite all the places I mentioned above having been part of Greater Britannia within the last century, in one way or another. Still heavily invested in the old idea of history as a straight line, in Britain we make the mistake of ignoring many of the shifts that the world has been through since the end of empire. The boomerang is most dangerous when you aren't looking at it, and don't know that it's hurtling back towards you.

Denial and Decolonisation

In 1997, Britain's new prime minister, Tony Blair, travelled to Hong Kong, having just won a landslide election victory the previous month. He arrived in Britain's last major colony to oversee its handover to China, a day many saw as the full stop on the British Empire's long goodbye. Standing solemnly during the handover ceremony, as the blowing of trumpets accompanied the lowering of the Union Jack and the raising of the red flag of China, Blair admitted to feeling 'a tug of, not regret, but nostalgia for the old British Empire'.[14] Later that evening, he went to a hotel lit up by Chinese lanterns to meet Jiang Zemin, the Chinese president. Blair was immediately shocked by Jiang's ability to talk 'with greater knowledge about Shakespeare' than he himself could ever hope to muster. He then described how

Jiang confessed to hoping that the Hong Kong handover could act as a 'new start in UK/China relations and from now on, we could put the past behind us'. Blair would later admit, 'I had, at that time, only a fairly dim and sketchy understanding of what that past was. I thought it was all just politeness in any case. But actually, he meant it. They mean it.'[15]

This little vignette, just a throwaway story from Blair's autobiography, is an encapsulation both of Britain's relationship to its imperial past and how this past impacts on the country's ability to navigate the world. The history that the Chinese president was most likely speaking about was the devastation of the nineteenth-century Opium Wars, when Britain attacked the Chinese Qing dynasty for having the audacity to ban the British opium trade within their country. In China, the Opium Wars, which ended with the ceding of sovereignty over Hong Kong to the British and the 1860 burning of the Old Summer Palace in Beijing by British troops, are known as the start of 'a hundred years of humiliation'.[16] The wars were, by any standards, world-changing events. Yet here was a boarding school and Oxbridge-educated British prime minister who seemingly had never heard of them or bothered to read up on them before going to complete the handover of Hong Kong. (What Blair thought were the reasons Hong Kong had become a British territory in the first place, one can only guess.) If, while on a trip to Britain, a French president casually admitted to knowing little about the Napoleonic Wars, the mockery they would receive from our press would never end. Yet not only does Blair hold a similar level of ignorance regarding Britain's history with the world's upcoming superpower, he also feels comfortable enough to write about it in his autobiography. Moreover, despite knowing nothing of one of the most significant moments in British history, Blair maintained a general nostalgia for empire. His description of the handover captures the double-edged sword of Britain's relationship with its past – we don't feel we have to know the details of the empire to know it was a good thing.

It says a lot that Tony Blair, the prime minister whose government proclaimed that 'we are all middle class now', would display such unapologetic amnesia about the legacy of empire. He represented a belief in the uplifting power of globalisation that relied upon an erasure of all histories of empire. Not that the prime ministers who have come after Blair have been much better, right up to and including Boris Johnson. In 2018, Johnson seemed to forget about 500 years of conflict between England and its first colony, Ireland, when he compared the tensions over the border between Northern Ireland and the Republic of Ireland to the difficulty of managing the border between Camden and Westminster.[17] On another occasion, while on a trip to Myanmar when foreign secretary, he needed a horrified ambassador to inform him why walking round audibly reciting Rudyard Kipling's poem 'The Road to Mandalay' was, in fact, 'not appropriate', considering that the poem romanticised Britain's imperial history with the very nation they were visiting.[18] Back in 2002, Johnson wrote about Africa, arguing that 'the problem is not that we were once in charge, but that we are not in charge anymore.'[19] This quote came back to haunt him when he later became prime minister and sought to establish trading relationships with the countries in the region with which Britain had 'historical ties'. Johnson expressed a desire to turn the Commonwealth from a 'great family of nations into a free trade zone' after Brexit. Perhaps, like the government officials who nicknamed the plan for Britain's role in the world after Brexit 'Empire 2.0', Johnson forgot that for many Commonwealth countries, the Commonwealth might not hold the same romantic memories of the nineteenth century as it did for him.[20]

Our leaders' ignorant and arrogant attitudes towards the subject of empire contrast sharply with the attitude that has been taken by many of Britain's younger generation, who, over the past few years, have become louder and louder in calling for a reckoning with its aftermath. In summer 2020, during the claustrophobic midst of the coronavirus pandemic, these calls reached boiling point. In the UK, the Black Lives Matter protests moved quickly beyond calls for police accountability and prison reform to focus on much broader conversations about the 'decolonisation' of the public understanding of British history. The death of a black American, George Floyd, at the hands of the Minneapolis police had inadvertently opened the lid on the long-suppressed legacy of the empire across the Atlantic Ocean.

However, the response in the national press stretched from apoplectic rage to outright ridicule. These calls to revisit the aftermath of empire were dismissed as mere 'sophistic absurdity' that aimed to 'demoralise and divide' the country.[21] Student-led campaigns asking for educational institutions to 'decolonise' their curriculums were described by the government's minister for universities, Michelle Donelan, as a project of 'Soviet Union-style' censorship.[22] Exactly how a request to learn about long-overlooked topics of study functioned as Soviet censorship was left unexplained. As the debate moved beyond spaces of formal education and into cultural and heritage sites, the anger continued to escalate. When the Royal Botanic Gardens in Kew talked about trying to 'decolonise' their collections by highlighting how the study of plants from across the world was influenced by empire, they were attacked in the press as having become so 'woke' that they were now obsessing about the racism of plants.[23] The debate around decolonisation was relegated to being just another frontier in the culture war, and it was being caricatured as perhaps this war's most frivolous frontier at that.

In contrast to this supposedly petulant, disrespectful focus on irrelevant issues of empire, opponents called for the country to pay attention to the far more serious matter of the fate of the communities who have been 'left behind' in Britain over recent decades. Talk of 'levelling up' Britain's forgotten regions and investing in working-class communities was suddenly coming from the mouths of politicians and journalists who just a few years earlier had supported the imposition of brutal austerity policies on these very same places. Now, they were worried about how unequal Britain had become. Across the media and mainstream politics in Britain, the discussions around empire have been dismissed as something that, at best, doesn't concern the country's working-class communities or, at worst, actively harms them. Demands for racial equality and decolonisation were not embraced as an opportunity to change how our world works, but disregarded as simply just another performance of 'the identity-obsessed politics advocated by young social justice campaigners' that aims only to 'fuel the fires of division'.[24] Perhaps all these people talking about empire were just stuck in the past, unable to face up to the challenges of the twenty-first century; perhaps this call for 'decolonisation' was just the latest in a long list of never-ending complaints made by angry racial justice campaigners. Either way, the message was clear. Talking about empire belongs to the pantomime world of student politics, where cancel culture and micro-aggressions matter more than wealth inequality or urban deprivation. Ideally, everyone should just ignore the whole conversation because, according to academic Matthew Goodwin, 'once you leave university campuses or the Twitter bubble', nobody cares about bizarre issues such as 'decolonising'.[25]

There are several assumptions that underlie this commonly held position. First, there is often an assumption that the aftermath of empire only effects racial groups who are visibly descendants of Britain's colonial legacy – in other words, talking about empire is just another attempt by resentful black people to impose white guilt on those who are doing better them. Darker, now unspoken ideas of superior and inferior groupings of humanity simmer underneath this argument. Perhaps racial minorities want to 'decolonise the curriculum' because they need it dumbed down to their level of scholarship? Even when calls for 'decolonising' education are defended, the defence often carries a little hint of this same worldview – supporters will argue decolonisation matters because it is important for racial minorities to feel represented, that it helps make studying more accessible. Vary rarely does the conversation consider how *all* of us are bound up in and impacted by the aftermath of empire, in our own ways.

Second, the irrelevance argument suggests that empire is something that happened hundreds of years ago. The amnesia about British Empire imposes an exaggerated historical distance between our lives today and the period of imperial rule. Empire becomes just about plantation slavery and indigenous communities being chased from their lands by men in red coats with smoking muskets and, yes, while everyone now accepts that this wasn't the nicest way to behave, can we really be surprised that people in the distant past had different ideas from us? It was all so long ago, wasn't it? But the end of empire is anything but ancient history. For most adults in Britain today, the main period of decolonisation in the 1950s and 1960s occurred while they or their parents were alive. Yet despite how recently it took place and the scale of its global importance, the decolonisation of the British Empire is not seen as a significant moment in the nation's history. Unlike, say, the Tudor dynasty or the Gunpowder Plot, the end of empire and the questions it threw up is presented as being of little relevance to our lives today.

Finally, the entire debate around decolonisation in twenty-first-century Britain operates as if the legacy of empire is almost entirely carried within the symbolic and cultural register. Decolonisation becomes about whether streets are called Diversity Grove or Kitchener Road. Or whether schools should have to fly the Union Flag. Or if the BBC should have to delete old episodes of *Fawlty Towers*. Street names and statues obviously carry a certain importance, but by keeping the conversation at that level only, the legacy of empire can be presented as existing separately from the material problems that are plaguing so many communities across Britain today. The aftermath of empire becomes something that has no impact on the unemployed former industrial worker or the single mother stuck on a zero-hours contract that doesn't pay enough to cover childcare. Conversations about law, economics and the systems that produce wealth inequality and financial insecurity are supposed to be the issues that matter to the real world. And, currently, we act as though these issues are, somehow, wholly disconnected from the very recent, and very live, aftermath of empire.

A New World

Moving across the old empire, we can see that inequality has not only been spiralling in the UK over recent decades but has been growing around the world. Inequality is also the story of the African continent after empire, especially in the twenty-first century. The Live Aid/Comic Relief picture of sub-Saharan Africa as a desolate place 'where nothing ever grows' and desperate people all fight to eke out impoverished lives belongs to another epoch. Accra today is making more millionaires than any other city on the continent.[26] The turn of millennium has brought with it a transformation of the city's skyline, with multistorey office blocks and upscale apartment complexes shimmering along its Atlantic Ocean coastline. It is an extremely young city, populated by armies of tech-savvy, fashion-conscious teenagers moving seamlessly from shopping for kente cloth at the fabrics market to buying covers for their MacBooks at the local Apple store.

But is the ability to go to KFC or Pizza Hut on a Saturday night the realisation of the dreams of development that Ghanaians hoped for after empire? Accra is a city that, like our planet, remains unbalanced. We still live in a bifurcated world, but this division no longer runs so smoothly between what we once called the 'First', 'Second' and 'Third Worlds'. In the twenty-first century, there are many pockets of the First World within the Third World, as well as vice versa. Go to the gilded mega-mansions on Lagos's Banana Island or to the seven-star hotels of Dubai and you will find yourself standing at the very cutting edge of global luxury consumerism. Today, the so-called 'developing' world contains many of the planet's most reverential temples to capitalist grandeur, and is home to a number of multibillionaires who rank among the world's richest people – tycoons like Mexico's Carlos Slim or Nigeria's Aliko Dangote. Accra reflects this new globe. It has now morphed into a global hub littered with sparkling new designer supermalls and luxury hotels where Naomi Campbell or Jay-Z and Beyoncé stay when they are in town. But amid the city's gated communities and commercial centres persist the same slums, sewers and streets laden with potholes that have been ignored for decades. Like many a metropolis in the developing world, Accra is awash with new wealth but also blighted by an extreme inequality; there isn't a simple, happy fairy tale of 'Africa rising' to be found here.[27] The story of development my grandfather told me to expect has mutated. There are private gyms and nightclubs where hospitals and schools were expected. Everybody in Ghana seems to have a mobile phone, but there is a shortage of functioning ambulances.[28] How did 'development' develop in such a way that if you happen to fall ill, your best bet is to order an Uber through your iPhone to take you to a private hospital?

To start to answer these questions, we have to step away from the belligerent idea of African cities like Accra as being outside of time. For too many, Africa can never be a place where you look in order to gain insights into the modern world, because it is locked outside of the modern world. Instead, the continent is still used as a lazy shorthand to convey a stock picture of famine, disease or poverty; any problems it might have faced were not part of any wider dynamics occurring across the world, but confirmation of the intrinsic inability of savage people to look after themselves. Increasingly, when some unexpected social or economic crisis erupts in Britain or America, commentators have a habit of trying to emphasise the seriousness of the issue by saying 'this is like Africa, this is like a Third World country'.[29] When a hospital is overrun or protests get out of control or an authoritarian nationalist is elected in London or Washington, politicians and journalists are quick to declare, 'This shouldn't be happening here, it is like we are in Mogadishu.' Or 'Kampala'. Or 'Lagos'.

Such statements should really raise a whole other set of questions, but never do. Like *why* did cities like Mogadishu or Kampala or Lagos, all part of the British Empire just a few decades ago, become bywords for chaos? Why were we happy to tolerate the 'chaos' in these cities, all still supposedly part of our great Commonwealth? Why does this 'chaos' now feel like its drifting towards Britain and across the West? These questions can't be answered by clinging on to ideas of a natural order and hierarchy across the globe; the belief that the world is divided into places where crises should happen and places where they should not.

Without asking these questions, we can't understand the crises Britain is faced with now. Things are falling apart and the centre cannot hold. Prices are rising, wages are stagnant, services are being cut and, for many, the feeling of security has become a half-remembered dream. Parents and grandparents are witnessing their own offspring struggle to maintain a lifestyle that they once took for granted. These trends are only set to accelerate with the growth of automation, machine learning and robotics. A third of jobs in Britain are currently at high risk of being replaced by artificial intelligence in the near future.[30] And in the jobs that remain, ever-intensifying systems of digital surveillance are increasingly being used to make sure employees work harder and harder for their static wages. The shift to automation is also likely to heighten Britain's geographic inequalities, with the jobs that are most at risk concentrated in the former industrial heartlands. Not that Britain's disintegrating middle classes are going to be insulated from these changes. Lawyers, accountants, engineers and financial advisers are going to increasingly find that skills they spent years cultivating are being made superfluous by new technology. These once-lucrative forms of employment are not the ticket to security they once were. Conditions of work are worsening across the board. Pensions are being watered down, collective bargaining power is being weakened, casualisation has become rampant. Professions that not so long ago cast a pitying eye towards striking miners, dockers or steel workers are now embarking on their own industrial actions. Doctors, barristers, professors and pilots are finding out now, rather belatedly, that they too are workers and the lowering of labour conditions across the board will not leave them untouched.

This dynamic can't be reconciled with the old story of development that I learned as a child. We lose sight of the global economic changes now boomeranging back on us when we insist on viewing British history as, in the words of Michael Gove, an 'island story', an insular tale of an island that led the course of human development through its own innovation.[31] Simply declaring that Britain must be proud of its history or blindly insisting that everything that the country does is 'world-beating' isn't enough to address the very real questions that people are facing in the great age of divergence. Will waving the Union flag or singing 'Rule Britannia' help a family forced to queue at a food bank each week?

For decades now, communities have been feeling the constraints on everyday life getting tighter and tighter. In 2018, Philip Alston, UN special rapporteur on extreme poverty, reported that a fifth of Britain's population now live in poverty, with child poverty potentially to increase to as high as 40 per cent by 2022. And this was before anyone had heard of Covid-19. In Alston's words, 'for almost one in every two children to be poor in twenty-first century Britain is not just a disgrace, but a social calamity and an economic disaster, all rolled into one.'[32] In looking around to see the widespread precarity, skyrocketing income and wealth inequality, an eroded welfare state and a hollowed-out political system, it is possible to recognise the disjuncture between the romantic 'island story' we have been told and the world we actually live in. The current crisis is not something that has arisen over the past few years. For the past century, the ground has been shifting under all our feet. But by pathologically avoiding one of the major events of this era, the ending of empire, we have been overlooking essential questions about the machinery of how the world works. What was the British Empire? Where exactly did it stretch to? How did it start? How did it end? Which elements of it died away with decolonisation? Which elements adapted and remade themselves in the aftermath? To face the problems of today and tomorrow, we must rethink which stories we assume to be relevant for understanding our world in the present day.

A Tour of Empire's Afterlife

This book is just a small part of the growing interest in the legacy of empire in Britain that has started to enter the public's consciousness. A number of books published recently have explored how Britain's unresolved imperial afterlife continues to impact on race relations, and have posed questions about the identity and the general national culture of contemporary Britain.[33] The backlash against these books has tried to relegate the whole issue of empire to just another topic in an ongoing culture war, framing the issue around topics guaranteed to generate clicks for a dying tabloid industry. Is it right or wrong for students to take down a picture of the Queen because of her colonial associations? Is Winston Churchill a national hero or a colonial tyrant? The point is to drown the issue of empire in a cacophony of noise. Empire can then be dismissed as just another culture war issue. Just another 'black' issue. And while the discourse of race, which formed such an essential part of the imperial project, will weave in and out of my narrative, it is also important to remember that empire is about more than just the way racism continues to inform life in Britain. Other authors have already written about the deep, interpersonal experience of racism in a better way than I could. This book will instead go back to the source of the issue and remind us that racism grew out of colonisation, not the other way round. The painful, personal experience of racial discrimination only carries power because it sits against a background of deep, structural inequalities. Britain's vast wealth inequalities are only amplified when we look at the racial breakdown of the data: households measured as having more debts than assets being twice as likely to be 'Black African and Other Asian' families than white families.[34] Empire carries an economic legacy, not just a cultural or racial one.

As important as ideological justifications for racial hierarchies became to the project of colonisation, the British Empire was not just a five-hundred-year world tour of being mean to brown people. It was about extracting resources and hoarding wealth. It was a global system of cultivated and coordinated armed robbery. And while Britain no longer exercises sovereign control over large parts of the planet, many of the legal and economic structures put in place to facilitate the imperial system of wealth transfer still drive our world. In fact, as people across the colonies focused on winning back their sovereignty after the Second World War, seduced by its grandstanding world of flags and anthems, a counter-offensive was underway. Over the later decades of the twentieth century, the power of sovereignty was watered down as another realm of legal control was reinforced instead – the private realm that operates away from the cameras, a world of property and contacts, of debt and of capital.[35] Without appreciating the significance of this element of empire's afterlife, it is difficult to understand how global capitalism operates today.

The struggles at the end of empire set the tone for the world that we all live in, and it's time for us to think about the aftermath of empire not only in terms of identity but also in terms of wealth and economics. Decolonisation means confronting many of the forces that are driving inequality and insecurity in the world today, both in Britain and abroad. This book has been written and structured in a particular way in order to illustrate a resonance between the era of decolonisation and the present day, between the contestations that occurred throughout the globe during the end of empire and the contemporary challenges facing our un-balanced, unequal world.

When talking about the triumph of capitalist globalisation following the end of empire, we often centre the role of the USA, and understandably so. With its military and economic might,

America served as the irresistible force that bent so many newly independent governments to its will during the final decades of the twentieth century. However, another protagonist in this story is the British Empire, or what it left in its wake. From English laws of property to the global spread of the commercial corporation; from the financial reach of the City of London to Britain's overseas territories – like the Cayman Islands and Bermuda – being used to hoard wealth 'offshore', the afterlife of Britain's Empire has played a crucial role in shielding capitalist interests from the threat of democracy over the past few decades. It has become so good at this job that it has left millions of British people wondering where their own sovereignty has gone.

This book explores the material aftermath of the British Empire over the last century not only through the experiences of the UK, but in connection to the stories of Ghana, India, Singapore and Jamaica, among other territories that grew out of the empire's collapse. The structure will follow a bending of time rather than the traditional assumption of a linear history of progress. Zipping back and forth between then and now, each chapter starts with a different scene from the breakdown of the British Empire and examines how its afterlife continues to inform the structures that still govern our world. The boomerang will provide a moving metaphor across the chapters to trace how the consequences of the dying days of empire are now blowing back across the developed world. The overall picture will be a collage showing how the material challenges that are being faced by the 'left behind' in the UK are not divorced from the afterlife of the British Empire, but are part of the same story.

Chapter 1, 'The State', begins with the failed attempt by the British West African colonies to demand self-government after the First World War, before expanding to consider how the importance of sovereignty has ebbed and flowed over the intervening century. Chapter 2, 'The Company', travels to Iran in the aftermath of the Second World War to revisit the conflict between nationalist leader Mohammad Mosaddegh and the Anglo-Iranian Oil

Company. We will see how the outcome of this conflict propelled us towards today's world, where the multinational commercial corporation appears to have become omnipotent. Chapter 3, 'The Border', starts with Britain's response to the independence of India and the inevitability of a world of empires becoming a world of nations. We will learn how Britain's response to losing its most populous colony involved the implementation of an unprecedented level of border control for people while simultaneously advocating for a world of 'no borders' for the movement of money.

Chapter 4, 'The Debt', looks at Jamaica's brief foray in leading a Third World economic revolution during the 1970s, before it was undermined by the twin spectres of sovereign debt and loan-restructuring agreements. Here we see how phrases like 'debt crisis' and 'austerity' were commonplace in the Third World decades before the 2008 financial crisis. Chapter 5, 'The Tax', moves across the Caribbean to the Cayman Islands in order to trace how British overseas territories have driven the global proliferation of the offshore economy since the end of empire. And finally, Chapter 6, 'The City', looks at the specific economic path that Singapore took following its independence from the British Empire and the lessons that it holds for those who dreamed of a potential 'Singapore-on-Thames' economic model for Britain.

Through these various scenes, we will engage with some of the most significant figures trying to remake the world after empire, from Jamaica's Michael Manley to Singapore's Sinnathamby Rajaratnam, from Ghana's Kwame Nkrumah to Britain's Margaret Thatcher. All students at British universities in the 1940s and 1950s as the empire started to collapse, these key characters would travel across the world over the decades that followed with vastly different visions for the world after empire. Through the ideas and events that surround this interconnected group of politicians and intellectuals, this book will tell a new story of Britain over the course of the twentieth century.

For our starting point, we will go back 100 years to the end of the First World War. At the start of the twentieth century, 'to be born English was to have won first prize in the lottery of life'.[36] England was the centre of the largest empire the world has ever seen – the British Empire, an empire remarkable not only for how it expanded across the globe but also for its unprecedented wealth and population.[37] The Royal Navy was the world's most feared military force and the British pound was the global reserve currency. A century later, has this lottery ticket expired? In a 2018 BBC survey, only 17 per cent of English people still believe that the country's best days are yet to come.[38] How did the world change in the intervening period? What are the forgotten stories of the twentieth century that could help explain our contemporary situation? With the United Kingdom of Great Britain and Northern Ireland now in the midst of a turbulent period, the need to look at this question fearlessly and honestly is more urgent than ever.

I

The State

In June 1919, seven months after the armistice had brought an end to fighting, the Treaty of Versailles was signed, officially bringing the First World War to an end. The British Empire had emerged from the war battered and bruised but victorious, and the treaty ensured that the spoils went to the victors. The terms of the Treaty of Versailles would help the British Empire expand even further, as it absorbed colonies from its defeated Ottoman and German rivals. By 1920, with regard to population, wealth and land mass, Britain had the largest empire in human history. That same year, a handful of delegates from the National Congress of British West Africa (NCBWA) arrived in London on a dreary September morning to try and challenge the supremacy of this seemingly omnipotent empire.

Founded earlier that same year in Accra, the capital of the colony that Britain called the Gold Coast after the region's prosperous gold mines, the NCBWA had come together in the wake of the Versailles peace talks to work towards a new vision for the African continent. As an organisation, its goal was to bring together the most influential West Africans of the time to make a collective case for legal and political emancipation. By the time they set sail for Britain, the leaders of the NCBWA were well armed with as much educational artillery as Africans in the early twentieth century could acquire. The party included Cambridge-educated lawyer Joseph Casely-Hayford and the Sierra Leonian physician Dr Herbert Bankole-Bright, who gained his medical degree at Edinburgh University. Confident that history was on their side, the merry band of high society West Africans, hailing from Nigeria, the Gambia, the Gold Coast and Sierra Leone, embarked on a press tour as soon as they arrived in London. Styled in the latest tailored suits, their public relations skills were impeccable as they set about challenging the stories of 'savage' people from 'dark' colonies that many British people had been told about Africans. They gave lectures to students, lobbied representatives from the League of Nations and even charmed a few sympathetic Members of Parliament.[1]

However, as the weeks turned to months, the delegates' initial optimism was gradually eroded. The group's demands were modest – they were not asking for full independence, only requesting that legislative councils be created in the West African colonies, where the locals could get a small share of sovereignty. Just half of the members of the proposed councils would be African, and they would still operate under the authority of the British governors who ruled the territories in the name of the Crown. The delegates also hoped that British West Africa might get its own court of appeal, and perhaps even a newspaper that could be shared across the region.

But these humble requests still proved to be too much. Though the group had managed to win a few hearts and minds during their stay, the reception they received from the Westminster government was as frosty as the London winter they were now enduring. Their hopes of discussing their proposals with the prime minister fell apart when David Lloyd George refused to meet with them.[2] They were further undermined by messages sent by the British governors that ruled the colonies they came from. The governors knew that their own continuing power and accompanying lavish lifestyles depended on discrediting this new pan-African organisation. The governor of Nigeria, Sir Hugh Clifford, and the governor of the Gold Coast, Sir Gordon Guggisberg, insisted the government should not take these over-educated elites, dressed up in the clothes and vocabulary of English gentlemen, as representative of the West African masses. Real Africans, they insisted,

were primitive, fiercely tribal and nowhere near ready to handle
the modern pressures of statecraft. Clifford openly ridiculed the
idea of there ever being such a thing as one single Nigerian
nation.[3]

In the end, the delegates requests to King George V for
increased powers of self-rule were rejected without even the courtesy of a meeting. The NCBWA appealed with a new submission,
asking to at least get a chance to state their case in person. Perhaps
if they got in the same room as the sovereign or senior figures
of government, they might impress them the same way they had
impressed students and journalists across the land over the past
few months. However, on 17 February 1921 the newly appointed
Secretary of State for the Colonies, Winston Churchill, wrote
a letter to the delegates informing them that the government's
decision was final, and that the case of African self-government
was closed.[4] The message from the British political class was clear
and simple – the empire was there to stay.

The discourteous dismissal of the NCBWA provides a small
glimpse into the state of the world just a century ago. To the
African delegates, the failure of their journey must have felt like
more confirmation of the overwhelming intractability of British
imperial power. Yet despite the empire's sun shining over more
parts of the world than it ever had before, it was, by the early
1920s, already deep into its twilight years. The Treaty of Versailles
had given to the imperialists with one hand while taking away
with the other; by setting up the League of Nations and its new
mandate system, whereby some colonies would be supervised by
international organisations, the treaty signalled a shift away from
a world of explicitly territorial European empires. And below the
institutional halls of international law, talk of anti-colonialism was
now bubbling up in the streets of cities across the world. The
Hapsburg and Ottoman Empires and tsarist Russian Empire all
crumbled during this period. Looking at the shift in atmosphere,
British politicians might have been wiser to take the NCBWA's
proposal a little more seriously.

The decade or so after the NCBWA's frustrating trip to London would see Ireland gain independence and the Statute of Westminster being passed, which granted legislative independence to the settler colonies of Australia, New Zealand, Canada and South Africa. The horror of the 1919 Amritsar Massacre inspired a rise in nationalism in India, setting it on its own path towards independence. The pound sterling began to fall from its position as the world economy's premier currency, and by the 1940s the US dollar had replaced it as the reserve currency used in international transactions. Ultimately, it would take a mere generation after the NCBWA set sail for London for the Gold Coast to become the first colony in sub-Saharan Africa to win complete independence, founding the sovereign nation state of Ghana in 1957. And Britain as a political entity would leave the twentieth century in a drastically different form from the way it had entered it.

Erasing Empire

Like millions of other people in Britain today, my family history and life story has been shaped by the break-up of the British Empire and the ramifications that followed. This is true not just of first-generation immigrants from Ghana, Bangladesh or Barbados, but also of families in Britain's port cities like Liverpool and Bristol, or financiers who work between London's Square Mile and the Cayman Islands. Yet there is a wilful amnesia about this crucial turning point of the past century. Without making sense of the end of the empire, not only can we not understand the changing complexion of this island, but we also cannot understand how multinational corporations have become so powerful over the last few decades, why tax havens are spread across the world, or why the UK is struggling with a constitutional crisis. The end of the British Empire is one of the great global changes of the last hundred years, the triumphs and tragedies of the process of decolonisation cemented as epoch-defining moments in many countries around the world. Yet Britain, the protagonist in the whole messy drama, has forgotten it was ever even on the stage.

Britain's present-day amnesia about decolonisation emerges, in part, from the confusion around the debate about decolonisation, which is reflected in the different ways the term is often used. In narrow, strictly legal terms, decolonisation is the process through which territories that existed under the colonial jurisdiction of another country receive their independence and are recognised as sovereign nation states. They receive the power to make and break their own laws, resulting in new heads of states, new national anthems and new passports for their citizens. In the middle of the twentieth century, whole swathes of the globe went through this process. Though there remains a sprinkling of small territories across the world still defined as 'non-self-governing' by international law, the era of decolonisation redrew the global map, as the French, Belgian, Portuguese and, largest of all, British Empires broke up into a collection of new nation states. After this process, many people considered the chapter on decolonisation to be closed – it was simply an issue of legal status and now it had been resolved. Nowadays, decolonisation is often discussed as a purely academic topic, something for historians to discuss among themselves. It is certainly not seen as a topic worth revisiting by those interested in addressing the contemporary political and economic challenges of our unequal, hyper-globalised world. But decolonisation wasn't just another administrative step along the linear path of development: instead, it represented a struggle to remake the world. It also required not only those who had been colonised but also those who had been doing the colonising to remake themselves.

The UK's twentieth-century transition from an empire state to a nation state was not accompanied by a comprehensive review of its constitution and state institutions. This is despite the fact that, for the bulk of its constitutional history, England and then Britain was an imperial realm, not just a national one. By the time of the 'Glorious Revolution' of 1688, itself part coup and part invasion, England had already established legal jurisdiction over Barbados (1627), Jamaica (1670) and the Virginia slave colonies in what would eventually become the USA, as well as having forts in what is today Accra, Ghana and Bunce Island, Sierra Leone, among others. Scotland had also embarked on its own fledgling imperial project during the seventeenth century, and when the country was finally pulled into a political union with England by the Act of Union of 1707, it was in no small part due to the opportunities for imperial wealth that such a marriage offered.[5]

In many ways, Britain's relationship with colonialism is older than Britain itself. Rather than saying Britain had an empire, it would be more accurate to say that the empire had Britain, as the British political entity was largely born of and sustained by its imperial project. Decolonisation, rather than being a bureaucratic transition that happened in distant, foreign lands, was a fundamental turning point in the history of Britain. As the historian David Edgerton explains, the United Kingdom of Great Britain and Northern Ireland emerged as just 'one of the new nations which arose from the dissolution of the one empire'.[6] To measure the full weight of decolonisation, it is necessary to understand the ways in which the state of Britain today is not the same as it was a century ago.

At the turn of the twentieth century, real questions were being asked by leading politicians as to what distinction, if any, existed between the British state and the wider empire. For some of the most influential figures in the land, Britain's future depended on its ability to turn the empire into a single, federal state. And in 1902, after the long reign of Queen Victoria had come to an end, the crowning of a new British monarch was seen by Britain's colonial secretary at the time as an opportunity to remake the state structure of the anglosphere. With representatives from across the empire coming to London to pay their respects to the new king, colonial secretary Joseph Chamberlain looked to open discussions about subsuming parts of the empire into the British state.

Described by Winston Churchill as the man who 'made the weather' in Britain, Chamberlain was a businessman who had become rich during Birmingham's industrial revolution before becoming a politician.[7] He had started his career as a Liberal but changed his allegiances following Liberal Prime Minister William Gladstone's decision to grant the Irish home rule in 1886. Fearing a decline in British power, Chamberlain threw himself into the imperial cause, becoming the colonial secretary for the Conservative government in 1895. Though he himself wouldn't be prime minister, his son Neville would famously occupy the office at 10 Downing Street, with history generally unforgiving of the results. Chamberlain senior's legacy is more convoluted. Still cited as a personal hero by politicians like Theresa May, Joseph Chamberlain's mid-career transition to 'first minister' of the British Empire offers a preview of a path that the British state might have taken in an alternative history. Amid the pomp and ceremony of the crowning of a new king, Chamberlain hosted the 1902 Colonial Conference, where he proposed a pathway towards formalising Global Britain as a single jurisdictional sphere.[8]

The notion of creating an imperial federation, turning parts of the globe-spanning empire into a single federal state, emerged towards the end of the Victorian age to address the lack of representation for Britain's settler colonies within Parliament, the same issue which, a century earlier, had caused the British Empire to suffer its most expensive loss. Forced to watch the USA grow into a rival global power from what had once been Britain's thirteen colonies, leading nineteenth-century intellectuals, such as popular writers James Anthony Froude and John Robert Seeley, called for greater constitutional unity across the empire.[9] Both Froude and Seeley wrote best-selling books arguing for what Chamberlain's great political ally, Sir Charles Dilke, had named *Greater Britannia* – a vision of Britain that included colonial territories as full parts of the Union.[10] Seeley's 1883 book *The Expansion of England*, in particular, influenced a generation of intellectuals by arguing that the separation of the British state and wider empire was a form of denialism, a nation pretending: 'we seem, as it were, to have conquered and peopled half the world in a fit of absence of mind'.[11] For Seeley, the empire was a natural outgrowth of England's path of development which would, one day, lead to 'the foundation of Greater Britain', stretching all across the globe.

The year after Seeley's book was published, the idea of a Greater Britain began to solidify into concrete proposals through the foundation of the Imperial Federation League. This organisation, which founded branches in Australia, New Zealand, Canada, Barbados and British Guiana, as well as the United Kingdom, looked to bring these geographically disparate colonies into a single jurisdictional federation, similar to Germany or the USA. There was talk of a new Act of Union with the colonies. Britain's leading constitutional experts of the age recognised that the UK's 'unwritten' constitution had already been shaped by the pressures not only of facilitating the union between England, Scotland, Ireland and Wales but also of meeting 'the wants of a large empire' and being able to 'control in different manners and in different degrees colonies and dependencies'.[12] After all, if the empire had no constitution that was distinct from the British Constitution itself, why not unify it into a single coherent body?[13] Other organisations joined the call of the Imperial Federation League, including the British Empire League, the Imperial Federation (Defence) Committee and the Round Table movement.

These federalists came from both ends of the political spectrum and imagined creating an expanded parliament that could include members representing at least the settled, white-dominion colonies of Australia, Canada, New Zealand and South Africa, alongside MPs for Bristol West or Edinburgh South. A large element of the imperial federation movement was explicitly white supremacist, imagining the new transoceanic Greater Britannia state as an umbrella for inevitable global triumph of the Anglo-Saxon race. However, the successes of Indian-born MPs like Dadabhai Naoroji and Mancherjee Bhownagree in the House of Commons at the end of the nineteenth century encouraged some federalists to imagine non-white subjects might also be represented, leading to the debate about the imperial federation being extended to India and the West Indies. Such was the optimism around the transportation and telecommunication advancements of the turn of century that supporters of the federation believed the geographic hurdle of whole oceans separating the territories could be overcome. In an 1885 lecture for the Imperial Federation League, the writer Edward Ellis Morris argued that it was as easy in his time to travel from Melbourne to London as it had been to get to London from the islands off northern Scotland at the time of the 1707 Act of Union.[14] The motto for the campaign for a unified British imperial state was 'federate or disintegrate'; to avoid the trauma of decolonisation Britain had to constitutionally accept that it was, and always had been, an empire.[15]

Powell and the Forgetting

A federal British empire would never come to pass, of course. By the time the politicians in Westminster took the idea seriously, the direction of travel for its colonies was already towards independence. The island of Britain that sat at the heart of this vast empire would need a new identity. Having flirted with the idea to make the empire a single state at the turn of the twentieth century, by that century's midpoint Britain's political class was denying not only that the empire had mattered but, in some cases, that it had even ever existed. The figure who best embodies this shifting mindset was another Midlands-based politician who is often spoken of alongside Joseph Chamberlain as one of Britain's most significant politicians not to have become prime minister – Enoch Powell.

Powell's life spanned Britain's transformative twentieth century, just as his career spanned the far corners of the empire. Often photographed sporting a top hat, cane and a moustache rumoured to be modelled on Friedrich Nietzsche's, Enoch Powell is one of the most controversial British figures of the last century.[16] His name is now synonymous with the 'Rivers of Blood' speech that brought his serious political career to a stuttering halt in 1968, placing Powell in the rogue's gallery of far-right, explicitly racist British politicians with the likes of John Tyndall and Nick Griffin. But Powell enjoyed an influence among the British establishment that the figures he is grouped with could only imagine. A Cambridge-educated classicist, Powell was a leading figure within several Tory governments, often seen as the prime-minister-in-waiting, and he remains an intellectual inspiration for politicians to this day. His obituary in the *Daily Telegraph* declared he would 'survive more surely than any other British politician of the twentieth century except Winston Churchill'.[17]

Powell's legacy continues to hang over conversations about immigration, nationalism and even economics in Britain. And all of these aspects of his thought sat underneath the umbrella of his attitude to the afterlife of empire. For the first half of his life, Powell had been a proselytising devotee of the British Empire. Having served as a secretary to the Joint Intelligence Committee for India, his fascination with the 'jewel of Britain's empire' turned him into a parody of the pith-hat-wearing British colonialist. Dressing in the clothes of a viceroy in the making and adamant about Britain's everlasting jurisdiction over the colonies, Powell believed that 'in its widest sense, the nation is the empire'. His election address when becoming an MP in 1950 stated plainly, 'I believe in the British Empire. Without the Empire, Britain would be like a head without a body.'[18] But this illusion was already crumbling – when he learned his beloved India was to throw off colonial rule in 1947, Powell described it as 'a shock so severe that I remember spending the whole of one night walking the streets of London trying to come to terms with it.'[19] Yet, a few years after that first speech, the same Enoch Powell was writing that the British Empire that he had been so committed to protecting had, in fact, never existed.

In his 1965 book, *A Nation Not Afraid*, Powell shared his ideas about Britain's destiny for the rest of the century. To start with, he wanted readers to recognise that 'the myth of the British Empire is one of the most extraordinary paradoxes in political history.'[20] Like a cheap magician trying to stuff the rabbit back into the hat, Powell's new position was that Britain had never had an empire, that the idea of the 'British Empire' was simply 'an invention', cooked up by latter-day intellectuals to make sense of something that had happened before their time.[21] Britain had not set out to conquer the world – the colonies were just things that the country had been 'landed with'. [22] Britain had been trying to get rid of these expensive burdens but, like newborn babies clinging onto their mother's bosom, the dependant colonies wouldn't let go. Now they had finally been shaken off, Powell insisted that the colonies and their loss should be forgotten about as quickly as possible.

To him, the Commonwealth was 'essentially a sham', a way for colonies to keep riding on the motherland's coat-tails without paying the due respect.[23] Britain, on the other hand, had barely been affected by having an empire at all, according to Powell. The other European imperial powers and their people may have been fundamentally changed by their imperial adventures, but because Britain's empire had not really been an empire in the first place, it could move on without so much as a backward glance.[24] From saying that Britain without the empire was like a head with no body just a decade earlier, Powell was now insisting that decolonisation had no impact on Britain whatsoever. For him, the only reason why anyone thought the empire was important in the first place was because of the work of Joseph Chamberlain.

Powell presented Chamberlain's campaign for an Imperial Federation as being the moment that the British Empire was 'invented'.[25] According to Powell, when Chamberlain and others were debating whether or not the empire should be united into a federated state at the turn of the twentieth century, they made the mistake of accepting the presumption that there was such a thing as a 'British Empire' at all. By overvaluing the importance of the empire, Powell felt Chamberlain and his allies were missing an even more remarkable story; the tale of an adventuring, pioneering island where the laws, constitution and systems of government had been 'unbroken' for over 'a thousand years'. Casting aside his previous life as a devotee of the empire, Powell found comfort in the story of Britain as the exceptional nation state, a country 'unique in history' for being uninfluenced by the outside world.[26]

A Nation Apart

Despite spanning across the globe and being the largest empire in history, the British Empire has been relatively easy to delete from the official national narrative after decolonisation. In its place stands the story that Powell turned to in order to ease the trauma of decolonisation: the tale of Britain as an independent, pioneering state that always stands alone. The empire and its aftermath become unimportant if you understand Britain as just being, in the words of leading Conservative politician Liam Fox, 'a small island perched on the edge of the European continent [that] became a leader of world trade'.[27] The narrative of Britain as an island state that does things its own way has been embraced by leaders from across the political spectrum. At his first Labour Party conference after being elected prime minister, Tony Blair proclaimed to his audience, 'we are one of the great innovative peoples . . . we are by our nature and tradition innovators, adventurers, pioneers'.[28]

Turning Britain from a global empire into an island of explorers helps to maintain the image of history moving in a singular, straight line. If Britain was never really an empire, then decolonisation is an insignificant event and everything continues to operate as it was. Powell's vision of Britain as a paradisal land, 'unique' in being undisturbed by the upheavals that befell others, took on a quasi-religious tone at times. To Powell, Britain's 'unwritten' constitution was not just ancient or mysterious but also miraculous: 'institutions which elsewhere are recent and artificial creations, appear in England almost as works of nature, spontaneous and unquestioned'.[29] Parliament, the monarchy, the common law, the constitution – in other countries their equivalent institutions reveal themselves as man-made creations of the state whilst on this island they appear as more like acts of God. To avoid, or at least minimise, the significance of decolonisation, Powell paints a picture of the British state being born of immaculate conception, growing organically and uninterrupted by outsiders for over a millennium.

However, today faith in Britain's innovative spirit or ancient institutions is starting to wane. Recent political upheavals in the UK have led to increased interest in daily parliamentary goings-on and the public has not been overly impressed with what it sees. A 2019 survey showed that one of the few things that united 'leave' and 'remain' voters in the UK was being unhappy with the current state of the UK's democratic system.[30] From newspapers across the spectrum, headlines called for the country to reconsider whether institutions like the parliament, the judiciary and the 'unwritten' constitution were up to the task. During the Brexit debates, the Speaker of the House of Commons became a national hate figure and Supreme Court judges were denounced as 'enemies of the people'.[31] Brexit was driven by a stated desire to reclaim the powers of sovereignty, but the subsequent years of political wrangling did more to damage public confidence in the British state than all the years of membership of the European Union. Then, just as it seemed that the pressure Brexit had placed upon Britain's political institutions was going to ease, at least for a short while, they would be hit by a public health crisis that would expose the state's shortcomings to an extent previously unseen. The decentralised nature of the British Empire left an indelible mark upon the Westminster state that had developed at the heart of it. The reason why the state was able to dismiss the significance of decolonisation is the same reason why, today, the state is pre-programmed to contract out its response to a global pandemic: Westminster emerged during empire as the centre of an outsourced imperial project.

The State of Outsourcing

Even now, the outsourced state continues to boomerang back on itself. By early March 2020, it became clear to most people in Britain that the government would have to take some drastic action to avoid being overwhelmed by the coronavirus pandemic that was now sweeping through the European continent. The governments of France, Italy and most other European states had implemented strict lockdowns of their populations, with all large public gatherings cancelled for the foreseeable future. Even in the absence of state instruction, across the UK organisers began to cancel their events, aware that large congregations of people provided the ideal environment for the virus to spread. This was not the decision that the board of the Jockey Club came to, however. In the midst of the rising panic, this organisation, which runs Cheltenham Racecourse, chose to push forward with the Cheltenham Festival, the annual meeting that comprises one of the highlights of the racing calendar. The festival opened on 10 March, with about 150,000 people in attendance over the four-day event, all in close quarters, shouting, cheering and hugging each other as their favourite horses galloped through to victory. After the festival, the attendees returned to their homes across the country, taking with them whatever infections they had picked up during the festivities. In the months to follow, as Covid-19 devasted Britain, the Jockey Club's decision to continue with the Cheltenham Festival at the outset of the pandemic was widely condemned and blamed for having accelerated the spread of the virus.[32] Yet it would be a member of the board of the Jockey Club who would go on to be selected to lead the UK's effort to track and stop the spread of Covid-19.

Baroness Dido Harding, herself a former competitive jockey, had been born into the fast track of life. The granddaughter of Field Marshall Lord Harding, the governor of Cyprus during the Cyprus Emergency and adviser on Britain's brutal response to the Mau Mau Uprising in Kenya, she was made a member of the House of Lords by her old university friend, David Cameron. In 2010, the same year Cameron had become prime minister, Harding had just become the first CEO of the new telecommunications conglomerate TalkTalk. Her tenure there would prove to be dramatic. At TalkTalk, Harding presided over a data breach that resulted in the personal and banking details of millions of customers being exposed. The company was criticised for having failed to implement the most basic cybersecurity protections and Harding stepped down from her role eighteen months later.[33] Fortunately for Harding, she was able to move into the public sector, becoming a Conservative life peer in 2014 and being initially tasked with overseeing a programme of 'improvement' in the NHS. Then, in May 2020, she was put in charge of Britain's programme to test its citizens for Covid-19 and trace who they had been in contact with. It was labelled the 'NHS' track and trace system, but, in practice, it wasn't run by the government or its National Health Service. Harding immediately outsourced the management of this programme to a group of private companies, including the company that, in recent years, has emerged as among Britain's most prolific collectors of government contracts, Serco.

Serco's role in managing Britain's test and trace programme was just the latest step in its takeover of many aspects of the day-to-day operation of the British state. The company's website takes pride in proclaiming that it is 'Shaping UK Public Services', with its work spreading across an array of areas including 'Defence, Justice & Immigration, Transport, Health and Citizen Services'.[34] However, Serco's growing influence over everyday life has been anything but smooth sailing. The prisons it runs have been criticised by inspectors for keeping inmates in alarming conditions, its out-of-hours healthcare services have been condemned as being substandard and its contract with the Ministry of Justice was submerged in scandal when the government discovered that it had been paying Serco for electronic tagging devices that the company never delivered.[35]

Yet Serco's most controversial outsourcing project has been its management of the Yarl's Wood Immigration Removal Centre. A corrugated-iron imposition on the Bedfordshire countryside, Yarl's Wood warehouses hundreds of foreign nationals while they await deportation, with the vast majority of detainees there being vulnerable women. In 2015, two campaigning organisations, Women Against Rape and Black Women's Rape Action Project collaborated on a dossier chronicling the stories of sexual harassment, abuse and rape of detainees at Yarl's Wood.[36] Asylum seekers, many already survivors of sexual violence, found themselves being propositioned and pressured for sex by the guards who ran this detention centre. Male guards were able to subject female detainees to humiliating strip searches and watch them as they went to the toilet. Women who had endured perilous journeys from as far afield as Cameroon or Lesotho reported having to give sexual favours to guards in order to speak to their families or to get their case advanced. The same year the dossier was published, Rashida Manjoo, the United Nations Special Rapporteur on Violence against Women, criticised the UK government for refusing to grant her access to Yarl's Wood during her fact-finding trip to the UK, comparing it to when she was denied entry to a Bangladeshi refugee camp.[37] Despite preaching the gospel of outsourcing, it seemed that the government was shy about showing off its benefits to the world. Serco's tenure at Yarl's Wood has been a stalked by scandal after scandal, but that didn't stop the government rewarding the company in 2020 with a £200 million contract to run two more detention centres.[38]

No obstacle appears to be able to slow down Serco's outsourcing machine. Even Covid-19 just became another opportunity for the company to secure further government contracts, with Harding recruiting the firm to manage regional test centres and run aspects of the telephone contact-tracing system. The resulting system was widely criticised as being a failure. An end-of-year report from the National Audit Office found that the UK's test and trace system was missing the targets it had set itself for returning tests and contacting people who might have been infected. Call handlers were being paid to spend whole days sitting in call centres that were receiving next to no calls. The system also failed to anticipate the increased demand it would face when schools and universities reopened after the summer break.[39] Despite recognising that most of the countries that had already built up successful test and trace systems had done so through state provisions and without extensive use of outsourcing, Harding's team had insisted that turning to the private sector was the only way to scale up a British version at speed.[40] As a result, by November 2020, the government had signed 407 contracts worth £7 billion with a number of different organisations. An estimated 70 per cent of these contracts were, like the contracts received by Serco, directly awarded to hand-picked companies without any competitive process.[41] Friends of government ministers were able to have their companies fast-tracked towards lucrative agreements to provide personal protective equipment for hospital staff or to supply food to vulnerable families. At the outbreak of the pandemic, the World Health Organisation declared that the key to suppressing the virus was establishing a successful test and trace system. The UK's outsourced system proved incapable of stopping the virus, contributing to the record death rate suffered in the country. Meanwhile, at the end of 2020, Serco happily announced that its profits for the year had exceeded all previous expectations.[42]

Covid-19 revealed the inbuilt faith in the private sector that underwrites many of Britain's political institutions. There is a long history of politicians pushing a vision of the British state as concerned with *enabling* rather than *providing* services for its citizens.[43] The actual work of government is assumed to be best done by those motivated by profit. Over the past few decades, governments formed by both the Labour Party and the Conservative Party, as well as the coalition of the Conservatives and the Liberal Democrats, have all, to a greater or lesser extent, advanced the cavalry of private companies undertaking state projects. Politicians have preached that outsourcing state responsibility to the private sector increases efficiency and encourages innovation. The competition between the different companies looking for government contracts was supposed to drive down the cost to the state while improving the quality of the services that the public ultimately received. Outsourcing promised to take the question of healthcare provision, prison supervision or education supplies out of the realm of politics and make them matters of cold, financial calculation, ensuring that the country always got the best deal. But instead, decades of actively whittling down the state's capacity to provide for its citizens meant that the British government was initially ill-equipped to confront the immense challenge posed by the Covid-19 pandemic without turning to corporate friends.

Around a third of all public spending in the UK takes the form of contracts given to private companies like Atos and Serco in order for them to perform functions that would once have been done by the state itself.[44] On the surface, it often still looks like it is the state providing these services. But across the country, intermingled with genuine public services are private companies who are running immigration detention centres, providing school meals, managing homes for vulnerable children and administrating mental health services, all with the aim of raising their own share prices.

Where did the British state's addiction to outsourcing come from? It is no accident that the UK, alongside the USA, is the world's largest outsourcing market.[45] The British instinctive reliance on the private sector to do the job of government is not only a result of contemporary fiscal pressures but is also connected to deep assumptions about the role of the state, partly formed through the imperial project. The imperial federalists sought to close the gap between the Westminster state and the global business of empire; however, this gap was not resolved with a constitutional union but was bridged by private enterprise, a conveyor belt of companies doing much of Britain's colonial heavy lifting over the centuries. The relationship between outsourcing and the British state has deep roots that connect our contemporary governments' dependence on private companies, even in the midst of a pandemic, to the history of private profiteering that drove the British Empire.

Outsourcing Empire

The rise of outsourcing in Britain is often traced to the public reforms that swept through the country in the 1980s courtesy of Margaret Thatcher's government.[46] However, if the frame is expanded to take in the full breadth of Global Britain, then the history of outsourcing becomes much older, predating even the unification of the United Kingdom. Across the world, first the English and then the British Empire relied on partnerships with private companies to extend power into new territories. As early as the sixteenth century, the English state had already entered into agreements with private companies like the Muscovy Company and the Levant Company to advance the state's interests across western Asia. By the time the East India Company emerged at the turn of the following century, England was spearheading the model of 'outsourcing' its imperial adventures. Elizabethan colonial corporations did not have to worry about maintaining their honour in the same way state representatives did, enabling companies to feign deference to a local ruler or commit horrific acts of violence in a way that might bring shame on national soldiers but not on privateers.[47] The colonial corporation was a tool also used by other European empires, but nowhere else used as many private companies in its imperial effort for as long or as successfully, with only the Dutch East India Company being possible competition to the production line of British imperial trading ventures. From the sixteenth-century Levant Company to the Royal Niger Company of the late nineteenth century, much of the dirty work of actually administrating Britain's vast empire was outsourced to private corporations.

This outsourcing of empire has aided the contemporary amnesia we have about the British Empire. After decolonisation, the likes of Powell were able to deny British imperialism because, even at its Victorian peak, the empire often remained one step removed from the minds of everyday British people. It wasn't that the empire didn't matter, but rather it mattered too much in the eyes of the country's elite to be left to the whims of an unpredictable, uneducated general public. In their specific modes and with varying degrees of collaboration with the state, the colonial companies were able to keep much of the project of empire encased within the domain of private enterprise. Vast territories of the globe became company property; human beings dying on board a slave ship became lost merchandise that the owners could claim on insurance. The outsourcing of empire continues to have a neutral-ising impact on our collective memory of the imperial period, shrouding the racism and violence that took place across the empire under a cloud of technical legalese. After all, account books and financial interests are boring and private, not topics to be discussed openly in polite society. Few want to read about the contracts and title deeds of the East India Company or the African Company of Merchants. We all tend to try and avoid thinking about the nuances of ownership in property law or the binding force of contractual terms until they affect our own lives. Therefore, with so much of the empire managed by corporate interests, moments of conquest or defeat could slip quietly out of the public's national memory and into the accounting files of back-room company offices.

The Private over the Public

The story of Serco's skyrocketing pandemic profits is just the latest chapter in the much longer tale of the intimate relationship between the British state and private corporate power. Contemporary outsourcing speaks to the way in which the British state evolved to privilege private fields of law over the laws of the state. Victorian constitutional jurist Sir Henry Maine once proclaimed that the development of societies followed 'the movement from Status to Contract' – in other words, the shift in social relations from hierarchy to reciprocity. Undeveloped societies care about centralised authority, the hoarding of power within a single sovereign; civilised societies recognise the benefits of dispersing power through exclusive agreement. This was the genius of the English legal tradition in the eyes of the finest legal minds of the empire – the use of the contract as a more sophisticated mechanism of conquest and control. The English legal system emerged to provide strong protections for property owners and merchants from the interventionist tendencies of the Crown; these protections could be used to subdue foreign rulers as well. Legal agreements were mobilised to give acts of coercion the sheen of legitimacy and the thirst for profit used to entice private actors to travel to the tropics and take on the responsibility of governance.

The anti-statism of the English legal system and outsourcing of the British Empire helped build the scaffolding of global capitalism over which much of our contemporary global economy continues to hang. So much of the empire was produced not by marauding army generals or fanatical missionaries but by those most unglamorous of people, the private lawyers, sitting in dusty basement offices across the British Empire and connecting its wealth across borders. If poets are called the unacknowledged legislators of the world, as the writer Samuel Taylor Coleridge famously declared, then lawyers are the unacknowledged 'wealth-creators'. Where others might focus on the statesmen who draft grand constitutions, England has always privileged the private lawyer who, through their penning of contracts, property deeds and wills of inheritance, can turn an object into an asset, the inanimate into income, possession into capital. The private lawyer is the alchemist who can turn property into wealth. As legal scholar Katharina Pistor has shown, whether that property is land, an idea or a promise to repay a loan, it will need a system of law that recognises the exclusive claim of the asset owner in order to be of value.[48] And, across the world, the chosen system of law for asset owners has been English common law. Not only does this legal system echo throughout the world thanks to the imperial legacy, but in England, the private lawyer has been able to cannibalise more of the public realm than in any other jurisdiction.

Part of the counter-offensive against the demands of decolonisation that emerged in the middle of the twentieth century was the recruitment of a great army of private lawyers to protect the flow of property claims across the world from the grasping hands of the new sovereign governments. The job of this army was to shepherd the movement of property, copyright, shares, stocks and credit swaps across the whole world, but many of these lawyers are still stationed in London, in the financial and commercial centres of the Square Mile and Canary Wharf. The number of solicitors has grown exponentially in Britain over the past fifty years, outpacing the growth of the wider population. While the total national population grew by around 9 per cent over the past thirty years, the number of solicitors working in England and Wales has grown by over 300 per cent during the same period.[49] The UK also has more accountants per capita than anywhere else.[50] In 2019, disputes between foreign companies made up 70 per cent of the cases heard in London's Commercial Court.[51] Thanks to the generous leeway that the British state has long granted the private sector, much of the world's assets are traded through this country's legal and financial system. Give companies the choice of which country's legal system they want to govern their contract, and they will choose England's. This may be great news for the bank balances of City traders, lawyers and accountants, but has it benefited the country as a whole?

Coming back to the image of history not as a line but as a boomerang, the failings and limitations of the British state today reflect the consequences of the logic of outsourcing that for so long it exported around the world. The commercialised structure of British imperialism impacted not just the places it was tested out on across the world but has also stunted the development of the state back home. Many of the elements of the British state that Enoch Powell presented as evidence of its unique providence, as signs that this state was organic where others were manufactured, are actually just examples of the remnants of feudalism that had survived beyond their expiry date thanks to the distractions of empire. The anomalies of the British state betray its history as a compromise between medieval political authorities and private capitalist interests rather than showing it as a standard of a modern, democratic nation state. The upper chamber of Parliament, the House of Lords, is still among the least democratic legislative houses in the world. Hereditary legislators were removed in most places in the early twentieth century, but still sit in the Lords. Britain is also the only country to still offer automatic seats in Parliament for religious clerics other than the theocratic Islamic Republic of Iran. The financial district of London, better known as 'the City', enjoys a jurisdictional quasi-autonomy reminiscent of feudalism, even having a permanent, unelected representative seated in Parliament to protect its interests – the ominously named Remembrancer. The head of state and the head of the Church of England are same person, the ruling monarch, meaning there is no formal separation between the church and the state. If, at the time of decolonisation, the former colonies had introduced many of the quirks of Britain's constitutional system into their state structures, they would have been taken as evidence that these places are still not yet fully 'developed'.

After the empire's abrupt end, the likes of Powell sought to downplay its impact on Britain. Powell's onset of imperial amnesia proclaimed that 'the nationhood of the mother country remained unaltered through it all, almost unconscious of the strange fantastic structure built around her'.[52] Yet the anomalies of Britain's state system start to become clearer when we appreciate that the UK was itself a product of the empire, not just its possessor. If we insist on viewing history as Powell's continuous line in which Britain is leading humanity along the path of development, then an honest examination of its state institutions suggests that the pioneer strayed from the path during its imperial adventures, leaving it with a political system that is, in many ways, stuck in transition. Britain's early conversion to nation state form, combined with imperial riches, meant that – like the classic Hollywood child star – it was stunted in its overall development, shielded by early wealth and privilege from the growing pains that other countries had to endure to form their own state.

The Boomerang of the Outsourced State

The commercial opportunities of empire brought the British state together in the first place. Scotland's national poet Robert Burns famously decried the noblemen who had signed the Acts of Union as having been 'bought and sold for English gold', because it was only after their own colonial company had failed to establish the colony of 'New Caledonia' in what is now Panama that they embraced unification with England and its own burgeoning empire. To Burns and other Scottish nationalists, their colonial investors had accepted the jurisdiction of Westminster so they could write off their own financial losses – the Union offered them the perfect insolvency insurance policy. Once the British Empire ended, the glue that had first held the Union together was lost, and the distinct nations of the Westminster state have been drifting further and further apart ever since. On 6 September 2014, the country opened newspapers and turned on televisions and was shocked to see the UK facing a terminal diagnosis. The poll numbers for the Scottish independence referendum, which the unionists expected to be to a comfortable victory, showed that the campaign for independence now held a slight lead with just over a week to go before voting.[53] A sigh of relief flowed through the halls of Westminster when the unionists were able to eventually gain victory in the referendum held the following week, albeit with a narrower margin than expected at the start of the campaign. But it would prove a pyrrhic victory, as the years that followed have intensified the tensions between Scotland and England, Brexit having increased the political distance between the two countries. At the time of writing, in May 2021, the Scottish people had elected a pro-independence majority to the Scottish Parliament, with the ruling Scottish National Party promising to pursue another referendum.

When, at the start of the twentieth century, Joseph Chamberlain called for an imperial federation to transform a decentralised and outsourced empire into a single state, he did so out of concern not just over Britain's ability to hold on to its overseas territories but over its ability to keep its own union together. Calls for 'home rule' were already coming from the Celtic nations of Britain. With the structure of an imperial federation, Westminster could have granted Scotland, Ireland and Wales their own federal autonomy alongside the settler colonies, keeping them within the Union but at a greater distance. The United Kingdom of Great Britain and Ireland had come together over the past few centuries through a process of absorption rather than federation – each constituent part had been fully absorbed into the whole, with all sovereignty stripped from each individual country once it became part of the Union.[54] Yet tensions between the unified projection of Britishness and the centralisation of all sovereignty within the English parliament at Westminster would occasionally erupt, in moments like the Scottish Highlands clearances or Irish rebellions of the late eighteenth century. By the late nineteenth century, it had become clear that calls for greater self-government threatened the British system, not only in far-off colonies but on the islands of the Union as well. Chamberlain's deep opposition to Irish home rule came from his conviction that if one part of the British political project started to break off, then you would eventually see the dissolution of, first, the whole empire, and then the Union itself. On the other hand, if you wanted to bind the different parts of the British nation state together, then you also had to include the other, far-flung territories that had been co-constituted with the Union from its very beginning.

If there is any doubt about the importance of the empire to Britain's internal coherence, we need only observe the difficulty with which the state once known as the United Kingdom of Great Britain and Ireland has been struggling to hold itself together without it. Enoch Powell considered the devolution of power to Scotland, Wales or Northern Ireland to be 'constitutional nonsense', fearing it would lead to Britain becoming a federal state and a Supreme Court being established that could challenge the supremacy of Parliament.[55] After fighting so hard to save the empire, Powell also insisted that Britain cut ties with former colonies after independence and not engage with the Commonwealth system that came afterwards, or it would stunt the development of true British nationalism.[56] Britain had to erase all traces of the empire in order to not face the trauma of the break-up, and for Powell, the Commonwealth was but a sad reminder of all that once was. Today, Powell's fears for the Union appear to have been well founded. The Republic of Ireland was the first to flee the Union in the aftermath of the First World War; the rest of the twentieth century saw Northern Ireland plunged into a bloody civil war as it fought its way to a compromised position of autonomy within the Union, around the same time that Wales and Scotland were also gaining their own parliamentary bodies to take a large amount of the governing power away from Westminster.

Devolution of power to each individual country in 1998 was supposed to stop the breakdown of the Union, but it only seemed to fuel nationalist passions further. The crisis of Brexit has also opened the possibility of a final severing of ties between Northern Ireland and the rest of the Union. After decades of conflict, the Good Friday Agreement allowed an uneasy peace to settle in Northern Ireland, at least until the decision taken by the rest of the Union to leave the EU raised significant questions for the country, which shares a land border with the EU. The disruption has led to growing pressure for the question of whether Northern Ireland should be in Britain or Ireland to be settled once and for all, with a 2019 poll showing that there is a slight majority in favour of Irish reunification among the population of Northern Ireland, including nearly one in five people from unionist backgrounds saying they think Brexit strengthens the case for Northern Ireland to leave the Union and rejoin the rest of Ireland.[57] The feeling appears to be mutual, with a majority of British people now saying they no longer care if Northern Ireland stays in the Union or not.[58]

The Return of Sovereignty

At the start of the twentieth century, while dreaming of bringing about a federal Greater Britain spanning the globe, Joseph Chamberlain proclaimed that 'the day of small nations has passed away; the day of Empires has come'.[59] The weight of his statement must have felt heavy to those frustrated delegates from the NCBWA sailing back to West Africa after their unsuccessful 1920 trip to London.

Yet Chamberlain's vision had completely misread the shifts and tensions that the coming century would bring. Chamberlain died in 1914, the first year of the First World War, which would help to call time on the world of empires. After the First World War, support for the imperial federation declined and although proposals kept on being discussed by British politicians up until the Imperial Conference in 1937, it was no longer a serious prospect. Contemporary champion of the British Empire, Niall Ferguson, has even gone as far as describing Britain's entry into the First World War as 'the biggest error in modern history'.[60] Following the war, calls for greater self-government heightened the pressure on the British system. By the last decades of the twentieth century, *Greater Britannia* had disintegrated into a plethora of independent nation states, almost entirely disconnected from each other politically outside of the paper-thin binding of the post-imperial organisation known as the Commonwealth.

While the NCBWA's trip to London ended in disappointment, it would have an abiding influence on the city. The student groups delegates spoke to took up the cause of self-government for the colonies.[61] Four years after the NCBWA sailed home, the West African Students Union was founded in London. In the aftermath of another world war, the union's vice-president was a young West African autodidact recently arrived in London. Born in a village to a largely illiterate family from the Gold Coast, by 1945 Kwame Nkrumah was travelling to the capital of the British Empire to undertake a PhD at the London School of Economics. An intense and impatient young man, in the UK Nkrumah found himself immersed in a community of young radicals who had also travelled to Britain from the colonies. His circle included George Padmore, a future legendary Trinidadian writer, and Jomo Kenyatta, an anti-colonial activist who would go on to become the first president of Kenya after independence. Together they analysed the similarities in their experiences of life as black men under the British Empire, even though they had grown up oceans apart. Like Froude, Seeley and Powell, Nkrumah noticed the dispassion and disinterest with which most people across the country appeared to view their own empire. He describes how 'there was nothing to stop you getting on your feet and denouncing the whole British Empire'; even if they knew what you were talking about, nobody cared.[62] When he travelled to Manchester in October 1945 to attend the Fifth Pan-African Congress he had organised with Padmore, Nkrumah was shocked that this meeting of what would become anti-colonial leaders was wholly ignored by the British press.

Nkrumah would never complete his PhD. While in London, he was invited back to the Gold Coast by J. B. Danquah, himself a protégé of Joseph Casely-Hayford and the NCBWA. Danquah was part of a group of lawyers, academics and politicians who wanted to finish the job the NCBWA had started and had formed the first political party in the Gold Coast in an attempt to pressure Britain into granting more powers of self-rule to local leaders. However, having seen the disintegration of the NCBWA a few years earlier, Danquah wanted to avoid the same mistake of being unrepresentative of the general population, so he looked to appoint someone from outside the elite families of the colony, who might be able to communicate their message to the masses. Nkrumah was chosen to serve as Danquah's general secretary, and in 1947 he returned to an Accra saturated by the atmosphere of rebellion, to join a growing campaign calling for 'self-government in the shortest possible time'. Nkrumah's initial message to the masses was that whether you were a farmer, a teacher, a nurse or a gold miner, all your problems would be solved with self-government. He told them to 'seek ye first the political kingdom and all things shall be added unto you'.[63] The assumption behind this statement was that power lay within the realm of sovereignty, within the power to make laws, elect politicians and have your own state. This power was being denied by the British imperial presence. Statehood was to be the salvation; sovereignty would open the door for a new Africa to emerge.

First the NCBWA and then Nkrumah's calls for powers of self-rule point to the shifting form of sovereignty over the past century. When the NCBWA set sail for London, sovereignty was the key to being able to decide your own fate in the world. Sovereignty was a treasure jealously guarded by Britain and a small group of world powers. Today, politics in Britain, as in much of the developed world, is driven by its own search for sovereignty. Britain is supposed to sit at the core of the world system, a permanent member of the exclusive club of nations that are actually able to exercise power in the world. Yet even the old imperial heartland is now beset by a real feeling that, as a collective, we have lost the ability to determine the destinies of our lives. Anger and frustration are heightened as this is not the way we expected the world to be thanks to the narrative of history-as-a-line we were raised on. Nkrumah's journey once he returned to the Gold Coast opens up a different story about sovereignty. After eventually leading the African continent in the process of decolonisation, he like many others of his generation, would be forced to wrestle with the realisation of just how much the power of empire lay not in the hands of sovereignty but within the private realm of capitalism – in property deeds, contracts and trusts. Taking sovereignty back from Westminster only opened up new points of conflict: this time with the multinational corporations to whom Britain had always outsourced much of the imperial project.

2

The Company

In the first decade of the twentieth century, a burly, moustachioed British businessman called William Knox D'Arcy began an audacious search for oil in Persia. After raising money from investors at home, D'Arcy was able to get a contract from the Shah of Persia for the right to explore for oil across 480,000 square miles of land (around five times the size of the UK) for sixty years, in exchange for £20,000 and 16 per cent of the profits he would make from any oil found.[1] With his contract in hand, D'Arcy sent his team of engineers into the desert to search for his fortune. Initially, his efforts appeared fruitless, and by 1908 his financial partners' patience was exhausted. He was told by his financers that if the engineers had not found any oil by the time that they reached 1,500 feet below the surface, then they would be pulling their money out and the search would be abandoned. As D'Arcy was losing heart, at 4 a.m. on 26 May 1908, one of his drills finally hit oil at 1,179 feet. British imperial soldiers were immediately called to surround the area and protect this new treasure trove from any local threat.[2] That day, the first of the great Middle Eastern oilfields was born – and the river of black gold has not stopped flowing since. The personal rewards for D'Arcy were immense – soon afterwards he became the director of a new company that would one day become Britain's richest corporation. Originally known as the Anglo-Persian Oil Company, D'Arcy's oil discovery was the birth of British Petroleum or, as we call it today, BP.

BP currently bestrides the globe as one of the largest multi-national companies in the world, but a century ago, it was just an ambitious private initiative, albeit one working in tandem with British imperial policy. The birth of the Anglo-Persian Oil Company epitomised the spread of enormous oil and gas companies that have come to dominate the world's energy market, but it began life as just the latest in a long line of corporate bodies that played a key role in extending Britain's imperial reach across the globe. Its operations in Persia served to solidify Britain's influence in an area that was home to one of the oldest civilisations in the world. During the First World War, Britain occupied much of the country, and while it didn't become a formal colony, as part of what was called 'Britain's informal empire' Persia remained a key part of the British world system. On Winston Churchill's recommendation, the British government bought a percentage of the firm. The government's stake came in useful to power the country's war efforts. The alliance between the British state and the Anglo-Persian Oil Company once again highlights the importance of corporate power to the structures of British imperialism, even deep into the twentieth century.

Colonialism and the Birth of the Commercial Corporation

Of all the inventions the British Empire gave to the world, perhaps the most significant, despite being rarely mentioned, was the modern, commercial corporation. A corporation can be generally defined as an entity, created by law, to exist as a separate thing to the individuals that created it. The corporation has a legal life, not a natural one. Like the monarchy or the church, it is something different to the individuals who make it up – a shareholder is not a company just as the Queen isn't the monarchy. The corporate model is the ideal legal structure to allow an organisation to outlive its members and, in turn, allow the members to be protected from being personally liable for the actions the organisation undertakes. In the medieval age, corporations were mainly bodies created for a social purpose – churches, charities and other organisations committed to a collective, long-term social good. Corporate charters allowed the organisation to continue with its benevolent work long after the founders were willing, or able, to pursue it.[3]

However, as Europeans began to embark on imperial explorations, the corporate form became the ideal organisational vehicle for those who wanted to enjoy the riches of empire but be protected from the risk. The joint-stock corporation began to emerge through imperial voyages, where the 'stock' that would be carried back on the ship would be shared among the corporation's owners. The first joint-stock corporation in England was the Muscovy Company, which was granted a royal charter of incorporation in 1555 by Mary I. Bringing together the corporate legal structure and the older idea of a company – a collection of people coming together to break bread among themselves – the early imperial age solidified the idea of the commercial company, with the Levant Company receiving its charter in 1592 and the East India Company in 1600.[4] Investors did not even have to leave the comfort of their own homes to get a taste of the bounty that these companies were plundering across the seas. From 1571, a 'share' of the company's 'stock' could be bought on the London Stock Exchange, allowing investors to simply stay at home and wait for their share of the colonial pie.

Sitting in grand mahogany offices across the cities of Britain, men who were, until very recently, memorialised as entrepreneurs and philanthropists – like Royal African Company Deputy Governor Edward Colston or South Sea Company shareholder Thomas Guy – were able to profit from colonial expeditions while remaining removed from the bloodshed and brutality being visited upon men, women and children in foreign lands in order to guarantee a return on their investments. Yet, as shown by the history of outsourcing, despite the legal structure marking these commercial corporations out as private initiatives, there was never a clean separation between the British state and these colonial companies during the age of empire. Company directors would often also be sitting as Members of Parliament, and the state would look to these companies to make philanthropic donations and build infrastructure back in Britain. This is why, even in twenty-first-century Britain, so many of the buildings, schools and concert halls that we walk past every day carry the names of these colonial companies or their directors.

In June 2020 the national myth of liberal, tolerant Britain and the legacy these colonial companies left behind collided, resulting in an eruption of tension when a statue of Edward Colston in the centre of Bristol was torn down by Black Lives Matter protesters, before being thrown into Bristol harbour. Colston had been a prominent member of the Royal African Company (RAC), which was incorporated in 1660 and enjoyed a monopoly over the English trade in slaves from the West African coast to the Americas. It is estimated that during Colston's time at the RAC, 84,500 men, women and children were taken by the company's ships from their homes in West Africa to suffer a life of slavery in the New World, with a quarter of them not even surviving the journey, so horrific were the conditions aboard ship.[5] The image of Colston's statue being thrown in the river by a multi-racial group of young protesters has become a symbol of a new generation's demand for Britain to finally reckon with its suppressed colonial past. The outpouring of rage witnessed in the Black Lives Matter protests provoked local authorities and public institutions across the country to reconsider the names that make up the public spaces of Britain's cities.

This event provoked a backlash from critics who accused the protesters of erasing history. They pointed to Colston's reputation as a great philanthropist, someone who, in donating to schools, churches and charities across the city of Bristol, did a lot to help the poor of Britain, even if he enriched himself through the dehumanisation of Africans. This argument, often provided when-ever a challenge to the legacy of these old colonial companies is offered, not only draws a false equivalence between the value of buildings and the value of massacred men, women and children but also misunderstands the role of the commercial corporation in the age of empires. Before the passing of the Registration Act of 1844 and the Joint Stock Company Act of 1856 ended the requirement for firms to be incorporated by the ruling sovereign, colonial companies needed to be granted a royal charter to exist, and in order to get that charter they would have to show they carried some sort of social purpose, however broadly defined, similar to the charitable idea of the corporation that had existed in the medieval age. This is why the East India Company or the Virginia Company would speak so fondly of social benefit and the good of the nation.[6] The Hudson Bay Company donated money to charity hospitals across London and took apprentice boys from orphanages not simply out of a passionate concern for the offspring of the poor, but because its founding charter tied its trading monopoly to a commitment to 'promote all Endeavours tending to the publick Good of our People'.[7] The 'philanthropy' of colonial companies and their directors wasn't simply an attempt to do social good to help balance out the bad things, it wasn't even a cynical public-relations attempt at what we today might call corporate social responsibility. Rather, their charity was a necessary requirement to be able to sin in the first place, some-thing you had to commit to if you wanted to receive the right to incorporate and profit from lucrative trading monopolies. Celebrating the philanthropy of the old colonial companies and their directors is the equivalent of celebrating a plane hijacker for having bought a flight ticket beforehand.

The scale of these colonial companies grew to such an extent that they became a new type of global power; by the start of the nineteenth century, for example, the East India Company commanded a private army that was larger than the British army at that time.[8] Earning its epithet of the *company-state*, the East India Company functioned as the de facto sovereign on the Indian subcontinent for nearly two centuries, before Westminster took control of the region after the Indian Rebellion of 1857.[9] The Hudson Bay Company in North America also served as a quasi state, as did the Royal Niger Company in West Africa for a period of time. All these corporations at their height owned vast swathes of territory, wielded huge military forces, made and enforced laws, collected taxes, wrestled with questions of population governance and had an effect on world-historical events, such as the Opium Wars or the 'Scramble for Africa.'[10] The royal charter of the Royal Niger Company gave the company 'powers for the purposes of government, preservation of public order, protection of the said territories'.[11]

Today, we think of colonialism as this bloodstained history of conflicts between nations or even a clash between 'races'. However, it was to a large extent a corporate endeavour, with private companies serving as makeshift state governments across the world. When the colonies began to gain their sovereignty in the middle of the twentieth century, the stage was set for a clash between the power of Britain's colonial companies and the power of newly independent nation states. Whose claim to ownership of the lands that underwrote the global market would prevail in this new world of nations?

The Company in the World of Nations

The end of the world of empires and the rise of nationalist leaders across Asia and Africa left firms like the Anglo-Persian Oil Company facing a troubling future. In 1951, rising tensions came to a head for the company in an early example of the conflict between multinational corporate power and what would become known as 'Third World' nationalism. The spark was the election of Mohammad Mosaddegh as prime minister of the country which had renamed itself Iran. Mosaddegh's political programme of nationalisation meant a clash with British oil interests was inevitable. The Anglo-Persian Oil Company felt that they alone had been responsible for nurturing the oil industry in the region and that the company's property rights to its oilfields should be respected, despite the sovereignty being claimed by the new Iranian government. The company had changed its name from Anglo-Persian Oil to Anglo-Iranian Oil in 1935 to reflect the changing times, but beyond this rebranding they weren't giving up anything else, least of all the profits they were enjoying. The year before Mosaddegh's election win, the Anglo-Iranian Oil Company (AIOC) registered profits of £170 million (around £5 billion in 2020). Yet they were unwilling to renegotiate the terms of their deal with Iran, not even in light of the recent agreement by the American-owned Arabian-American Oil Company to a fifty-fifty split with Saudi Arabia.[12]

Frustrated by the failure of negotiations with the company, Mosaddegh decided to tackle them head-on. He decided to nationalise the oil industry and expel foreign companies from the oil-producing city of Abadan.[13] On 1 May 1951, Mosaddegh seized the assets of the AIOC. His justification for this action was that, if sovereignty was going to mean anything in the new world of nations, then the oil produced on land within the sovereign state of Iran belonged first and foremost to the people of Iran. The plan for nationalisation included a provision for the Iranian government to give 25 per cent of the profits they made from the oilfields to the AIOC as compensation for their loss. For the directors of the company and their allies in the British government, this offer of compensation was just a further insult. Britain immediately used its global influence to put pressure on other countries so that they would not accept the oil being produced by the Iranian government. To the British, Iran nationalising the oilfields was theft of property, plain and simple; for Mosaddegh's government, all they were doing was returning property back to its rightful owners.

The Coup

The Westminster government in charge at the start of the Abadan crisis was the same government that is now widely canonised as the most progressive in British history. With the empire disappearing in the aftermath of the world wars, Prime Minister Clement Attlee's Labour government led the reorganisation of the country. This included embarking upon an expansion in unemployment insurance and council housing, and giving birth to the National Health Service. Part of this project included the nationalisation of private industries. Over the course of just one term in office, Attlee took into public ownership the essential but fiscally unproductive industries of gas, electricity and coal and the railways.

Given the circumstances, the Attlee government might have been expected to have some understanding of Mosaddegh's desire to use his nation's resources to invest in the education, health and welfare of his citizens. Yet, if the Iranians were expecting sympathy from a progressive Labour government, they were soon to be disappointed. The government's first instinct upon hearing of Mosaddegh's nationalisation was to launch a military invasion of Iran to take back the oilfields by force. Labour's Foreign Secretary, Herbert Morrison, grandfather to Peter Mandelson, had been a conscientious objector during the First World War, but in the face of this brazen display of Iranian muscular sovereignty he transformed into a war-mongering hawk, calling for some old-fashioned gunboat diplomacy to deal with the upstart natives.[14] However, with the UK still counting the costs of the Second World War and already committing military forces to support the USA's campaign in Korea, a full-on military invasion would have been an expensive endeavour.

As an alternative, the Attlee government imposed a naval blockade and economic sanctions on Iran, blocking Iranian industries' ability to access key British exports, like steel, and freezing Iranian bank accounts held with British banks. Britain then submitted a formal complaint to the recently formed United Nations, claiming that Iran's nationalisation actions had placed world peace at risk. To the shock and embarrassment of the government, they were unable to secure enough votes in the UN

Security Council to support their claim. They then took Iran to the International Court of Justice, where the Iranians used Britain's old 'separation' of official foreign policy and British corporate interests, which had previously aided imperial power, against them. International law could only intervene in a dispute between two sovereign nations like Iran and the UK, not in a dispute between Iran and a private corporation. If the AIOC was just a private company separated from the British state, as Britain had always claimed of its colonial companies, then there was no need for international law to get involved.[15]

With legal routes exhausted and the military option seemingly unviable, the British government eventually turned to more under-hand options for dealing with the Iranian problem. As the crisis dragged on, Attlee's Labour government was replaced by the Conservatives in October 1951, ushering back into power an old ally and one-time paid consultant of the AIOC, Winston Churchill. Churchill's government mobilised the anti-communist fears of the USA and, in 1953, with new president Ike Eisenhower and his administration fearing that Mosaddegh's success could inspire even more radical policies by governments across Asia, Latin America and Africa, American support for drastic action in Iran was secured.[16] Documents declassified in 2017 detail the precursor meetings held in 1952 between Sir Christopher Steel of the British Embassy in Washington and the US Assistant Secretary of State Henry Byroade in order to organise a coup against Mosaddegh in Iran, codenamed Operation Ajax.[17]

In August 1953, the USA and the UK teamed up with wealthy Iranian military general Fazlollah Zahedi to stage a riot that led to Mosaddegh being removed from office and placed first in prison and then under house arrest. He would stay under house arrest until his death in 1967. Zahedi succeeded Mosaddegh as prime minister, and with a new pro-Western administration in place, the AIOC regained its oilfields. Of course, as any good businessperson knows, the best way to rescue a brand damaged by controversy is to change the name, so following the coup, the

AIOC rebranded itself as British Petroleum. Though it was still the main producer of Iranian oil, British Petroleum now had to share its resources with American oil companies as the USA collected its pound of flesh for having rescued Britain. Britain had essentially sacrificed its oil monopoly in south-west Asia in an attempt to smother this outbreak of Third World nationalism in its crib. The USA took the opportunity to supersede Britain as the dominant foreign power in the region. But British Petroleum had emerged victorious from this early confrontation between the old colonial company and new sovereignty. The coup in Iran set the tone for how threats from democratically elected Third World governments towards transnational corporate interests would be dealt with in the world after empire.[18] The tragic fate of Mosaddegh was a warning to all people across the world excited by the promise of decolonisation: be careful, sovereignty is not the saviour you think it is.

The Age of Sovereignty

On the day of the Brexit referendum, a Lord Ashcroft poll recorded that nearly half the people who voted leave said they did so because they felt that Britain was losing its sovereignty.[19] The winning slogan of 'take back control' captured the feelings of frustration of many people across the country. For years, there had been an increasing feeling that Britain's ability to determine what goes on within its own national jurisdiction had somehow been stolen. A number of culprits were blamed for this theft, from the opaque European institutions in Brussels deemed too far removed from British life to the immigrant, religious or racial minority communities who, in the eyes of many, were now far too close. But rarely included in this line-up of suspects for the crime of 'stealing democracy' were the multinational companies that had dominated the world economy over the past fifty years. Erased from the Brexit narrative was any analysis of how the corporatisation of life after empire had helped to create a world in which the movement of wealth was independent of the potentially turbulent will of the demos. Different states still wield unequal levels of power in our world, but the triumph of the transnational corporation in the aftermath of empire has led to the value of national sovereignty in relation to the economy being watered down across the board. The tale of Mosaddegh and the AIOC prophesied the world of recent years, where the ability of nation states to use sovereignty as a shield against global corporate power feels increasingly weak.

The failure of Mosaddegh's plan was not inevitable. At the time, all talk was of national sovereignty, a concept that millions of people across the world were using to mobilise their claims of freedom. The new institutional home for international law, the United Nations, was founded on the principle of sovereign equality.[20] Alongside the UN came rising trends towards decolonisation, Keynesian economics, the Bretton Woods currency exchange system, and the European welfare state, all of which, in different ways, pointed to the ascendency of the independent nation state in the age of sovereignty. In 1951, *Time* magazine celebrated Mosaddegh as the man of the year, so much did he seem to represent the coming future.[21]

Yet Mosaddegh, like many other Third World leaders at that time, had made the mistake of falling for the fairy tale. Sovereignty did not equal control. Much like today, the focus on seizing and wielding the instrument of sovereignty in the world after empire underplayed the enduring power of the realm of private law, contracts and property. If the conflict between Mosaddegh and the AIOC exposed the limitations of sovereignty back in 1953, how should we understand the same concept in the twenty-first century? If sovereignty was unable to bring to heel the corporate power of the AIOC, what does it mean in a world where, with the touch of a keypad in Frankfurt, Shanghai or Tokyo, jobs can disappear and factories can close in Sunderland, Stockport or Milton Keynes?

In his classic 1957 text *The King's Two Bodies*, the political

theorist Ernst Kantorowicz describes our most common understanding of sovereignty – to have supreme authority over a clearly
defined territorial boundary.[22] But, crucially, this authority also
relies on being recognised as such by other sovereign authorities.
For example, many a leader of an indigenous American community in the sixteenth century found there were dangers in facing
invading Spanish conquistadors who did not recognise their sovereign authority over their land. In terms of international law,
sovereignty depended on reciprocity. You were sovereign not just
because you were the ultimate authority within your land, but
also because other sovereigns recognised you as their counterpart.
And for centuries, European empires only recognised *each other*
as fellow sovereigns. The Westphalian Peace of 1648, the agreement
that ended religious war in Europe, became the template for the
international mutual recognition of sovereignty. Of course, this
system didn't always hold together in practice, as the world wars
make clear. Still, until the mid-twentieth century, the recognition
of sovereignty was a luxury beyond the reach of the majority of
the world's people. Then decolonisation began, suddenly expanding
the narrow list of who counted as a sovereign.

At the time of its creation, the United Nations did not necessarily
expect to be the institution that would rubber stamp the process of
turning the colonies of the world into independent nation states.
The UN charter of 1945 was weaker than its predecessor, that of
the League of Nations, in confronting the issue of empire, and
did not suggest any moves towards decolonisation, nor to subject
colonial territories to international oversight, as the League had
done. All the charter asked of the great empires was to agree to
promote the 'well-being' of the inhabitants of their colonies.[23]
In the lead-up to the San Francisco Conference where the UN
was created, Britain had influenced the USA into abandoning its
initial proposals to let the UN enjoy supervisory powers over all
colonial territories.[24] The UN was established as the foundational
institution of the world of nations but it was also supposed to
protect the old privileges of the world of empires. Yet, as more

and more countries fought for and won their independence, the balance of power within the institution began to tip away from the former imperial powers. The new nations began to pressure the UN into taking a bolder position on decolonisation. In 1960, the UN General Assembly adopted resolution 1514 (XV), better known as the *Declaration on the Granting of Independence to Colonial Countries and Peoples*, a resolution which enshrined the UN's support of independence, self-determination and decolonisation. The following year, the UN created the Special Committee on Decolonisation, completing its transition from being an institution that began life as a wartime alliance between Britain, America, France and the Soviet Union into the vehicle through which peoples from Africa, Asia and the Caribbean could ensure that their revolts against colonial rule were legitimised by international law.

Of course, despite its stated commitment to sovereign equality, the UN was not a wholly egalitarian institution. Its structure revealed underlying hierarchies still existing between member states, most visibly via the UK, America, France, Russia and China having permanent seats on the Security Council. Furthermore, the UN's concepts of key legal principles like sovereignty were drawn from the political traditions of only a few countries, with Britain's idea of parliamentary sovereignty being among the foremost influences. The transition of places like Sudan, Nigeria and Kenya to being sovereign entities in their own right was limited by pressure for newly decolonised nations to meet a standard of state infrastructure that was determined by their former European colonisers, even if the Europeans didn't always follow these rules themselves. In the new world of the UN, every state should have one nation; every nation should have its own state; and each nation state should resemble the European nation state that had previously colonised it as closely as possible. Having struggled so hard for their independence, the former colonies were now free to do as they were told.

By effectively forcing 'new' nation states to follow the model of parliamentary democracy, sovereignty in the decolonised world would give new strength to the idea of Westminster as the 'mother of parliaments', with the rest of the world following its example in one unbroken line. In addition, the people who headed up many of these new, decolonised governments had often been schooled in Britain. The first prime minster of India, Jawaharlal Nehru, had studied at the University of Cambridge and Inner Temple. Hastings Banda, who led Malawi to independence, was once a medical student at Edinburgh University. The leader of independent Tanzania, Julius Nyerere, also attended Edinburgh and, as previously mentioned, Kwame Nkrumah of Ghana and Jomo Kenyatta of Kenya had first become friends in London, where both had been students at the London School of Economics. Yet a sense of betrayal was felt by some British politicians at the sight of the 'native' elites that they had educated to run their colonies now turning against them. In 1931, Winston Churchill had dismissed Mahatma Gandhi as being 'a seditious Middle Temple lawyer, now posing as a fakir of a type well-known in the East, striding half-naked up the steps of the Viceregal Palace, while he is still organising and conducting a campaign of civil disobedience'.[25] Churchill's statement reveals an anger at not just what Gandhi was doing but also at who Gandhi was. Britain's imperial project had brought figures like Gandhi, Nehru, Nkrumah and Nyerere over to its elite universities in order to turn them into a comprador class – a section of the local population who saw themselves as being closer to Britain than to their countrymen and, therefore, would help sustain British rule for another generation. But following the end of the world wars, when the order of the international community started shifting, it became clear that the British Empire had inadvertently trained its own gravediggers.

The Wind of Change

A few years after the dispute between the AIOC and Mosaddegh, another crisis erupted in the region concerning state national-isation of British company property. In 1956, Gamal Abdel Nasser of Egypt announced the nationalisation of the Suez Canal and froze all the accounts of the Suez Canal Company. The Suez Canal, known as the highway to India, was key to British trade routes to and from the east. The new Conservative prime minister, Anthony Eden, damned Nasser as a 'Muslim Mussolini' and feared his brand of pan-Arabian nationalism could spread across the Arab world, undermining British interests in Iraq, Jordan, Saudi Arabia and beyond.[26] However, while the British government secured French and Israeli military support for their confrontation with Nasser, the USA turned their back on their old ally and refused to back the attempt to recapture the canal. As Enoch Powell feared, the USA had used its support of Britain against Mosaddegh to usurp Britain's role in the region and was now using its new-found global power to erase the last remnants of its former parent country's military strength.[27]

Britain's painful retreat from Suez sounded the death knell for Eden's premiership. His successor, Harold Macmillan, decided it was time to accept the terminal condition of the British Empire. On the 5 January 1960, at the start of the most tumultuous political decade of the century, he arrived in a freshly independent Ghana to curry favour with the man seen as being at the forefront of this rush of new African nations.

By the time Macmillan landed in Accra, Kwame Nkrumah was a world away from the penniless LSE student he had been just over a decade earlier. Having been recruited from university to serve as an organiser for the first political party in the Gold Coast, Nkrumah decided that the group of high-society lawyers, doctors and businessmen he was working for would never be able to organise the masses. He broke off and formed his own political party, the Convention People's Party (CPP), focused on inspiring the working people of the colony with the slogan of 'Self-government Now!' – independence would not wait any longer. In December 1949, Nkrumah wrote to the British colonial authorities declaring that if they would not respond to the growing demands for self-government then he would bring the country to a standstill by calling for a general strike.

Believing that Africans lacked the organisational capacity to pull off such a feat, the British authorities ignored Nkrumah's warnings. What the colonial administration didn't realise was that the CPP had already been asking the women who ran the bustling markets of the Gold Coast to spread the word of the strike to everyone who came to their stalls. Thanks to the hard work of these women, families across the country had already been hoarding food and money to see them through the hardship of a strike for weeks before it was announced.[28] By promoting the strike, the market women had strengthened the connection between the people, the different labour unions that would be organising it and Nkrumah's political party. On 8 January 1950, Britain's golden African colony went into shutdown. The cocoa farms and goldmines that created such healthy profits for the colonial companies who owned them lay empty as workers refused to report for duty. Nkrumah was immediately arrested and imprisoned by the authorities but, a year later, while still sitting in his prison cell, he was elected by the people to serve as the head of the new legislative assembly that had been created to quell tensions in the colony. On 12 February 1951, Kwame Nkrumah was a prisoner hated by both the British and local elites in the Gold Coast. The very next day, he was invited to Christiansborg Castle, a former slave fort that was the seat of British power in Accra, and asked by the British governor Sir Charles Aden-Clarke to serve as the prime minister of the Gold Coast.

A few years later, the Gold Coast became the independent nation of Ghana and Nkrumah the first black African president of a sovereign nation state. When Macmillan embarked on his tour of the African continent in 1960, it only made sense that he would start his journey there. The type of labour strikes that had carried Nkrumah to power in the Gold Coast had become an increasingly popular tool for trade unions and women's organisations across the continent to use in the service of gaining greater political power. The colonial fantasy of Africans as living in exotic tribal communities, free of the types of class consciousness that could be seen across Europe at the time, fell apart. If the workers of the Gold Coast had been able to bring about their own state through organised labour struggles, the British authorities realised that it wouldn't be long before people in neighbouring African colonies began to follow suit. With the increasing militancy of the local populations, the cost of maintaining the empire was starting to outweigh the benefits.[29] Despite appearing to be just the latest gentleman imperialist coming through an Eton–Oxbridge–Conservative Party production line, as prime minister, Macmillan differed from his predecessors in deciding to submit to the tide of independence movements rather than drown himself trying to swim against it.

A few days into his stay in Accra, Nkrumah hosted Macmillan at a giant state banquet. For all the diplomatic pleasantries, the air was thick with tension as attendees waited to see how the British prime minister would respond to the dramatic changes taking place on the continent. It was at this dinner that Macmillan gave the first clear indication that the British government was giving up the fight against decolonisation. Though he is more famous for giving what became known as the 'Wind of Change' speech in South Africa at the end of his tour a month later, Macmillan gave the original version in Accra at Nkrumah's state banquet. It was here that the British prime minister announced that 'the wind of change is blowing right through Africa. This rapid emergence of the countries of Africa gives the continent a new importance in the world.'[30] Today, it is really only the version of the same speech that Macmillan gave in South Africa that is remembered. The Cape Town version has come to represent the British government 'speaking frankly against the country's system of apartheid', as the BBC would say in 2005, distancing the UK from the system of violent racial segregation that survived in its former colony of South Africa up until 1994.[31] When the speech is relocated to its original site, the image of Macmillan talking about the 'wind of change' on a sweltering Accra evening makes the prime minister look less like a courageous opponent of apartheid and more like the exhausted representative of a disintegrating empire.

Nkrumah was only further encouraged in his campaign for pan-African sovereignty by Macmillan's words of concession. Towards the end of that same year, Nkrumah would strike a similar note in a speech he made to the United Nations General Assembly in New York. While addressing a packed hall filled with world leaders, what Macmillan had called 'the wind of change' Nkrumah renamed 'the flowing tide of African nationalism', which he saw as coming to transform global order.[32] A few years later he would draw on this moment even more explicitly, writing, 'The wind of change blowing through Africa is no ordinary wind, it is a raging hurricane against which the old order cannot stand.'[33]

Confidence in the world-changing potential of African sovereignty was sky-high at the start of the 1960s. Fourteen new African nation states had been born in just the nine months between Macmillan's address in Accra and Nkrumah's message to the United Nations. Today, our abiding images of revolution in the sixties may be Martin Luther King declaring 'I have a dream' on the steps of the Lincoln Memorial or the burning Vietnamese monk, Thích Quảng Đức, self-immolating in protest, but the sight of Kwame Nkrumah standing on the United Nations podium at the end of 1960, dressed not in a suit but wrapped head to toe in traditional Kente cloth, appeared to be just as transformative.[34] By then, Nkrumah was being referred to across the world by his nickname, Osagyefo – the Redeemer – and seemed to represent the coming order of global sovereign equality. Nkrumah himself had great faith in the promise of the UN to serve as midwife to this new world. In his speech, he declared 'I look upon the United Nations as the only organisation that holds out any hope for the future of mankind.'[35] With the UN supporting decolonisation, the optimism of independence leaders, who felt like they had the weight of history and international law behind them, was understandable. However, in the balance of power between sovereignty and property, major problems loomed on the horizon for the African nationalists, even at their zenith.

The Company and Decolonisation

In elevating the importance of seizing the state, Nkrumah underestimated how important the commercial element of colonial power had been to the British Empire. The economic benefits the Gold Coast provided Britain were illustrated by the colony's very name. Gold mines across the country produced enormous riches for British companies, with none more powerful than the Ashanti Goldfields Corporation, founded in 1897. By the time Nkrumah was heading towards power, the chairman of Ashanti Goldfields was the eccentric former British major general, Sir Edward Spears. A former wartime spy, a friend of Winston Churchill and once a Member of Parliament himself, Spears hoped that, like the Anglo-Iranian Oil Company, the Ashanti Goldfields Corporation could rely on the British government to protect it from the aggressions of the likes of Nkrumah, whom he dismissed as a firebrand agitator, not truly representative of the mass of Africans he presumed to lead.[36]

Spears initially hoped that he could secure formal representation for British business interests within the new, independent Ghanaian government as it was being created, similar to the way the City of London enjoys its own distinct representation in Westminster. When that was unsuccessful, he then tried to further the divisions between Nkrumah and the local Ashanti chiefs, hoping the classic divide-and-rule tactic that was used to isolate the NCBWA from the wider public at the turn of the century might put paid to Nkrumah's fledging state.[37] Spears' friend and former director at the Ashanti Goldfields corporation, Duncan Sandys, was the only member of the UK Cabinet to stand against the Gold Coast gaining the right of self-government in 1956.[38] But when Nkrumah eventually did become president, the Ashanti Goldfields Corporation was now faced with the problem that the AIOC and many other colonial companies had to confront – how would the old colonial company survive life in the decolonial state?

As it happened, Nkrumah was more cautious with regard to expropriation than Mosaddegh had been in Iran. The very small number of foreign firms that were nationalised following Ghana's independence were companies already failing, something that the Ashanti Goldfields Corporation was not in danger of. Even at the end of Nkrumah's reign, in 1966, the company was still posting pre-tax profits of over £3 million – equivalent to £56 million in 2020.[39]

Gold was not the only natural resource the Gold Coast held in abundance. Britain also exported diamonds, timber and, most profitably, cocoa from the colony to trade across the world. Nkrumah had been as easily seduced by the promise of sovereignty and development as many of his peers, and embarked on a programme to exploit those natural resources. The economy was moved away from its over-reliance on exported raw materials and towards state-led industrialisation; no longer would the country just send out raw cocoa; rather it would have its own cocoa-processing factories and sell the finished chocolate bars for a far greater profit. Ghana would also engage in huge state-led development projects, like collectivised rubber farms and the building of the Volta River Dam, an ambitious, long-planned hydroelectric scheme which created the largest artificial body of water anywhere in the world. To undertake this massive shift towards industrialisation, Nkrumah increased taxes on the business interests operating in his country. But he sought to avoid seizing the property of overseas companies – the old colonial companies could continue to profit in the new independent Ghana, but they would have to pay for the privilege.

While the Ghanaian government may not have been expropriating property, according to Spears, the tax burden it was placing on companies like the Ashanti Goldfields Corporation was 'crippling'.[40] Nkrumah also began to drift away from the more neutral position he originally took up in the Cold War.

By the mid-1960s, he was openly advocating for socialism and cultivating closer diplomatic ties with the Soviet Union. He was also becoming increasingly enamoured of his new-found powers of state. A new constitution in 1960 gave Nkrumah greater powers as president, which he used to dismiss members of the judiciary and armed forces who displeased him. The interests of the trade unions and women's organisations that had propelled him to power were sidelined in the name of loyalty to the new nation. By 1963, Nkrumah had gone from being heralded around the world as the leader of a new Africa to being damned as a 'Black Stalin' by the *New York Times*.[41] He stopped talking to members of the Western press and as his paranoia grew, so did his appetite for authoritarianism, with political opponents being detained indefinitely and public dissent suppressed.

Eventually, despite not following Mosaddegh's path of directly confronting the hangovers of corporate imperialism, Nkrumah would ultimately suffer the same fate as his Iranian counterpart. In 1966, he was overthrown by a military coup while he was on a state visit to Vietnam and China. He was replaced by a collection of army officers and police chiefs who styled themselves as the National Liberation Council (NLC). While Nkrumah was travelling abroad, Spears landed back in the country and immediately reached out to the leaders of the NLC to congratulate them.[42] To his pleasure, the NLC greatly reduced the tax burden on corporate dividends and also devalued Ghana's currency to reduce costs for foreign traders.[43] The new leaders of Ghana would follow guidance they had been given by the International Monetary Fund (IMF) and liquidate the state projects that had been so central to Nkrumah's plans for long-term economic security, selling those industries to private enterprise. Over a decade before Thatcher and Reagan brought privatisation to the Anglo-American world, the first independent sub-Saharan African nation state had experienced its own moment of 'selling the family silver', a story that would become more and more familiar over the subsequent decades.

Nkrumah had preached the gospel of sovereignty, convinced that once Ghana had gained the legal right to self-government, it could use its resources and wealth to 'catch up' with its former colonial motherland. For all his commitment to creating a distinctive pathway for a new Africa to emerge, Nkrumah's imagination was still contained within the story of development that saw former colonies following Britain's mythology: first, you gain sovereignty, then you invest in industrialisation, and that is the way you become a developed nation. But the backlash against the new-found sovereignty of the former colonies started almost as soon as Nkrumah sat down in the presidential office. Over the course of his time in power, Nkrumah witnessed how self-determination could be challenged by multinational companies invested in his ostensibly independent nation state.

Nkrumah noted that the core failing of a new nation state like Ghana was that while it may have 'all the outward trappings of international sovereignty', in practice its 'economic system and thus its political policy is directed from outside'; life was dependent not on government decisions but on external forces.[44] A fluctuation in the price of cocoa on the international markets or an executive decision made in a London boardroom by shareholders who had never been to West Africa could be enough to throw the whole country into disarray. By the time Nkrumah wrote about his disappointment with the promise of national sovereignty in his 1965 book *Neo-Colonialism: The Last Stage of Imperialism*, it was already too late. The next year he would be removed from office and would spend the rest of his life exiled from the country he had led to independence.

The Power of Property

The independence leaders who pursued sovereignty focused on just one part of the Anglo political tradition. Overlooked by the new nations coming out of the dissolution of the British Empire was how dependent the British state had been on its external advantages. Britain's liberal democracy, with its unwritten constitution and elevation of the private right to property, thrived when the state was 'expanding', but it was not the ideal model for newly independent countries looking to develop themselves. To focus on sovereignty as the key to political control is to underestimate the immense role that the private right to property played in creating the world of empire. Perhaps the independence leaders had read too much political theory and not enough literature. From Charles Dickens' *Bleak House* to Jane Austen's *Sense and Sensibility*, the most beloved stories of the British canon often make clear the deep connection between property and power on this island. The common law's prioritisation of the security of property has been weaponised against state authorities in England repeatedly over its history, from the English Civil War to the American Revolution. Perhaps inevitably, it would be wielded against those parts of Greater Britain who in the mid-twentieth century broke off and sought to claim sovereign power for themselves.

From the seventeenth century onwards, English political writers worked to define the question of individual property, with perhaps the most influential description coming from the philosopher and early investor in the Royal African Company, John Locke.[45] If we start with the idea that all humans began with common ownership of the earth, similar to how we still see the oceans, then how do we arrive at a place where land can become a commodity that certain individuals or corporations can claim private ownership over? Locke explained that this transition had happened because some people had mixed their labour with land. They had worked on a piece of land, they had developed it and, in so doing, had turned it into their individual property, to the exclusion of all others. As a result, to own property became both a marker of status and the surest guarantee of your wealth accumulating over time. As Britain moved into the eighteenth and nineteenth centuries, land ownership was no longer the preserve of the aristocracy but increasingly resided in the hands of an upwardly mobile capitalist class. Property and land overlap but are not the same thing: while the Victorian colonists claimed more and more territory for the empire, they increased the use of other forms of property that could outlive the land if necessary. By the twentieth century, rural land was being overtaken by abstract assets like stocks, bonds and other financial products as the most valuable store of property.[46] Yet the traditional rules regarding property didn't change. The same laws of private property that emerged from a compromise between the feudal aristocracy and the rising capitalist class in early imperial England, which encouraged companies to undertake imperial voyages confident that whatever treasures they plundered would belong to them to the exclusion of others, still serve as the model for transnational derivative trades, credit default swaps, claims to intellectual property, debts or digital codes today.[47]

The culture of respect for property rights became celebrated as one of Britain's great contributions to the world of nations. The model of private enterprise, underwritten by security of property, is presented by our politicians as a blessing that the British Empire bestowed on its children in a way that the French or Spanish Empires did not.[48] This line of thought holds that when the East India Company, the Anglo-Iranian Oil Company or the Ashanti Goldfields Corporation insisted on their property rights, it wasn't just for the benefit of their own profit margins, it was also actually for the benefit and development of the societies in which they were operating. By claiming ownership of invaluable resources and excluding the people who actually lived upon the land, they were teaching the locals about the sanctity of property.

Of course, the Nkrumahs and Mosaddeghs of the world were not convinced. Not only does the narrative of property rights as the unique, benevolent creation of English common law ignore the various forms of property tenure and use that indigenous communities across the world practised before colonisation, it also overlooks how property rights have been used to impoverish and dispossess people through the centuries. The history of property is also the history of transatlantic slavery, land appropriation and gentrification.[49] Property has, in practice, been mixed with ideas of race, gender and class to serve as a framework of domination – women assumed to be the property of husbands, slaves the property of their masters. Following decolonisation, a narrow conception of property was mobilised to protect crucial global resources like oil and gold from the hands of mobilised populations across former colonies who might get over-excited with their new powers of democratic government. In order to safeguard the ability of corporate interests to accumulate wealth across borders, the legal principle of sovereign equality began to be diluted. Instead of the proliferation of sovereignty resulting in the weakening of global capital, the undermining of sovereignty has created a world in which nation states compete in a race to the bottom to provide ever-kinder environments for corporate interests.

The Boomerang of Corporatisation

The multinational company is one of the earliest examples of the boomerang effect that this book highlights. Even though the likes of the Levant Company and the East India Company were established in England, their effects were first felt in the colonies. Only with the 1844 passing of the Registration of Joint Stock Companies Act did the commercial corporations sail back to their country of birth and turn themselves from being colonial monopolies into the juggernauts we see today. Thanks to this piece of legislation, the establishment of a corporation was no longer reliant on the grant of royal charter from the ruling monarch, with all its attached obligations to furthering the public good. Now corporations would be created through a two-step, independent registration process. With the liberalisation of the laws governing incorporation, the commercial corporations began to spread and grow across society to become the primary vehicles for delivering goods and services in almost every corner of the world in the late nineteenth and twentieth centuries.

Yet, throughout this period, the corporate takeover of life on earth was generally seen as a positive step in human development; in Britain, there was a presumption that what is good for the corporate world is inevitably good for the people. As late as the turn of the millennium, the corporate capture of states or the curse of having a resource that attracted attention from multinational companies were still generally seen as problems for troubled, 'emerging' nations, not as something that needed to concern an advanced economy like the UK. Today, there is less confidence in the idea that unfettered corporate power will shower blessings on most people living in Britain. The epilogue of the conflict between Mosaddegh and the Anglo-Iranian Oil Company points to this shift. At the time of the crisis, Ludwig von Mises, one of the godfathers of the economic idea now described as 'neoliberalism', which propelled the current triumph of corporatisation, understood the hypocrisy of Britain undertaking 'nationalisation' at home but defending the AIOC in Iran. He wrote, 'If it is right for the British to nationalize the British coal mines, it cannot be wrong for the Iranians to nationalize the Iranian oil industry.'[50] Of course, for von Mises, the solution was not for the British to recognise Iran's right to nationalisation. Instead, the way to correct this hypocrisy was for Britain to accept greater domestic privatisation and, over the coming decades, this vision came to pass. In 1987, as part of a great rush to privatise as many state resources as possible, Margaret Thatcher's government sold its final shares in British Petroleum, the company for which Britain had, just a few decades earlier, risked international embarrassment to protect. In 1998, British Petroleum completed a merger with the American oil giant Amoco, creating BP Amoco, or just BP for short, and became one of the largest companies in the world.[51]

Long-term, what was the reward Britain received for throwing its weight behind the Anglo-Iranian Oil Company in the 1950s? In its current incarnation as BP, the company has been consistently cited as one of the UK's biggest tax-avoiding firms. In 2018, BP was reported to have made profits totalling £5.6 billion but still managed to end up receiving tax credits from the British state, meaning the taxpayer paid them an extra bonus worth up to £134 million.[52] Today, BP and the other descendants of Britain's old colonial companies are no longer as dependent on the power of the British state as the AIOC once was. They are still interwoven with the British state, of course, but now it is the multinational company that holds the power. A revolving door between the neo-Gothic spires of Westminster and the glass and steel offices of Canary Wharf skyscrapers has helped ensure that British government policies remain generally corporate-friendly. The British businessman John Browne is a prime example of this process in action. He was the chief executive who oversaw BP's merger with Amoco in 1998, ensuring that it would enter the new millennium with more power than it ever had before. After he finished making BP the world's largest oil company again, Browne entered the hallowed halls of Parliament, becoming Lord Browne of Madingley in 2001. From the House of Lords, Lord Browne would help to increase the influence that the business community enjoyed within government by over-seeing the formal inclusion of corporate leaders on the boards of every government department.[53] In June 2010, he was invited by the government to become its new 'super-director', to help the government ensure that a business-friendly ethos was maintained across all state departments.

Just a couple months before Lord Browne's appointment to the role, his former company, BP, had caused the largest oil spill in history, devastating the Gulf of Mexico.[54] The oil spill, known as the Deepwater Horizon disaster, caused around four million barrels of oil to leak into the ocean basin, damaging marine wildlife and taking the lives of eleven people employed at the rigs.[55] This environmental disaster was widely blamed on a failure of governments across the world to adequately regulate the safety practices of oil companies. Then London Mayor Boris Johnson immediately leapt to the defence of BP, claiming that attacks on the company were 'anti-British'.[56] But this appeal to patriotically defend a multinational oil company fell on deaf ears – in Britain and across the world, people were outraged at the scenes of dead wildlife being pulled out of a blackened sea. Questions were being asked about how this had been allowed to happen. Why had state after state failed to stand up to the oil companies?

Regulators had been competing with each other to maintain favour with companies like BP, prioritising the importance of appearing to be business-friendly over the environmental safety of their own citizens. In Britain, critics pointed out that for the government to hire Lord Browne, who had presided over his own environmental disasters at the company, including the 2005 Texas City refinery explosion and a 2006 oil spill in Alaska, immediately after the Deepwater Horizon disaster, hardly encouraged confidence that oil companies would now face a reckoning.[57] Their fears were proven right. BP received little more than a slap on the wrist for Deepwater Horizon, and has continued to use its weight to weaken regulatory control over its actions. In 2013, it successfully pressured the EU into abandoning its proposed environmental protections and, in 2018, it lobbied the USA to weaken a landmark piece of environmental legislation.[58]

By siding with the AIOC and corporate interests generally, Britain helped set the global economy on a path where corporate power was increasingly estranged from democratic control. In the world of nations, former imperial powers like Britain treated corporations like a beloved family dog that was allowed to bite whatever it wanted outside the house but was expected to behave as soon as it returned home. Now, in the twenty-first century, Britain finds that the multinational company is no longer an obedient pet but a wild animal, leaving everyone, even those at home, terrified of what actions it may take next. Corporate lobbying, offshore tax evasion, the privatisation of public goods and government bailouts for corporate debts are now accepted as part of the normal economic and political process. Citizens across the globe, even in the former imperial core where the commercial corporation was born, have increasingly felt unable to offer any real challenge to the protective bubble within which corporate power is encased.

A New Hierarchy

Criss-crossing between the developing world and the developed world in the 1990s, as I did so often during my formative years, the shifting scales between multinational corporate power and state sovereignty were unmissable to me, even as a child. I would encounter the same brand names moving back and forth from Britain to Ghana, but in Ghana, the multinational company seemed to occupy the space in a different way, to mushroom to new levels of omnipotence. In Accra, the likes of Coca-Cola, Nestlé and Shell filled up not just billboards, as they might do in London, but covered taxis, homes and even human bodies. Semi-naked men stand at noisy traffic junctions, their bodies painted from head to toe in the orange of Fanta or the black and white of Guinness, the respective logo across their chest. They stay standing in this costume under the baking sun for hours on end, carrying a heavy crate of the company's products on their heads to sell to passing motorists. In cities like Accra, Lagos and Nairobi, it is not unusual to stumble across entire walls of houses or even whole township dwellings painted completely in blue, with the Pepsi symbol etched across the front. This scale of advertising imbues these companies with an almost supernatural ability to penetrate every sphere of private life in the developing world. The people living in these homes will have received little more than the free paint job as compensation, or maybe some free bottles of Pepsi if they are lucky.[59] When in Ghana, it always felt like the multinational company held more power than any other body of authority that you might encounter. The state, the church, NGOs;

all of them were subordinate to Vodafone or BP. If we were visiting the rural regions of the country, it could be difficult to access clean drinking water. But a bottle of Coca-Cola, Sprite or Fanta would always be available for sale nearby.

The triumph of corporate power in the decolonised state was not inevitable when Mosaddegh, Nkrumah and so many others seized the reigns of national sovereignty in the 1950s. But the watering down of the sovereignty of new nation states in order to protect corporate property rights has directly contributed to the mega-companies now exercising what American law professor Frank Pasquale refers to as a 'functional sovereignty'.[60] Taking us almost full circle to the quasi-state powers enjoyed by the East India and Hudson Bay companies at the height of British imperialism, the twenty-first century has seen giants like Amazon and Google emerge as no longer just companies competing in a free-market; rather, they are the market. They are the platforms upon which all other companies must hope to build and they set the rules through which others can be allowed to trade.[61]

States fall over themselves trying to provide ever-more favourable terms to attract these companies to their jurisdiction. Enticements have moved beyond simply offering to lower the tax burden, like the National Liberation Council did after the coup against Nkrumah – now countries are asking multinational corporations to take over the very practices of the state in an acceleration of the outsourcing phenomenon that Britain has experienced. Airbnb are not just pointing users towards holiday homes, they have now begun to take responsibility for the urban planning of declining towns.[62] Where the East India Company once used to run their own courts, now we have the likes of Amazon, who run their own de facto court system through dispute resolution schemes aimed at settling conflicts between buyers and sellers using their platform.[63] They may not have the military force of the East India Company, but today's multinational companies have the power to hoard unprecedented amounts of our personal data or control the distribution of a life-saving vaccine through their rights of intellectual property.

No longer can we pretend that only countries in the developing world have to bend the knee in the face of corporate power. Whether it is the Republic of Ireland with Google or the Netherlands with Starbucks, European nation states have found themselves adapting their tax, environmental or regulatory policies in order to please their corporate masters.[64] And with a legal, political and economic system already built to serve the interests of 'outsourced' corporate colonialism, Britain is particularly vulnerable in this world of multinational juggernauts.

Since the era of Mosaddegh, an international legal framework has emerged to ensure that any government that tries to undertake drastic action against multinational corporate interests will face brutal economic punishment. There is less need for a coup now, since a web of private courts like the World Bank's International Centre for the Settlement of Investment Disputes (ICSID) allow corporations to regularly successfully sue nation states that they feel have breached their property or contractual rights. Following the ICSID's ratification in 1966, investors have successfully sued countries such as Uganda, the Philippines and Ghana for undertaking government policies that harmed their profit margin. Now the UK is itself facing substantial threats of investor–state disputes from multinational corporations who are concerned about the economic fallout from Brexit. Furthermore, the terms on which Britain left the EU ensure that many future trading issues will be resolved by arbitration panels and private tribunals, which have historically been shown to favour corporate interests over those of the nation state. Brexiteers spoke a great deal about sovereignty, but is that what sovereignty looks like?

Through an affinity with corporate capitalism, successive British governments worked to contain the power of sovereign autonomy at exactly the moment it was spreading around the world through decolonisation. The sovereignty now being offered by Brexit does not mitigate the power of private corporate actors, who are now backed by an overarching web of legal protection. Power does not simply live within state houses, national flags and stirring constitutions, but also within the rights of property, in tightly drafted contracts and in corporate boardrooms. The nomadic nature of today's multinationals tears apart the already fragile connective tissue between wealth accumulation and social responsibility.

For multinational corporations to spread themselves freely across the world in the twentieth century, the mechanisms to facilitate the movement of their capital across borders would also need to be assured. Yet, as the rest of the century would show, the easy movement of capital also encourages the movement of people. If multinational companies were going to continue to extract wealth from the lands of the former colonies, then many of the people who lived there would, unsurprisingly, decide to follow the money.

3

The Border

In 1947, as India moved towards independence, Prime Minister Clement Attlee implored the Indian people not to forget the lessons that the British had given them during colonial rule. Standing up in the famous oak chamber of the House of Commons to read the Indian Independence Bill, Attlee proudly declared that 'India owes her unity and freedom ... to the British'.[1] His speech sought to calm the exuberance of the nationalists celebrating freedom in what had been Britain's imperial crown jewel, and to remind Indians that their pathway to becoming a civilised and successful independent nation state would ultimately depend on rejecting the superstitious delusions of their ancient cultures and embracing the principles that the British had kindly imparted upon them. Sounding more like a graduation speech given by a headmaster to his pupils than an acknowledgement of recognition from one sovereign nation to another, Attlee's parliamentary address on the eve of Indian independence shows how Enoch Powell's image of Britain as the reluctant, benevolent empire crossed political boundaries. According to Attlee, India had only become part of the empire in the first place because of the 'voluntary cession of authority to the British' by Indian people tired of their own 'anarchic' rulers.[2] The previous few decades of strikes, civil disobedience and outbreaks of armed resistance on the Indian subcontinent were swept under the rug. Apparently, Britain had, of its own accord, come to the realisation that India had finished its necessary period of apprenticeship and was generously granting the region its independence.

Attlee's government presented the separation of Britain from its most populous territory as no great loss. If anything, it was a relief. Britain could now finally put down the burden of having to tutor this ponderous subcontinent. Attlee's chancellor of the exchequer, Hugh Dalton, captured the disdain with which many British politicians publicly treated this world-changing moment, which created not just one but two colossal new nations as multiple borders were drawn across British India to create India and Pakistan. In the face of this redrawing of the global map, Dalton claimed, 'I don't believe that one in a hundred thousand in this country cares tuppence about it [India] so long as British People aren't being mauled out there.'[3] Attlee's government reframed independence as just another reinforcement of Britain's civilising power. In his words, independence was 'the fulfilment of Britain's mission in India', and all the events that had taken place on the Indian subcontinent over the past few centuries, from the Bombay plague to the Bengal famine, the land seizures of the East India Company's private armies, the Amritsar Massacre and the civil disobedience campaign that eventually made India ungovernable, had all been just 'steps in the road that led up eventually' to this preordained destination point.[4] The response to Indian independence set the tone for the prevailing British political response to decolonisation – insist that this was always the plan all along. As the vast, transnational empire began to splinter at an exponential rate over the next few decades, more and more people would be given the same parting message millions of Indians received in 1947: don't forget the lessons we taught you.

In 2012, British politicians were talking about India in a very different manner. That year, a group of then relatively obscure Conservative MPs published their vision for Britain's future in a book called *Britannia Unchained: Global Lessons for Growth and Prosperity*.[5] While the country's liberal press was celebrating the London Olympics, with its image of an all-singing, all-dancing multicultural Britain, this ambitious group of back-bench politicians sought to warn against a culture of laziness and narcissism that they believed was taking hold of the country. For them, Britain had become stagnant, slothful and self-obsessed, anaesthetised by an overgenerous welfare state and no longer competitive in the only sport that actually mattered – the global economy.

In order to jolt the country out of its daydream, these politicians called for the UK to follow the lessons offered by the 'developing world', especially the nation of India. Just sixty-five years on from Attlee warning a soon-to-be-independent India to remember its British training, India was now being held up as a model for Britain itself to follow. The authors argued that India was rising because 'in contrast to Britain's fame obsession, success in India is becoming a mid-trained computer engineer or technician'.[6] In their opinion, British workers had turned into 'among the worst idlers in the world. We work among the lowest hours, we retire early and our productivity is poor'.[7] The spoilt British youth could learn a thing or two from their Indian counterparts, because 'unlike those from the backstreets of Bangalore, low-income students in Britain do not see study as a way out of poverty'.[8] British students take easy degrees, fearing the rigour of science and technology, while 'youngsters in India and Mexico are queuing up to enrol on these courses'.[9] With money and capital now free to move across the globalised world as it wished, the authors of *Britannia Unchained* predicted that multinational corporations would be only too quick to relocate jobs from Britain towards the 'highly educated, tech savvy and low cost workers in Bangalore and Guadalajara', and rightly so.[10] The conclusion of this book was that the British economy was in desperate need of some shock therapy. In a rather crude example of the boomerang metaphor that moves through this book, here was a text openly arguing that the old imperial heartland needed to go through the same disciplinary processes that economies of the Global South suffered after decolonisation. For in the twenty-first century, 'above all Britain finds itself increasingly ill-equipped to take on the hungry and ambitious international economic competition from Asia to Latin America'.[11]

When the book was published, the authors, Kwasi Kwarteng, Dominic Raab, Priti Patel, Liz Truss and Chris Skidmore, were a relatively insignificant group of aspiring but inexperienced young politicians. Almost a decade later, they have risen to the very top of British politics and form the backbone of Boris Johnson's government. At the time of writing, Patel has become Home Secretary, Raab the Justice Secretary, Truss the Foreign Secretary, Kwarteng Minister of State for Business and Skidmore has served as Minister of State for Universities. As Britain took the dramatic step of leaving the European Union and becoming an 'independent' nation itself, the *Britannia Unchained* gang sat in offices that spread across the whole scope of the British state. In government, they have become simultaneously cheerleaders for Brexit and the push to control UK borders and the drivers of the campaign for Global Britain to go across the seas to 'lead the world' again.[12] This dual desire to both pry open and clamp down the borders of the nation state speaks to the challenges brought on by the afterlife of empire.

The Nation State and the Welfare State

The villain in *Britannia Unchained*'s story of sloth and stagnancy in twenty-first-century Britain is clear and obvious – the welfare state that Attlee's government cemented in place following the Second World War. Coinciding with the end of the empire and the creation of a new image of the British nation, the post-war welfare state has come to represent a key battleground for competing visions of what the country should be. Reforms to ease the harshness of life for working people began with the victories of organised labour movements during the 1920s and 1930s. The path for the welfare state was also cleared by a growing movement for women's rights in the early decades of the century, when activists pushed not only for the vote but also for better conditions to improve the health and welfare of women and children. But the nationalist, collectivist experience of war gave calls for a comprehensive welfare state new impetus. The war effort had already required the British state to take greater care of its people, with concerns about the population being too malnourished and sickly to fight leading to government support for maternity services and free school meals.[13] After the war, the feeling that the country now owed the people for the sacrifices they had made hardened the desire for a new social contact to be drawn up. In 1945, Attlee's Labour government was elected with a mandate to create a new kind of Britain. The welfare state gave Britain not just a new type of society but also a new form of identity. Despite having an empire entering terminal decline, the abiding public image of 1950s Britain that is remembered today is a country turning the enthusiasm of VE Day parades into a system of state-sponsored healthcare, housing and unemployment benefits.

A romantic mythology has grown up around the post-1945 establishment of the NHS, building of council houses and growth of social security protections. Through its associations with the legacy of all things Second World War, the welfare state has become the foundation for a particular story of the rise of social democracy in Britain. Yet, as the historian David Edgerton has shown, it wasn't just the generosity of the Attlee government that drove forward the reforms; the background noise to the creation of the welfare state was Britain's need to create a new nationalism as the old empire started to crumble all around its ears.[14] The welfare state was but one part of the wider emergence of a new politics concerned with the construction of a nation. In the Labour Party's 1945 election manifesto, this overarching concern for 'the nation' expresses itself clearly. The manifesto contains the word 'health' nine times, 'social' is mentioned sixteen times but the 'nation' is raised twenty-seven times.[15] The 'spirit of forty-five' became a key tool in the erasure of empire. By tying the story of the 'little island that had won the war' to the emergence of a new national framework of care and security, the welfare state helped to ensure that in the popular memory, the narrative of the 1950s and 1960s would not be decolonisation but the development of social democracy.[16]

As much as Attlee's speech tried to downplay its significance, the loss of India signalled the need to salvage a new national model of Britain from the imperial wreckage. This wasn't just the loss of a colony; this was the loss of *the* colony. The British Raj had been the fulcrum around which the whole empire turned. No politician was more aware of the significance of losing the Raj than Enoch Powell. His romance with India was well documented, with him proclaiming it 'the most striking frontispiece of the Empire'.[17] By the time Powell ended his war service in India, he was known to have said that he felt as much Indian as British.[18] On his return to the UK, Powell argued voraciously for Britain to retain some form of sovereignty over India. In his mind, without India, Britain would immediately lose much of its military and economic power in the eastern hemisphere. Powell tried to tell his colleagues that the 'centre of gravity' for British global power was not London, but New Delhi.[19] From India, Britain could spread its power across the Indian Ocean and the Arabian Peninsula. Without the empire, and without India especially, Powell feared the might of the USA and Soviet Union would crush little old Britain.[20] When it became clear that Winston Churchill and the Conservatives were not going to challenge Attlee's decision to allow Indian independence, a furious Powell resigned from his position on the Conservatives' India committee.[21] From then on, he would commit himself to the project of creating the British nation, a project that would diminish and deny the importance of the empire and its loss. If the empire was gone, it now had to be forgotten.

The New British Subject

The response of the British state to the problem of divorcing the nation from the empire can be seen in the wave of immigration and nationality legislation that was passed after the war. The end

of the British Empire precipitated the vast movement of populations around the world. Prior to this moment, a young
cotton-mill worker from Kolkata, India, was legally as British as
a young cotton-mill worker from Chorley, Lancashire. Movement
across the empire was still unequal, but this was not explicitly
translated in different citizenship categories. Britain drew heavily
on this global collection of imperial subjects to power the war
effort, with soldiers from Kenya and South Africa and airmen
from Canada and the West Indies all coming to the motherland's
aid. The two and a half million Indians that signed up to fight in
the Second World War composed the largest volunteer force in
human history. Then, the year after India became independent,
the 1948 British Nationality Act was introduced by the Attlee
government. With the loss of India, Britain's most populous colony,
the question gained new urgency of how bordering organised
the millions of people around the world who had been conscripted
into the British Empire over the past few centuries. The 1948 Act
created the new category of 'Citizen of United Kingdom and
Colonies', marking the first shift away from the common status
of 'British subject' that had, until then, been shared by all the
empire's people. Despite acknowledging for the first time the
difference between 'the United Kingdom' and 'the Colonies', the
1948 Nationality Act still granted all nationals of independent
Commonwealth countries and those of British colonies the right
to enter and settle in Britain.

The Act became an invitation for subjects from the wider
empire. The government's main target recruits were white subjects
from Australia, Canada and New Zealand, hoping to replace the
streams of British families going the other way to start new lives
after the war. However, the year 1948 also saw a ship called the
Empire Windrush sail into Tilbury Docks in Essex, carrying on
board a group of Caribbean workers who have become the lasting
metaphor for a whole generation of people from the non-white
colonies who came and settled in Britain after the war. Though
we often refer to the Windrush generation as immigrants, it is

important to remember that they were already British subjects when they landed, and were simply moving from the periphery of Britain's territory to the metropole. Technically, they were no more immigrants than someone moving from Bangor to Brighton would be. It is also vital to remember that they came because the British government had made it clear that it was desperate for a labour force to rebuild the country. The new, national welfare state desperately needed workers. London Transport recruited more than 3,500 people directly from Barbados alone between 1956 and 1966, often covering the costs of their travel to the UK, and then deducting that money back from their first pay cheques.[22] The NHS could never have been adequately staffed without extra workers from the colonies, which is why agencies were set up across the empire to select and recruit people to train as nurses in Britain.

However, these invitations to workers from the Caribbean, West Africa and the Indian subcontinent to come and rebuild war-ravaged Britain in the 1950s and 1960s was just that – an invitation to *work*. British governments presumed that only the amount of people from the colonies they needed to fill that labour shortage would arrive and, also, that these people were only staying long enough to fill this temporary gap. Politicians wanted to import labour, but what they received were living, breathing human beings. Many had already answered the motherland's call when they had served Britain during the war; migrating to the UK was, to them, just an extension of that same duty. To be travelling to Britain from Kingston, Bridgetown or Mumbai during this era would, in many ways, just be coming home. After spending their childhoods being schooled on Jane Austen and cricket and then having so recently sacrificed so much in the aid of Britain's war effort, families from across Greater Britannia were now travelling to a motherland they had been told was still in desperate need of their help.

Imagine their horror upon discovering that, to many of their new neighbours and work colleagues, they were not family but foreigners, dirty invaders just as unwelcome as the Luftwaffe bombers so recently repelled. Despite the massive contribution of black and Asian colonial migrants to the building of the welfare state, their ability to access the benefits of Britain's new social contract was limited by crude racism. An unofficial 'colour bar' existed when it came to housing and employment. There were no laws of segregation in Britain, but in many cases they weren't needed. Companies would just refuse to employ black workers and for those who did manage to get a job, some trade unions would refuse to let them join their ranks. Finding housing was even harder. Our abiding image of the bigotry that clouded the lives of the Windrush generation remains the 'no blacks, no dogs, no Irish' posters they reported seeing in the windows of pubs and rental properties. While the proliferation and indeed existence of these posters has been questioned by some historians, nobody questions that colonial migrants in the 1950s and 1960s were turned away by private landlords, rendered ineligible for council waiting lists and refused loans by reputable mortgage companies purely on the basis of the colour of their skin.[23] As a snapshot of how widespread this discrimination was, one in six adverts for rental accommodation in North Kensington, London, in late 1959 had some sort of 'anti-coloured' stipulation – a requirement worded variously as 'no coloureds', 'Europeans only', 'white people only' or 'English only'.[24]

In addition to these daily indignities, new migrants to Britain would also have to open their morning newspapers to see their communities being consistently associated with violence and criminality.[25] Politicians began to fight elections on explicitly racist grounds. Perhaps the most sinister of post-war Britain's racist elections was the 1964 election in the West Midlands constituency of Smethwick, where recent Commonwealth migrants, particularly Indians from the Sikh community, had settled. That election was won by the Conservative Peter Griffiths, who managed to attract enough working-class, traditional Labour voters to vote for him by convincing them that they were in competition with these new foreign migrants for dwindling resources. His campaign slogan was, 'If you want a nigger for a neighbour, vote Labour.'[26] However, the Smethwick by-election, ugly as it was, would be overshadowed by an event in the nearby city of Birmingham just a few years later. Twenty years after the *Empire Windrush* sailed into dock, Enoch Powell, at the time a respected if occasionally rebellious member of the Conservative Party and the British political establishment, travelled to Birmingham to make a speech that would cement his place as one of Britain's most infamous historical figures.

The 'Rivers of Blood'

Enoch Powell's name will now forever stand as a byword for the idea that migrants, especially migrants from Africa, the Caribbean or South Asia, can never truly be British. Powell's reputation as a maverick figure among the right-wing British establishment was already well established by the 20 April 1968, when he attended a Conservative Association meeting in Birmingham. That evening, Powell warned his audience that, thanks to immigration from the colonies leading to a race war, the rivers of Britain would soon be 'foaming with much blood'.[27] In what has come to be known as the 'Rivers of Blood' speech, Powell complained that the true victims of racism in sixties Britain were his white constituents, who, because of immigration, were now 'unable to obtain hospital beds', found 'their children unable to obtain school places', saw 'their homes and neighbourhoods changed beyond recognition' and were essentially being 'made strangers in their own country'.[28]

In many ways, the 'Rivers of Blood' speech was not just an attack on migrant communities but also an acknowledgement of their success over the two decades since the *Empire Windrush* had landed. The people who had moved to the old colonial motherland from Africa, the Caribbean and South Asia had not just sat idly by and accepted the discrimination they had been faced with upon arrival – they had organised and carved out a space for themselves within the country. A bus boycott in Bristol in 1963 had forced the city to accept black and Asian bus drivers, and in 1966 a Caribbean carnival was established in Notting Hill in opposition to racial attacks; the carnival has gone on to become Europe's largest street party. Figures like Claudia Jones, Olive Morris and Darcus Howe led campaigns against the prejudice their communities had to endure when applying for jobs, renting houses or using public services. Migrant communities did not arrive in Britain without a history and many had already been through the experience of campaigning for labour rights or political recognition from the British authorities back in the colonies.[29] Eventually, the pressure they generated resulted in the British government passing a Race Relations Act in 1965, and when that legislation proved inadequate, the government proposed another Race Relations Act in 1968 that would finally make it illegal for landlords and employers to discriminate openly against people on the basis of the colour of their skin. The Race Relations Act 1968 was, to many, more than just the formal granting of rights to oppressed communities; it was also a recognition that those communities were now here to stay. Britain would have to find a way to be a multiracial nation state.

Powell had once been one of the loudest defenders of the empire. Yet by the time of the 'Rivers of Blood' speech, he had adopted the defence of a jilted lover, proclaiming that Britain was better off on its own, that it was in fact colonies like India that had always been overly attached to the British, rather than the other way around.[30] Despite having been enamoured with Indian culture when he lived there, Powell was now warning his constituents that the 'influx of immigrants' from the Indian subcontinent had brought with them their backwards culture and age-old ethnic and religious conflicts.[31] The passing of Race Relations legislation made it clear to Powell that Britain's black and Asian population was planning to be here permanently, hardening his resolve to oppose them. As he stood up in a dusty conference hall at the

Birmingham Midland Hotel on 20 April 1968, Powell saw himself as the last line of defence for the pure British people, uninterrupted by outside influence for a thousand years. Now, he declared the British public feared that 'in fifteen or twenty years' time the black man will have the whip hand over the white man' in the UK.[32] Powell concluded his speech by calling on the Conservative Party to commit to a policy of 're-emigration' in future. The only way to stop Britain being swamped by inferior people of an alien culture was to send Commonwealth subjects back to where they had come from.

Conservative leader Ted Heath expelled Powell from the shadow Cabinet and he was drummed out of front-line politics for his 'Rivers of Blood' speech, but the speech had struck a chord with the nation, making him one of the most popular politicians in the land. A poll taken afterwards showed that 74 per cent of British people were sympathetic to his views.[33] Furthermore, though Powell was derided by the *bien pensant* political class, the goal of redrawing British citizenship along national and even racial lines was actually one that was covertly shared by successive post-war British governments from across the political spectrum. The 1948 Nationality Act was followed by a rush of other nationality and immigration acts that sought to separate British citizenship from the status enjoyed by British subjects around the world through a quiet but violent process of exclusion.[34]

In 1962, the Commonwealth Immigration Act was passed by the Conservative government, which ended the automatic right of people from the British colonies and Commonwealth to settle in the UK. Though it made all Commonwealth citizens subject to possible immigration control, the target of this law was not white people coming from New Zealand or Rhodesia. Conservative Home Secretary Rab Butler said that the Act's 'great merit' was that it looked like it would apply to all parts of the Commonwealth, when in reality the Act's 'restrictive effect is intended to, and would in fact, operate on coloured people almost exclusively'.[35] In 1968, the Labour Party continued the trend by updating the

1962 Act with the Commonwealth Immigrants Act which tightened controls further. Finally, the 1971 Immigration Act created the concept of the 'right to abode' – the right to enter and live in the UK – and tied that to British ancestry. This was an explicit move to restrict access to only white Commonwealth subjects, who were far more likely to have had a parent born in Britain. The immigration acts were reinforced by a new British Nationality Act in 1981, which not only repealed most of the provisions of the 1948 British Nationality Act but also largely closed the book on the recognition of Commonwealth citizens as British subjects. Following the 1971 Immigration Act, the 1981 Nationality Act tied citizenship as well as the right to enter the UK to whether someone had a parent born in Britain.[36] Britain, in terms of the law, was now presented as a fixed, bounded and bordered nation state; the empire disappeared not only from the scene but from the memory of the law.

Despite Powell's 'Rivers of Blood' speech being publicly met with disdain by establishment politicians, the legislative changes to British citizenship between the 1948 and 1981 Nationality Acts shared some ground, at least, with Powell's demands. In August 1956, Powell had proclaimed that 'a fundamental change in the law is necessary before there can be any limit to West Indian immigration. It would be necessary to define a citizen of the British Isles by his place of birth and his race.'[37] With each new immigration and nationality act, a fundamental shift in the structure of Britain was being snuck into the law of land, taking it from being a multiracial, global empire to an insular nation state without any substantial public recognition or constitutional reform that acknowledged the scale of what was happening. Step by step, the categories of citizenship were gradually remade so that people from St Lucia to Sri Lanka were not only marked as no longer British but seen as never having been British at all.

The Powell who preached the gospel of race war in the 'Rivers of Blood' is the same Powell who proclaimed the empire to be an 'an invention'. You can't get one without the other. By diluting the significance or even the existence of empire, Powell could downplay the horrific racism suffered by the first generation of black and South Asian migrants that had led to the passing of the 1968 Race Relations Act. He argued that there is no 'comparison between the Commonwealth immigrant in Britain and the American Negro' as the black population of America started out as slaves and had faced discrimination in the law.[38] Powell's argument here has become a common way of absolving Britain of its racial legacy by way of comparison with the USA; race becomes a specifically American problem, something that tolerant Britain has no relationship to. This reading conveniently edits out the extensive practice of plantation slavery in 'offshore' Britain, in colonies like Jamaica and Barbados, which had been a part of Britain before it even became one country. It also intentionally ignores the myriad of ways that institutional and interpersonal racism can be practised without the need for explicit discrimination set out in the law. And the wave of immigration and nationality laws that were passed in line with Powell's rhetoric obviously had the consequence of impacting black and Asian British populations to a far greater extent than it did their white counterparts.

Yet as much as Powell wanted to raise the drawbridge against his imagined foreign invaders, calling for not just Britain but all civilised nations to install strong borders against the global movement of people, he also wanted national borders weakened in another aspect. Decolonisation meant that once vast, transcontinental empires were now strewn through with sovereign border after sovereign border. For the corporations that had grown rich during colonialism, each new border presented another obstacle to be navigated in order to ensure business could continue as usual. This was not how borders should be used, in Powell's opinion. The other side of Powell's worldview was a fervent commitment to a global economy where money, property and assets were free to move as they wish.[39] Powell has now been memorialised as a nationalist, a man who wanted to draw lines on the map and contain people in their proper place. But, in a certain sense, he was also a globalist and wished to erase those lines when it came to the economy, calling for openness and flexibility for the global movement of money. At the time he was expressing them, Powell's ideas about the global free market were niche, even within his own party. Fortunately for him, he would find like minds amid a collection of intellectuals who, in 1955, had established an organisational home for themselves, creating Britain's first free-market think tank, the Institute of Economic Affairs.

The Institute

As the Second World War came to an end, a British RAF pilot called Antony Fisher came across the ideas of Friedrich Hayek, a radical Austrian economist based at the London School of Economics, inside perhaps the least radical of publications, the family magazine *Reader's Digest*.[40] The magazine contained a short-ened version of the argument Hayek was putting forward in his book *The Road to Serfdom*, which warned of how Europe's slow drift towards socialism would eventually lead to the death of freedom. Reading his copy of the magazine in which Hayek was featured, Fisher was struck by an epiphany: Hayek's words exposed how Britain's welfare state was not the benevolent gift to the working people of a war-torn country everyone was saying it was. It was just a further step on the road towards 'serfdom', the breakdown of all individual liberty and free will.

Fisher's post-war civilian life showed him the personal benefits that free-market economics could offer. He built up a fortune as Britain's first battery chicken farmer, and wished to bring enlight-enment to the rest of the country. Fisher tracked down Hayek and asked the economist the question that had been haunting him ever since he had read that issue of *Reader's Digest* – what could someone like him do to aid the wider fight against socialism?

Should he make a run at getting into Parliament? In a surprising response, Hayek told Fisher that becoming a politician was a waste of time. Rather, Fisher should focus on shaping public opinion outside of party politics. The idea of having a welfare state had become common sense in Britain, so Fisher was advised to bring together intellectuals and academics with politicians in order to change the idea of what was common sense.[41]

Fisher's conversation with Hayek inspired him to establish the Institute of Economic Affairs (IEA) in 1955 as a think tank independent of formal party politics, inspired by American examples such as the Brookings Institute or the Carnegie Endowment for International Peace. Fisher found two young free-market economists to head up his new project, Ralph Harris and Arthur Seldon. In a post-war Britain that had accepted the welfare state as being the best way to help those without means, Harris and Seldon came with the added benefit of both coming from working-class backgrounds, giving their critiques of the welfare state extra weight. The IEA quickly became a curious but compelling new force on the British political scene, but it was not until they gained Enoch Powell as their parliamentary torchbearer that they really began to make their presence felt.

Powell embraced the IEA at a time when most British conservatives considered the organisation's members to be marginal extremists. A level of welfarism and state control of the economy was seen as unavoidable. Yet, through his collaborations with the IEA, Powell became Britain's first significant politician to challenge this way of thinking, publicly calling for denationalisation of public services and the relaxing of government controls on money. The economic ideas Powell, Harris and Seldon promoted together – that 'free enterprise is the true counterpart of democracy'; that governments must 'obey market forces promptly and faithfully'; and that we must all 'accept the differences of wealth and income without which competition and free enterprise are impossible' – have become normalised in the twenty-first century, but they were out of step with the London of the Swinging

Sixties.[42] The post-war welfare state had been woven into the landscape of the new British nation, with public services like British Telecom, British Airways and especially the NHS becoming part of a new national identity that was meant to be separate from the history of empire (despite the make-up of its workforce). The IEA saw it as their sacred duty to turn Britain away from this state-sponsored cocoon and remind the country that its true identity lay in the buccaneering spirit of entrepreneurism. Harris encouraged Powell to return to his scholarly roots and start writing books for the IEA that would communicate the importance of free-market economics to the masses. In 1960, Powell published a book with the IEA entitled *Saving in a Free Society*, where he argued for governments to stop using their sovereign powers over interest rates to try and manipulate the economy.[43] After this book, Powell and the IEA worked hand in hand on conferences, symposiums and further publications to advance their great pushback against the belief that state control was good for the British economy.

The IEA remained loyal to Powell even after the 'Rivers of Blood' speech, when his allies in mainstream politics deserted him. Powell became so entwined with the IEA that by the time Antony Fisher died in 1988, just four weeks after Queen Elizabeth II had made him a knight of the realm, Powell was one of only two politicians to attend his memorial service, the other being his fellow conservative firebrand Keith Joseph. Coincidently, Joseph's political career would carry echoes of Powell's. Both were one-time potential leaders of the Tory party but torpedoed their career ambitions by making rogue speeches – in the same city. Only a few years after Powell signed his political death warrant by giving the 'Rivers of Blood' speech at a hotel in Birmingham, on the 19 October 1974, Joseph would travel to the UK's second city to give his own ill-fated and unprompted monologue. In his speech, Joseph focused not on immigration but on the breakdown of traditional conservative morals due to the welfare state. He argued that thanks to public money, poor mothers 'of low intelligence' could now produce endless 'problem children' that were threatening the country's future 'human stock'.[44] Joseph's eugenicist speech was greeted with a similar reception to Powell's – and he too watched with horror as the establishment press and mainstream politicians turned their back on him.

The Fixed Exchange Rate

By talking too much, Powell and Joseph managed to disqualify themselves from the leadership position many assumed was their destiny. Short on friends, they were fortunate to receive the ongoing support of the IEA, but few of their colleagues in the House of Commons would publicly show them sympathy. One of the few to still advocate on their behalf in Parliament was an ambitious rising political star called Margaret Thatcher. In 1974, when the establishment of the Conservative Party was falling over itself to put distance between the party and Powell and Joseph, recently deposed former Secretary for Education Thatcher wrote a full-page article in *The Times* defending both men as 'fine academic minds'.[45] For Thatcher, who had admired Powell for years and worked closely with Joseph throughout her political career, the more extreme views of either man should not override the fact that both had landed on the right answer to the main problem facing Britain: the economy.

Powell and Joseph, in collaboration with the IEA, had been pretty much the lone voices in the wilderness, shouting about the dangers of a planned economy. They brought the ideas of cutting-edge free-market economists like Friedrich Hayek to mainstream politics and to Thatcher's attention. One of the key changes they wished for was a change in the way money moved across the world, and it was on this issue, perhaps more than any other, that Powell would influence Thatcher. Alongside the IEA, Powell was committed to challenging the constraints that Keynesianism had put on the market at the global level. Often forgotten amid the cloud of controversy that descended on Powell in 1968 is that he gave another speech that year in which he laid out the 'no borders' side of his vision. Just a few months after he delivered the 'Rivers of Blood' speech, Powell spoke at a meeting of the influential Mont Pelerin Society. This speech, called 'The Fixed Exchange Rate and Dirigisme', might have a far less eye-catching title in the history books, but in its own way is just as significant for understanding the direction our world has taken over the past few decades.[46] For Powell, while borders needed to contain people within their proper place, capital should be free to move around the world as it wished.

Today, the Mont Pelerin Society has gained a reputation as a cloak-and-dagger organisation, an exclusive gentleman's club, that, like the archetypal James Bond villains, hid in the Swiss mountains while it plotted to take over the world. In reality, the society was not as secretive or as sinister as it is sometimes presented, but it was no less influential. Founded in 1947 by Friedrich Hayek at the eponymous resort in Switzerland, the organisation brought together academics, politicians and business leaders who agreed that the cause of the age was to fight the spread of socialism across Europe and the wider world.[47] It has included among its membership some of the most influential economists of the twentieth century – not just Hayek but also his mentor, the Austrian libertarian Ludwig von Mises, and the architect of Germany's post-war recovery, Wilhelm Röpke. The British contingent of this elite band of free-marketers included all the leading lights of the IEA – Antony Fisher, Arthur Seldon, Ralph Harris (who would briefly serve as the society's president) and the man who Hayek once described to Harris as the person 'it seems all our hopes for England rest now on' – Enoch Powell.[48]

From its first meeting, the Mont Pelerin Society aimed to challenge the creeping state control of economies that its members saw gaining strength at both national and international level. The era of decolonisation had been shadowed by wider changes in the international order, including the establishment of new institutions to govern global trade. The 1944 conference at Bretton Woods in New Hampshire, USA, gave birth to two institutions that were meant to be the financial pillars of the new, post-war international legal order – the International Monetary Fund (IMF) and the International Bank for Reconstruction and Development, which in 1946 would become the World Bank. Initially, the IMF was charged with securing monetary stability, guarding against the type of casino capitalism that had led to the Great Depression. The World Bank was tasked with helping to stop countries falling into financial ruin by ensuring nation states could have access to credit, even if the commercial banks were afraid of lending to them. Perhaps most controversially, the Bretton Woods system ensured that exchange rates between currencies were fixed, in order to avoid money fluctuating too much in value between countries and to control how capital could move through the world. Powell was an immediate critic of this attempt to manufacture stability among the world's currencies, which he referred to as an 'attempt at mass self-deception'.[49]

In short, the idea of fixed exchange rates was that countries around the world would fix the value of their currency to the US dollar, which had now overtaken the British pound as the world's global reserve currency. Then, in turn, the USA would tie the dollar to the value of gold, a precious metal that would always be in demand. Each country's central bank would stay within the range of the fixed exchange rate and the whole system would be overseen by the International Monetary Fund (IMF). With the world's currencies anchored together, huge spikes and crashes in the value of money would be limited; international trade would be less free, but it would be steadier. The fixed exchange rate system was only sustainable if governments could maintain some control over the money that was flowing into and out of each country. This meant that countries imposed capital controls – limits on the amount of money that individuals could take across its borders. In Britain, fixed exchange rates internationally were accompanied by the 1947 Exchange Control Act at domestic level, which limited the amount of money British citizens could take out of the UK or hold in overseas assets. As late as the 1960s, British people were limited to taking only £50 with them on an overseas holiday (equivalent to around £900 today).

Unsurprisingly, the fixed exchange rate and the accompanying capital controls inspired differences of opinion among economists and politicians. Even within the Mont Pelerin Society, the idea was a highly divisive issue. Hayek led a camp of older members, perhaps still holding memories of the great crash of 1929, that feared the instability that more flexible exchange rates might bring with them. They argued that rather than freeing up exchange rates, all currencies should be tied even closer to the value of gold, with confidence in money being the best path for encouraging capitalism and entrepreneurism. A younger cohort, headed up by the ambitious American economist Milton Friedman, argued instead that loosening currency exchange rates could make international trade more profitable, as mobile money could counteract the rising power of trade unions and socialist parties around the world.[50] Despite his personal admiration for Hayek, on the question of fixed exchange rates, Powell fell firmly into the Friedman camp, arguing voraciously that the market should be free to decide what different currencies were worth, not faceless national and international bureaucrats.[51]

Therefore, in 1968, in the shadow of the disastrous recent 'Rivers of Blood' speech, Powell made his thoughts on the fixed exchange rate clear in a speech to the Mont Pelerin Society. By tying together the fixed exchange rate with the idea of 'Dirigisme'– the French notion of a state-dominated economy that is the opposite to the idea of *laissez faire* economics – this speech made an attempt to connect the global currency control system with fears that many people still carried about state totalitarianism. Powell saw fixed exchange rates as not only artificially propping up of the value of money in lesser countries, but felt that as a system it gave governments the perfect cover under which to indulge in the type of 'state control, limitations of freedom, even acts of tyranny' that otherwise would be unacceptable.[52] National governments now had the power to control the freedom of private individuals and investors to move money across borders and, what was worse, because it was done in the name of global monetary stability, even capitalists had come to accept this clear infringement of liberty. For Powell, through the veneer of having to guard against economic crashes, politicians and bureaucrats had 'been able to turn free men into slaves and rational beings into obedient cattle'.[53]

Powell claimed that it was because the fixed exchange rate was such a good vehicle for totalitarian state control that parties like Labour didn't call for an end to it, despite often talking about challenging systems of international finance. Even when inflation might have encouraged Labour governments to want more freedom to play with the value of the pound, 'instead they demand more and more controls, controls over imports, over private expenditure, over trade, over movement of capital. Why? Because a fixed exchange rate is the supreme commanding height of a controlled economy.'[54] In Powell's eyes, with fixed exchange rates, governments were free to increase taxation, nationalise private industries and embark on even more draconian actions, because they knew it was legally difficult for wealthy citizens to take their money and run to a different country. By controlling where people could move their money, politicians were able to sneak in socialist authoritarian control of the free market through the back door, using supposed international economic stability to justify their power lust. The two strands of Powell's thought can be summarised as a vision of the world where borders were for people, not for property. The sphere of human movement was to be a space divided up by fences and high walls, keeping each person in their natural place; the sphere of capital movement should be lush, open meadows, an inviting global terrain where wealth was free to graze as it wished.

Powell delivered his speech to the Mont Pelerin Society at a time when the debate on this idea was still so divisive, it was

tearing apart long-standing friendships between the members.
However, over the coming years the proposal to move from a
fixed exchange rate to a floating exchange-rate system began to
gain influence across Europe and North America. Milton Friedman,
the leader of this campaign, started to become an increasingly
prominent intellectual and then, following the election of Richard
Nixon in the USA, developed a close professional relationship
with the new American president. Economists from the Friedman
camp took up influential state roles, such as Gottfried Haberler
becoming the chairman of President Nixon's Task Force on US
Balance of Payments Policies.[55] As the 1960s gave way to the
1970s, the argument to leave the fixed exchange rate began to be
repeated by politicians, bankers, newspaper journalists and business
owners across the West. They were supported in their efforts by
a network of think tanks such as the American Enterprise Institute
in the USA, the Walter Eucken Institute in West Germany and,
of course, the IEA in Britain, who hosted conferences and put
out publications arguing for the creation of a floating exchange
rate. In 1971, this transnational campaign achieved its goal when
President Nixon decided to unilaterally untie the US dollar from
the value of gold, effectively ending the system of fixed exchange
rates. With the US dollar no longer tied to a fixed value of gold,
it made no sense for the world's other currencies to remain tied
to the value of the US dollar at a fixed rate. Other governments
across the world quickly followed suit and detached their currencies from the US dollar, creating the conditions for a new golden
age of hyper-financialisation. Corporations could operate across
borders with ever greater ease, leading to an increasingly globalised
marketplace. The value of each nation's currency would now
fluctuate up and down depending on the demands of the market,
just as Powell had envisaged in his speech. Exchange controls
began to be relaxed, and the wealthy were able to start looking
at the whole world as their playground again.

In Britain, exchange controls were abolished in 1979 as one of
the first actions of Prime Minister Margaret Thatcher on entering

10 Downing Street. When the action was announced, Powell, still an MP but no longer a member of the Conservative Party, stood up in Parliament and confessed how much 'envy' he had for the Thatcher government that they had 'the opportunity and the privilege of announcing a step that will strengthen the economy of this country and help to restore our national pride.'[56] The leash was taken off Britain's financial institutions, who had already been working to undermine international attempts to control the global movement of money by coordinating a burgeoning offshore economy with Britain's remaining colonial outposts. With capital flowing freely across borders, the City of London re-established itself as the sorting office for many of the new asset and debt exchanges that proliferated over the next few decades. In 2020, London's banks were noted to have far more cross-border exposure than any of the world's other financial centres, including those in Switzerland, Singapore and the USA.[57] Rather than the immigrants Powell feared, it was Britain's financial industry that emerged to truly hold the whip hand over the country by the start of the twenty-first century.

Precarious Lives

The two speeches that Powell gave in 1968 work best when read together. By combining the 'Rivers of Blood' with the 'Fixed Exchange Rate and Dirigisme', a picture of a planet where free-market economics and anti-migrant nationalist politics walk hand in hand starts to emerge. Far from being a tragic imperial nostalgist pining for a world that had passed, Powell's writings on economics show him to be looking towards the coming world of profits versus people.

In subsequent decades, Powell's image of a 'River of Blood' resurfaced every time another politician warned that Britain was supposedly being overwhelmed by migrants. In 1978, ten years after Powell's speech, Thatcher described her fear that with increasing Commonwealth migration, Britain was being 'swamped by people with a different culture'.[58] Her one-time protégé William Hague would repeat the trick during his unsuccessful 2000 election campaign, when he argued that Britain was being 'flooded' with fake asylum seekers.[59] In 2007, the *Sunday Times* published an article calling for Britain to 'Hold back the immigrant flood'.[60] In 2015, just one year before the Brexit referendum, Nigel Farage stoked fears about how Islamists 'wanted to flood' the UK and Europe.[61] For the lineage that connects Powell to Farage and his followers today, the only solution to this supposed 'flood' is for Britain to impose ever harder border controls. In this worldview, people do not come to Britain because empire created links with so much of the globe or because the post-imperial protections of property rights and the mobility of capital made life more precarious in so much of the 'developing' world. No, people only come to Britain because it is a soft touch – a country of porous borders and generous welfare provisions for all. Yet the rest of the world sees a completely different picture, with Britain commonly understood to have the toughest immigration laws in Europe.[62] To see just how lax British immigration laws are, we can look at the story of someone like Jimmy Mubenga.

Jimmy Mubenga arrived in the UK from Angola in 1994. He was living with his wife and children in east London in 2006 when he was convicted of assault after a dispute on a night out. His sentence was two years' imprisonment. By the time of his release from prison, Mubenga's permission to stay in the UK had expired. Although he began the process of applying for permanent UK residency, due to the government's commitment to deporting foreign-born criminals, he was informed that any application would be futile and he was to be sent back to Angola. For the crime of assault, he would be made to leave not only his home for the past sixteen years but also his wife and five children.

On 12 October 2010, Mubenga was shepherded onto a British Airways flight from Heathrow Airport to Luanda, the capital of Angola, by three detention officers employed by G4S – the private company the British government had outsourced control of the nation's deportation process to. As in so many other deportations, Mubenga was taken on board a regular commercial flight. On any given day at Heathrow, heartbroken deportees board flights to Kingston, Karachi or Kinshasa alongside oblivious tourists, more focused on the in-flight entertainment than on the stories of banishment being written right beside them. Tragically in Mubenga's case, his co-passengers would become only too aware of his presence and that of the guards hired to expel him from the country. Mubenga and the G4S officers boarded the plane approximately ten to fifteen minutes before the other passengers, and initially all appeared calm. However, after he received a call from his wife, a struggle broke out between Mubenga and the officers, leading to Mubenga being handcuffed and restrained by them for about forty minutes. The other passengers heard Mubenga cry out 'I can't breathe, I can't breathe' as he was being restrained, eerily foreshadowing the final words of American victims of police violence, Eric Garner and George Floyd.[63] Medical assistance was eventually called for, but by the time it arrived, Jimmy Kelenda Mubenga was dead.[64]

Mubenga's death not only illustrates the harshness of immigration control in the UK but also shows the difference in global access now enjoyed by the world's haves and have-nots. Angola, like the rest of sub-Saharan Africa, is often associated with war and poverty, but the old picture of a society of blood diamonds and child soldiers is embarrassingly out of date. In 2017, Luanda was named as the most expensive city in the world, listed ahead of Hong Kong, Tokyo and Zurich in the globe's leading cost-of-living survey for 'expats'.[65] For comparison, London was placed in thirtieth position in this survey that compared the price of housing, food, transport and entertainment across all of the world's major cities. Oil wealth has sparked massive economic growth in the Angolan capital since the new millennium. However, this wealth has not been spread over the city. Shiny new beachside properties are rented for $16,000 a month while three-quarters of the city's population continues to live under corrugated-iron roofs in slum settlements that they have built themselves.[66] Rich 'expats' and local elites populate the flight from London to Luanda, travelling to the 'developing' world to enjoy exorbitant parties on the luxury yachts that surround the city's coastline.

We see a snapshot of our unequal world when we see Jimmy Mubenga dying on a British Airways flight heading to the most expensive city in the world. Today, borders no longer simply follow the lines on a map. Borders have been erected everywhere; at hospitals, schools, banks, or even on flights themselves. In first class, we might find an international heiress or a suit-and-tie-wearing businessman reclining his seat into a bed as he checks the day's oil stock prices. At the back of the same plane, we might find a forty-six-year-old father of five being suffocated by the private security guards hired by the British government to do the dirty work of putting a poor black life back in its proper place.

This division is absent within the seemingly endless talk of the immigration problem in Britain. Controlling the movement of those without means has been conflated with the idea of taking back control, of Britain regaining its independence. But hard borders do little to address how Britain's economy is orientated towards the interests of the international markets. Hard borders also do little to address how the global movement of money pushes people away from the places where they were born, to leave their spouses for years at a time or their children in the care of relatives, in an attempt to carve out new lives elsewhere. When market speculation crashed the global economy in 2008, in Britain the price was not paid by the banks or by individuals with capital but by the unemployed, the disabled and the immigrants. In the aftermath of the crash, the government committed to adopting a policy of turning Britain into a 'hostile environment' for those the government had deemed to be unwelcome in this country.[67] Measures were passed to make access to healthcare, housing, bank accounts and other necessary elements of daily life dependent on proving your up-to-date immigration status. Migrants were once again framed as intruders who were at fault for the austerity 'real' British people were enduring, with no reflection on how the same financial speculation that had caused the crash might have disrupted lives and pushed people across the world in the first place.

The Boomerang of Bordering

I am a child of the NHS. Not that I was born in an NHS hospital; it was the hot and dusty surroundings of Korle-Bu teaching hospital in Accra that delivered me into this world. But the NHS adopted me soon after. My parents, fleeing the economic hardship of Ghana's structural adjustment programme, both became new recruits in the army of immigrants that staff Britain's healthcare system. With them working around clock and around the country, the hospital became my and my sister's consistent childhood home. Its waiting rooms served as our playhouses; its unoccupied lab coats became our sleeping bags. Phrases like 'senior house officer', 'on call' or 'ward sister' became part of my vocabulary years before I knew what they meant; beepers and sirens became the soundtrack to my youth. What might sound like a lonely infancy was anything but. No matter which hospital we were at, there was already a ready-made group of playmates also camping out at the hospital while they waited for the nurses, doctors, cleaners, porters or paramedics they called mum or dad to come and pick them up. Many of those kids were also from Commonwealth backgrounds, from Egypt and Sri Lanka, Pakistan and Nigeria, and we would run around empty examination rooms together, blissfully unaware of the long history of empire that informed our little congregation.

It came as a shock to grow up and understand that, in the public imagination, the NHS was the quintessential British institution, a romantic testament to the national capacity for self-sacrifice that immigrants were nothing but a drain upon. After all, it wasn't like ours was an uncommon story. According to Britain's Office for National Statistics, nearly one in three doctors and one in five nurses working in the NHS are immigrants.[68] Yet politicians and journalists who have built their careers on stoking up nativist fears of being flooded by dangerous immigrants have always side-stepped what the NHS, from its very origin, has told us about Britain's reliance on migrant labour.

This isn't just the story in healthcare; it is the story in Britain's food preparation industry, its hospitality industry and its transport industry. Perhaps more than any other time in the post-war era, the Covid-19 pandemic has exposed the overlap between Britain's migrant population and its 'essential' workers. This did not shake up people's ideas of who they shared ties of obligation and commitment with. Instead, these communities of care-givers, healthcare professions and delivery drivers were shown just how willing many were to sacrifice them in the name of national well-being. In the midst of the coronavirus crisis, naivety might have led me to think that the prevalence of migrants taking up the essential jobs of food delivery, care work and healthcare while the rest of the country hibernated indoors might have dampened the anti-migrant rhetoric that has dominated politics in Britain of late. In the same way religious people argue that 'there are no atheists in a foxhole', so too might we expect that 'there are no xenophobes on critical care wards' – when you are fighting for your life on a hospital ward against a deadly new virus, do you really care about where the person treating you is from? It appeared that in Britain, for many the answer was a resounding yes. That all of the first eight doctors to die from Covid-19 were migrant workers did little to slow down the fear-mongering about migra-tion. Just a few weeks after reporting their deaths, newspaper headlines were filled with scare stories of what Nigel Farage called an 'invasion' of migrant boats landing at Dover, and immigration was once again presented as the biggest threat facing Britain, despite the virus burning its way through the population.[69]

Rarely has the opening up of the global money markets from the 1970s onwards been so connected to the increasing insecurity felt by so many in Britain. With controls over currencies now relaxed, the game has changed; money is made by scanning the world in search of ever greater returns on your investment. Now, wealth management is a global industry, where those with the means can dip in and out of countries from Singapore to Bermuda, the way drunken revellers might bar hop over an evening, always in search of a better atmosphere or conditions that might further their interests. Jurisdictions compete with each other to offer the most favourable terms in the hope of attracting assets, in a regulatory 'race to the bottom'. Human lives begin to be lived at the mercy of casino capitalism, as financial deregulation and speculation lead to increasingly frequent and increasingly destructive economic crashes. The financial world and the real world become more detached with each passing year.

Yet the disruption caused by the fluid movement of money across borders has often been obscured placing the emphasis on other 'public enemies'. Since the 1970s, politicians have consistently blamed immigrants for the corrosion of the welfare state. Arguments are made that welfare states are only possible in supposedly homogeneous societies like Sweden, not in ethically and racially diverse societies like the USA or the UK.[70] We are told that people don't want to pay taxes to help those they don't see themselves as being culturally similar to. Newspapers continue to run headlines about how 'sickly immigrants add £1bn to NHS bill' or calling for a 'crackdown on free access to NHS services for migrants'.[71] In 2015, the British government capitalised on this feeling to introduce the immigration health surcharge, which requires non-European workers in the UK to pay to use the NHS, despite already paying for the service through taxes like everybody else. This charge even applied to migrant NHS and social care workers. In 2020, at the height of the coronavirus pandemic, when foreign healthcare workers were sacrificing their time, energy and even their lives to try and protect the British public, Boris Johnson's government tried to increase the immigration surcharge that they faced.[72]

The hyper-financialisation of the global economy has meant that more and more people are being made surplus to the requirements of capitalism. The process of confining whole populations to precarious lives began in the post-colonial world but it is not staying there. This is not just because desperate people tend not to simply accept that they must stay put even if there are no opportunities there. Regardless of how strong border laws are made, people continue to risk their lives sailing across the ocean on a rubber dinghy or climbing on the back of lorries to try and find something better. However, it is not just precarious people who are now moving around the world, but the precarious life itself.[73] The decolonial project was defeated by the same tidal wave of financialisaton that has also eroded the welfare state 'back home' in Britain. Since Thatcher, successive governments of both Conservative and Labour iterations have pulled apart more and more of the social safety net in Britain. With money free to move to where labour costs are lowest and employee rights are weakest, even a former imperial superpower is now incentivised to ensure it remains attractive to global capital. Informal employment, insecure housing and personal debt traps are all on the rise in twenty-first-century Britain. The free movement of money has turned Britain's property market into an alternative bank account for the financial elite of Russia, China, the UAE and elsewhere, completely severing the connection between the world of work and the world of wealth.[74]

Britain's cities are now populated by a growing so-called 'precariat' class – informalized workers working without contract, without benefits and without any hope of being able to buy themselves some security. The precariat model of labour may be a recent phenomenon in Britain, but it isn't new to anyone who watched how globalisation impacted the former colonies after empire.[75] Informal and precarious work relations have long been noted as a significant element of the standard 'developing' world economy. However, economists usually explained this trend by reading it as another indicator that these economies were on the stepping-stones to full development. This was part of the linear path, and in time capitalism would eventually absorb the informal, precarious economy into the formal market. Yet today, not only is the informal economy thriving across the 'developing' world, it is now spreading to countries like Britain. Now, it is the period of the industrial welfare state that the Attlee government claimed as their proud invention, one that should be followed by departing colonies like India, that is looking like the exception, not the rule.

What the *Britannia Unchained* authors admire about India today is how it has combined its inheritance of British capitalist traditions with the precarious labour force and market-friendly conditions of the 'developing' world. India maintains a legal system based on English common law, with its privileging of property rights, while encouraging international investment through allowing companies to follow weaker regulations than they would face in Europe. In a 2016 meeting of the Treasury Select Committee, chief Brexit ideologue Jacob Rees-Mogg argued that India should be the standard for Britain's future environmental and safety regulations. When it came to things like checks and balances on the safety of new buildings or the required types of packaging that toxic substances must be transported within, Rees-Mogg suggested that Britain's position should be 'if its good enough for India, we will accept it here'.[76] Following Narendra Modi's election as prime minister in 2014, India's embrace of free-market policies, which had been increasing since the 1980s, has gone into overdrive. In 2018, the Institute of Economic Affairs excitedly promoted a potential free-trade deal between Britain and India after Brexit.[77]

The Twenty-first-century Windrush

Any future trading relationship with India will have to reckon not only with the historical legacy of empire but also with the question of how people can move between Britain and the world's second most populous country. Already talk of a trade deal has been held up by the issue of Britain's migration rules. The tensions between the dual projects of Global Britain and the 'hostile environment' are becoming clear again. The consequences of the financial crash of 2008 impacted not only people migrating to Britain at the time, but the Windrush generation that Powell's rage was directed at many years prior. In 2018, Britain was gripped by the revelation that hundreds of people had been wrongfully dragged from their homes, detained in immigration centres, interrogated by officials and, in some cases, actually deported from the UK under the 'hostile environment' policy. Because many of the victims had been part of the Windrush generation of post-war British subjects who moved to the UK from the colonies, this crisis came to be known as the Windrush scandal.

Dexter Bristol was one of the people whose final years were devastated by the Windrush scandal.[78] He had arrived in the UK from Grenada as an eight-year-old boy in 1968 to join his mother, a British passport holder who was working in the NHS as a nurse. Bristol was able to travel to Britain on his mother's passport as, at the time, Grenada was still a British colony. The Caribbean island did not become an independent country until 1974. After a lifetime of living and working in Britain, in 2016 Bristol was suddenly informed by the Home Office that not only did they not consider him to be British, but that he had no right to be in the country. He lost his job as a cleaner and was denied access to benefits, leaving him completely destitute. His immigration dispute continued until March 2018 when, tragically, he suddenly collapsed outside his north London home and died of heart failure. While heart problems were medically held to be the cause of death, his mother argued that the enormous stress created by the Home Office's denial of his citizenship rights brought on his collapse and early death.[79]

At a time when most people would expect to be enjoying the fruits of their long lives, grandparents from the British Caribbean community suddenly had to face being told that they were not welcome in the only country they had ever known, and would be sent back to places they often hadn't seen since they were barely old enough to walk. The same forces that created the Windrush scandal had also devastated the Caribbean islands from which the victims had arrived decades earlier. While Powell and the anti-migrant politics he inspired promoted an amnesia about Britain's historical relationship with the Caribbean, it would be there that the struggle of much of his economic vision would play out. As the sixties moved into the seventies, Kingston, Jamaica, the very place where passengers had boarded the *Empire Windrush* to change the complexion of post-war Britain, became the new battleground for competing visions of what the world after empire would look like.

4

The Debt

In 1976, on a hot and humid December evening, a crowd of around 50,000 people amassed at National Heroes Park in Kingston, Jamaica hoping to see a musician that nobody was sure was even still alive.[1] The son of sixty-year-old white English plantation supervisor Norval Sinclair Marley and an eighteen-year-old black Jamaican woman Cedella Malcolm, Robert Nesta Marley, against all odds, had risen to become an international superstar.[2] More than simply a pop singer, the music of the man known around the globe as Bob Marley had come to represent the pain and yearning of all downtrodden people, not only in his native Jamaica but across all of what was then called the 'Third World'. In a music industry dominated by American and British pop acts, Marley enjoyed a level of success for an artist outside of the Western world that was, and remains today, unprecedented. However, just as his representation of local reggae music and the Rastafarian religion began to turn the world's eye to Jamaica, the social and economic framework of Marley's young nation began to be pulled apart.

Political violence had gripped the island since its last election, in 1972. With the next election on the horizon, Marley tried to cool the atmosphere by organising a free public concert in the name of peace. The concert came to be known as 'Smile Jamaica' and was explicitly promoted as being non-political.[3] But due to presumptions about Marley's own political sympathies, observers suspected, not entirely unfairly, that the concert would serve as a rally for the country's incumbent prime minister, the democratic socialist and self-styled champion of the Third World, Michael Manley. This suspicion was only heightened once Manley announced that the 1976 Jamaican election would take place almost immediately after the concert. With so much violence surrounding politics on the island, even the country's most famous musician couldn't avoid being caught up in the bloodshed. Two days before the concert was scheduled to occur, as Bob Marley and his crew met at his house to practise, heavily armed men broke in and began moving from room to room, firing wildly. Marley had just finished rehearsing 'I Shot the Sherriff' when the gunmen shot him in the chest and the arm. Before they left, they also shot his manager, his bandmate, and even shot his wife Rita in the head.

A couple of days later, when the crowd gathered at National Heroes Park, people were unsure whether they were converging for a performance or a memorial. News of the shooting had spread throughout the island, but the conditions of Bob Marley and his entourage were still the subject of rumour. Miraculously, everybody survived the attack. Had Marley been inhaling instead of exhaling at the time the bullet struck his chest, it could have gone into his heart. But as the crowd waited in anticipation in Kingston, Marley discharged himself from hospital and sought refuge at a friend's house up in the hills outside the city.

Initially, he refused to attend the concert; with the gunmen still at large, his life was still very much under threat. However, with the prime minister and opposition politicians reassuring him of his safety, he decided to come down from the hills and perform just one song. By the time Marley sauntered onto the stage, trademark dreadlocks draped over his face, the sky was pitch dark. But if the audience had any doubt as to who was really in front of them, all questions were answered when Marley opened his mouth and released his unmistakable rasping wail into the microphone as the band kicked into gear behind him. In the end, with a bullet still lodged in his arm, Marley played a complete ninety-minute show, swirling and dancing around the stage like a man possessed as his music washed over the crowd. At the end of the concert, he lifted his shirt to allow the audience to examine his wounds, as though they were Doubting Thomas.[4]

In the aftermath of the Smile Jamaica concert, Prime Minister Michael Manley won re-election just as he hoped, and with that, a mandate to pursue an almighty confrontation between his version of Third World socialism and the international capitalist interests that were invested in the country. But Marley would not stay to see it. At that time, around 20,000 Jamaicans were leaving the island each year.[5] Most were heading to the old mother country of the UK. The morning after the concert, Marley joined the exodus of people, settling in London for the next two years. At the time of the concert and election, Jamaica had only been independent from Britain for fourteen years. Before independence, the island had been under British control for over 300 years, making it among Britain's longest continual colonial relationships. For a rough comparison, the period between Ireland's formal incorporation into Britain and its independence was only 122 years. Of all the national histories that shaped the structure of Global Britain over the centuries, few could claim to be more significant than Jamaica's. Yet it is a history that remains unknown, even to most of the Britons who travel to the country every year to enjoy luxury cruises or five-star beach resorts.

Jamaica is consistently one of the most popular destinations for Britons holidaying out of Europe, with almost a quarter of a million British nationals visiting the Caribbean island every year.[6] Holiday companies sell Jamaica to Britons as being a distant, tropical paradise, not a country whose history has been intimately interwoven with the development of their own for centuries – perhaps because the blood and violence of this history doesn't make the most pleasant reading for a holiday brochure. The Kingdom of England first gained control of the island of Jamaica from the Spanish Empire in 1660, formalised ten years later by the Treaty of Madrid. English merchants quickly began shipping slaves from West Africa to work on the lucrative plantations that were built. The money from the slave plantations in Jamaica became one of the key sources of wealth for the now growing English and then British Empire.[7] Then, in 1831, a rebellion led by an enslaved black man called Sam Sharpe, who was executed for his role in the fighting, ultimately helped to bring about the collapse of plantation slavery in Jamaica, and abolition was passed into law in 1834. Another uprising in 1865, the Morant Bay Rebellion, pushed Britain into formalising Jamaica as a crown colony, the most direct form of British constitutional colonial rule.

Independence from Britain came in 1962, but this did not suddenly facilitate a complete divorce between the fates of these two countries; the afterlife of empire in Jamaica would carry major implications for how our world works today. The Jamaica of the 1970s was able to produce a figure like Bob Marley not only because of its musical traditions but because the country was, at that time, at the epicentre of a global political and economic confrontation between the sovereignty of Third World nations and the property rights of multinational capitalism. There was a political culture as well as an artistic culture on the island at that time that lent itself to Marley's songs about 'burning and looting' in the 'Babylon system'. In many ways what happened in Jamaica in the early 1970s is the prelude to the story that in Britain we call 'neoliberalism'. When Margaret Thatcher popularised the slogan 'there is no alternative', this was a rebuttal to all those people across the world who were at that moment being inspired by a politician from Jamaica to imagine that there might be an alternative, another way to organise the global economy. The tale of Michael Manley and Bob Marley's Jamaica in the late twentieth century is the tale of a small island that escaped an empire only to fall into an impossible struggle with its economic aftermath.

The Third World

Today the label 'Third World' is most definitely meant as an insult, an offensive reminder of your place at the bottom of the global hierarchy. Being Third World means you are poor, you are dirty and you are backwards. But being Third World has not always been a negative slur. The dictionary definition of 'Third World' describes it as 'the developing countries of Asia, Africa, and Latin America'.[8] But can any single term accurately capture the various economies and societies of Asia, Africa and Latin America, not to mention the Middle East and the Caribbean, which are also often thrown in? A historical analysis expands the definition. The term was first popularised in 1952, when French demographer Alfred Sauvy described the post-war international order as containing 'three worlds' on 'one planet': the capitalist, American-led 'First World'; the communist, Soviet-led 'Second World'; and the exploited and leaderless 'Third World'.[9] In this framework, the inferiority of the Third World appears, at first, to be fixed. But Sauvy's description carried within it a warning for the complacent First and Second Worlds: his categorisation of the Third World was based on the similarities he saw between their position and that of the Third Estate in pre-Revolutionary France. Just as the peasants and labourers of France eventually stormed the palaces of aghast royals who presumed the underclass would forever accept their subservient condition, so too did Sauvy see the potential for an ambitious Third World to perhaps, one day, overturn the global order.

Over the course of the turbulent 1960s, the idea of the Third World was reclaimed by former colonial peoples to describe the alternative world they wanted to bring into being. Unlike the idea of the 'developing world' that replaced it, the Third World was reimagined as a destination in itself, an inspirational slogan and identity that was embraced not only by anti-colonial activists in Latin America, Africa and Asia but also by student protesters and New Left intellectuals in London, New York and Paris. To be a 'Third Worldist' was to be in solidarity with Kwame Nkrumah, Frantz Fanon and Ernesto 'Che' Guevara, as well as their First World collaborators; people like Jean-Paul Sartre, Angela Davis and Tariq Ali. As the 1960s gave way to the 1970s, Third Worldism matured into a coordinated and coherent political, economic and legal vision for remaking the world. Its battle extended to institutional forums like the United Nations General Assembly. At the heart of the Third World movement was a simple question: if international institutions were supposed to reflect a new world where each nation state was equal, and there were more nation states in the Third World than in the First or Second, then why were these institutions not being used to address the inequality embedded in the global system? During the 1970s, this question was asked most forcibly by the Third World's latest spokesman, a sophisticated Jamaican politician who strode onto the world stage like he was born to it. Because, in many ways, he was.

The scion of a famous political dynasty, Michael Manley could have easily become just the kind of establishment figure who could be trusted to take charge of a vital former colony without rocking the boat. His mother Edna was a famous artist, whose sculptures are now considered national treasures in Jamaica.[10] Born in Bournemouth at the turn of the twentieth century to an English cleric and his quietly mixed-race wife, Edna scandalised her family by embracing her secret 'black' heritage, despite being able to 'pass' as completely white. She ended up marrying her mixed-race Jamaican cousin, Norman Manley, after the two met when he came to study in England.[11] Norman took Edna back to Jamaica, where her art career flourished, while he became the leader of the People's National Party and the final premier of colonial-era Jamaica. As premier, Norman Manley helped to drive the island towards independence from Britain. But having set his country on the path to freedom, Norman wound up losing the election that would have made him the first prime minister of an independent Jamaica, and served out the rest of his political life as the leader of the opposition. Out of the two sons that Edna and Norman would have, it was the younger, Michael, who would follow in his father's footsteps.

Educated at exclusive British colonial schools, Michael Manley served as a fighter pilot in the Second World War, cultivating the image of a dashing hero that would lead to him being married five times during his life.[12] Tall and thin, with skin so fair he could also be confused for someone solely white, Manley could have used his background and appearance to enjoy a comfortable life as part of Jamaica's elite. In a country where almost all the population were black, the wealthy section of Jamaican society was still marked by skin colour, with the richest families being usually white or fair-skinned Jamaicans. However, like his mother before him, Manley claimed his black heritage with pride. Also, like fellow Third World leaders Kwame Nkrumah and Jomo Kenyatta, he took up his university studies at the London School of Economics, enrolling in 1945, just as the Attlee government began to establish its welfare state. The social democratic atmosphere in Britain at that time and the teachings of Marxist LSE professors like Harold Laski and Ralph Miliband made an impression on the young man. These teachings moved from theory to practice when Manley returned to Jamaica to inherit his father's leadership of the People's National Party and begin his own political journey.

While very much his father's son, Michael Manley sought to do politics in a different manner, looking to win over not only the educated people of Jamaica but also the masses of the country. He believed that the spiritual and mystical powers in Jamaica could be summoned to serve his earthly ambitions for political and economic change, and began to frame his rhetoric to resonate in particular with the religion that was popular with young Jamaicans at that time, Rastafarianism.[13] Years before he became the leader of his party, Manley travelled to Ethiopia to meet Haile Selassie, the Ethiopian ruler considered to be a living god by the Rastafarians.[14] He invited Selassie to come and visit Jamaica and, when the Ethiopian ruler arrived in Kingston in 1966 in front of awed spectators, he presented Manley with the gift of a white imperial staff. Manley and his supporters named this staff the 'Rod of Correction' and nicknamed the politician 'Joshua', after the man who had led the Israelites to freedom.[15] Now, like the Old Testament biblical leaders Jamaicans grew up learning about, Manley was in possession of a divine weapon with which he could chase corruption and greed from their paradisal Caribbean homeland. At his election campaign rallies, he would brandish the white staff and jubilant fans would call out 'Beat them with the rod of correction.'[16]

His championing of the common people quickly made Manley a popular politician, and he ascended to the premiership of Jamaica in 1972. Upon taking office, he began implementing one of the most ambitious programmes of social reform that has been tried in a former British colony. Manley created a national minimum wage for Jamaican workers a full quarter of a century before the National Minimum Wage Act was passed back in Britain. His government also passed laws to provide affordable housing and free primary, secondary and tertiary education for its citizens. But it was on the international stage that Manley would cause the biggest stir. For him, the arena of international law offered the perfect avenue to organise all of the recently decolonised countries into using their growing power to call for the global economy to be rebalanced, and pursue what he and his allies would christen a 'New International Economic Order' (NIEO).

By offering a vision of the NIEO, Manley's government became an inspiration for the rest of the Third World, which was struggling to see the value of recently won 'independence' in a world still controlled by private ownership. For Manley, to be Third World was not an insult but a mark of pride. In his words, the former colonial world had now 'proclaimed itself the Third World to mark its transition from an age of apology to one of assertiveness'.[17] Why should the Third World continue to simply accept the terms it was presented with? With more and more countries achieving independence from the old empires and taking their seats in the new world of nations, Manley realised that by the 1970s, the Third World was the global majority, and if it could be united, it could be a significant power block.[18] But, if decolonisation was to be completed, they would need to turn their focus away from independence and sovereignty and towards the economy.

The Dream of a New International Economic Order

In the three decades between 1945 and 1975, membership of the United Nations had grown from 51 nation states to 144 nation states. But the first generation of nationalist independence leaders like Nkrumah and Nyerere had already learned a painful lesson regarding the limits of sovereignty. Resource-rich 'independent' countries still found the rules of international trade weighted against them. When Michael Manley emerged as the leader of Jamaica, among his main ideas was to see whether the new nation states could collectively use their numerical advantage at institutions like the UN to readdress this unfair economic system. The demands of the NIEO were as simple but all-encompassing as the name suggests. These countries were asking for nothing less than a redrawing of the rules of global trade so that all countries could enjoy economic as well as political independence.

The campaign for the NIEO was the culmination of years of increasing collaboration between the newly decolonised nations in international settings. In 1955, the independent countries of Africa and Asia met in Bandung, Indonesia, for a conference that is now seen as the birth of Third World internationalism.[19] At this conference, the Third World made it clear that while the newspapers in Europe and North America were filled with tales of the escalating Cold War, the majority of the global population lived outside of these power blocs and were more concerned with protecting their new-found sovereignty. Then, in 1966, they met again, this time with the addition of countries in Latin America to make it the Tricontinental Conference. With eighty-two countries represented at this meeting in Havana, Cuba, the Tricontinental Conference gave the Third World a space to meet outside the UN, without the shadows of their old colonial masters hanging over them. The themes of this conference were not only the ongoing campaigns of anti-imperialism and national liberation, but also racial discrimination, opposition to nuclear weapons and questions of economic development.[20]

Upon his election in 1972, Jamaica's confident new president had quickly realised that any changes he wished to enact on his own island were largely dependent upon changes to the wider international order, and therefore Manley took up the position of spokesperson for the economic interests of the Third World. Then, in 1973, the Organisation of Arab Petroleum-Exporting Countries (OAPEC), a group set up to ensure cooperation between the oil-producing countries of the Arab world, placed an embargo on the handful of countries they saw as supporting Israel, including the USA and the UK. The embargo caused oil prices to skyrocket. This delivered two lessons for the rest of the 'developing' world. First, while the rise in the price of oil had a devastating economic impact on all countries, rich and poor, who had to import their oil, those with smaller economies felt the consequences of being so dependent on the international markets more acutely. Second, the oil embargo also showed 'developing' countries that if it they acted in a unified manner, they could wield some serious bargaining power on a global scale.

A year after the oil embargo, Manley published a book entitled *The Politics of Change*, where he wrote:

> Clearly Third World countries must evolve a strategy in foreign affairs that reflects their common problems and needs. Such a strategy must take into account the terms of trade, the movement of international capital, the applicability of foreign technology, patterns of international trade and the right of self-determination.

To achieve his goals, Manley looked to the UN, for he believed that despite 'all its institutional limitations', the UN still represented 'the highest aspirations of mankind' and remained 'the most efficient instrument that man has devised to translate these aspirations into reality for the benefit of all'.[21]

With his allies from the formerly colonised world, Manley mobilised the numerical advantage they enjoyed in the UN to pass a resolution in May 1974, that still reads radically even today: the *Declaration on the Establishment of a New International Economic Order*. The UN Declaration contained a commitment to ending all waste of food products, a recognition of the right for countries to enjoy full permanent sovereignty over their own natural resources and, perhaps most strikingly, a provision which reinforced the power of national governments to control 'the activities of transnational corporations by taking measures in the interests of the national economies of the countries where such transnational corporations operate'.[22] For multinational capital, this declaration that global companies could only operate by the grace of the sovereign nation states they were invested in threatened to turn the UN into a forum for the enemy.

Just as the declaration was passed in the UN, the UN Commission on Transnational Corporations was established to analyse and oversee the actions of corporate interests across the globe.[23] The following year, the UN held a special session focusing on 'Development and International Economic Cooperation', which focused on trying to 'eliminate the economic imbalance between developed and developing countries'.[24] For a moment, it appeared as though the structural changes that Manley and his allies had been pushing for were starting to be realised. But as all the attention was focused on the UN, changes to the political landscape back in the old centre of the world – Westminster, London – would soon have major consequences for the dreams of the Third World.

The Rise of Thatcher

Around the same time that the NIEO was gaining influence at the UN, a political earthquake was occurring in the UK. The Britain that Bob Marley and so many other Jamaicans moved to was going through its own epochal shift at the end of the 1970s. After the failure of free marketeers like Enoch Powell and Keith Joseph to seize control of Conservative Party, in 1975 a green-grocer's daughter called Margaret Thatcher succeeded where they had failed, and after a few years as party leader on 3 May 1979 she became the first woman to be elected as the prime minister of the United Kingdom of Great Britain and Northern Ireland. Two weeks later, she sent a letter to the presidents of the Institute of Economic Affairs, Arthur Seldon and Ralph Harris. In this letter, Thatcher made clear who she believed had undertaken the intellectual heavy lifting that had made her victory possible:

> thank you for what you have done for the cause of free enterprise over the course of so many years. It was primarily your foundation work, which enabled us to rebuild the philosophy upon which our Party succeeded in the past. The debt we owe to you is immense and I am very grateful.[25]

The next month, Thatcher chose Ralph Harris to be the first peer appointed during her administration, making him Baron Harris of High Cross.[26] With one of its figureheads now firmly implanted in the House of Lords and a sympathetic prime minister residing in Downing Street, the IEA was in a position to see some of the policies it had dreamed up since 1955 become reality.

Thatcher was only too eager to oblige, confronting the power of the labour unions, relaxing capital controls and moving the UK towards being a more market-orientated country than it had been at any time since the end of the Second World War. Today, the story of Thatcherism is well established, a constellation of striking miners, nouveau riche yuppies and riots from Brixton, Handsworth and Toxteth in 1981 to Trafalgar Square in 1990. But, like its forebear Powellism, Thatcher's vision for change stretched beyond a domestic project. Too often we think of Thatcherism separately from the global context in which it arose, but the same economic theories that drove Margaret Thatcher to break the unions and deindustrialise the UK were also used to disempower the Third World governments of Africa, Asia and the Caribbean, which, with their moves to establish a new international economic order, were just at that moment threatening to gain real power over the fate of global capitalism.

Thatcher's project was not just about restoring Britain's economy but also about Britain's role as an international leader. Uncomfortable with aligning herself too closely with Europe but also chafing at the idea of Britain's complete subservience to the USA, Thatcher, who wore the accusations that she was a Victorian throwback with pride, looked to bring back the global influence Britain had been slowly losing since the turn of the twentieth century. As Manley and his allies ran around the UN frantically trying to show that there was another way that the world could work, the intellectual networks that produced Thatcherism were also busy trying to popularise their own version of a new international economic order, only this time with capital mobility, protection of foreign investment, deregulation and privatisation of state industries taking centre stage.

By 1970, Antony Fisher, the founder of the IEA, had grown weary of England following the decline of his battery chicken-farming business and the experience of a painful divorce. He first tried to replicate his farming model with turtles on the Cayman Islands, but pressure from environmental groups who opposed the breeding and harvesting of turtles for meat drove this project into insolvency.[27] Fortunately for Fisher, at a meeting of the Mont Pelerin Society in 1975 he met Dorian Crocker, a widow with deep pockets and an even deeper interest in the cause of saving the free market. They would soon be married and Fisher moved to North America, where he would be embraced by a new generation of economists, politicians and businessmen who shared his vision for an emboldened global free market. Fisher not only ended up living in the same San Francisco building as Milton Friedman but became such a close friend that after Friedman received the 1976 Nobel Prize in economics, he would often take press interviews at the Fisher house because he and his wife felt the Fishers' apartment was better decorated.[28] With the financial support of his wealthy new wife, Fisher was also able to elevate his project to new heights.

After the success of the IEA, the next step was to go global and create copycat institutions across the world. In 1981, Fisher founded the Atlas Economic Research Foundation. Whereas the IEA had been swimming against the tide when it started, Atlas arrived as the tide was turning, at the start of a decade in which capitalist interests would make substantial gains in the effort to rewire the global economy. Atlas set about becoming the mothership connecting all these new versions of the IEA (it is now known as the Atlas Network), providing the seed money to get like-minded organisations off the ground, connections to future donors and guidance about what steps these new organisations needed to take to gain influence within their own countries.[29]

Through the 1980s, Atlas sponsored trips by Friedrich Hayek and Milton Friedman to countries that had been targeted for new think tanks, financed translations of their writing into local languages and hosted workshops where their expertise could be shared.[30] From 21 to 26 April 1987, Atlas even took up temporary residence in Montego Bay, Jamaica, sharing technical expertise and offering institutional support to committed free-market warriors working across Latin America and the Caribbean.[31] Fisher's goal of duplicating the IEA across the world has been remarkably successful. By 2020, the Atlas Network included 446 institutions in 95 countries, a constellation of free-market garrisons now spread across every continent of the world, from the Nassau Institute in the Bahamas to the Centre for Public Policy Research

THE DEBT

in India and the Institute for Liberty and Policy Innovation in Ghana.[32]

Fisher and the IEA didn't forget about Britain, supporting the creation of new think tanks such as the Centre for Policy Studies in 1974, with Keith Joseph and Margaret Thatcher as co-founders. Thatcherism didn't just remake Britain – the ideological milieu from which it emerged also helped to remake the world. Upon hearing of the creation of Atlas, Margaret Thatcher, still early in her first term as prime minister, wrote to Fisher not only to underline her 'admiration for all the IEA has done over the years' but also to 'applaud' these new plans to extend its network 'further afield', concluding the fan letter by declaring to Fisher, 'I am one of your strongest supporters'.[33]

The End of the Third World

With Thatcher and her allies spreading the gospel of the free market across the world while Manley and his allies gained increasing influence within the UN, it was clear that a confrontation on the international stage was inevitable. Thatcher's position was greatly reinforced by the 1980 election of Ronald Reagan as the new US president – Reagan was equally committed to dismantling the restrictions placed on the market. The Anglosphere had taken this decisive ideological turn just in time for tensions between the 'developed' and 'developing' worlds to come to a head. In 1981, twenty-two heads of state from across five continents met for the first and only 'North–South' conference. The world leaders gathered at the Cancun Sheraton, looking out over the coast of Mexico towards the crisp Caribbean Sea, an idyllic setting in stark contrast to the tension that underpinned the power struggles taking place.

Those in attendance included Thatcher, Reagan, President François Mitterrand of France, Prime Minister Pierre Elliott Trudeau of Canada, President Julius Nyerere of Tanzania and

Prime Minister Indira Gandhi of India. Michael Manley and his efforts with the NIEO had helped pave the road to Cancun. Prior to this main summit meeting, Manley had hosted a mini summit between the 'developed' world and the 'developing' countries in 1978. While he was unable to secure the attendance of the major Western countries at his preliminary meeting, Manley was able to bring the leaders of West Germany, Australia, Canada and Norway together with the leaders of Nigeria and Venezuela for a conference in Jamaica that proved to be a productive discussion on how global trade between the countries could be improved.[34] However, the year before the Cancun conference took place, just five days before Reagan won the vote in the USA, Manley lost one of the most bitter and conflict-ridden elections to have taken place in the western hemisphere.[35] After a bloody contest marked by politically sponsored violence, Jamaica had elected a new president – the 'business-friendly' Edward Seaga, a politician known to opponents as 'Edward CIAga' due to his perceived closeness to the USA.[36]

Life on the island was changing. Just a few months before the summit in Cancun, Bob Marley, the man many saw as the prophetic voice of the 'Third World' struggle, died of cancer aged only thirty-six. The millions across the world who had sought solace in his music while suffering through the failed dreams of decolonisation could have been forgiven for reading Marley's death, on top of Manley's defeat, as an omen of another coming tragedy. When the Cancun conference commenced, other countries like Tanzania and Ghana tried to take up the role of confronting the British and American leaders, now that Jamaica was under the control of a government much more agreeable to Western capitalist interests. But with the wind of change now firmly blowing back in their direction, Thatcher and Reagan had little reason to compromise anymore, and casually dismissed them. Instead, Thatcher took the opportunity to tell the Third World that the solution to its problems was simply to open up the international markets even further – it wasn't that countries didn't need help, but first they needed to help themselves.[37] When Third World governments complained about the 'structural adjustment policies' the IMF and World Bank were imposing on them in exchange for loans (more on which below), the UK's representatives responded that, as they were also in the midst of a process of privatisation and deindustrialisation, haemorrhaging jobs across the automobile and steel industries, they knew 'quite a lot about structural adjustment' themselves.[38] The Third World countries needed to stop looking for sympathy and instead start looking at the opportunities that privatising their economy and opening up to foreign investment could provide.

Thatcher and Reagan shot down the idea of a UN Bank to lend to developing countries at better rates than the IMF and the World Bank, with Thatcher declaring that such a bank couldn't succeed within an institution like the UN, where developing countries held the numerical advantage. According to her, 'there was no way that I was going to put British deposits into a bank which was totally run by those on overdrafts'.[39] Thatcher believed that 'the primary responsibility for development rests with the developing countries themselves' and that it was incumbent on them to 'pursue policies that would attract private investment' rather than try and gain the means to exert control over the rules of global trade.[40]

Ultimately, the meeting in Cancun ended in frustration for those hoping for the birth of a new international economic order. No new laws or plans for action were agreed by the time attendees boarded their flights back home. When Thatcher returned to face the British Parliament at Westminster, she justified her obstruction tactics in Cancun by claiming: 'I think that there was a lot of misunderstanding about the purpose of the conference. I think that hopes were artificially raised.'[41] She argued that 'the United Nations resolution itself is very vague' – in effect, the commitments to a new international economic order that Manley and others had worked so hard to draft should be dismissed as empty platitudes that had no real meaning.[42] The dreams of the NIEO lay in tatters and would never recover.

Over the following decades, Manley's dream of 'developing' countries being able to exert control over the multinational corporations that operated within their borders drifted further and further away. The ambition of securing a binding international treaty that could hold corporations to a fixed set of international controls would never materialise. One of the central aims of the NIEO – for the world's governments to agree a United Nations Code of Conduct on Transnational Corporations – broke down during the 1980s, as the Thatcherite/Reaganite revolution shifted the emphasis of negotiations from protecting countries from potentially predatory corporations to protecting corporations from potentially greedy governments.[43] Then, in 1993, the UN Commission on Transnational Corporations was collapsed into the UN's Trade and Development Forum, where it would be reimagined as the UN Commission on Investment, Technology and Related Financial Issues.[44] The message was clear – controlling corporations was out, inviting foreign investment was in.

After nine years out of office, Manley would eventually be re-elected by the Jamaican people in 1989, but the change in global context meant that his second stint as prime minister would look very different from his first. When Manley re-entered office, the Cold War had just ended and the 'end of history' was being proclaimed – many were putting their faith in the new age of globalisation. The radical Third World leaders who had supported him in the 1970s had either given in, gone away or been killed. The Bretton Woods controls on finance were now a distant memory and financialisation was in the ascendency as money became more flexible than ever before. For those who were horrified by the spectre of a new international economic order emerging in the 1970s, perhaps the sweetest revenge was in watching Manley, as he returned to office, having to embrace many of the free-market reforms that he had spent so much of his first premiership opposing. He immediately devalued the Jamaican currency and imposed austerity measures on the economy in order to try and satisfy a new IMF agreement that Seaga had negotiated.[45] By the end of his second stint as prime minister in 1992, Manley was pushing the Caribbean states to get behind the American-led North American Free Trade Agreement.[46] That brief moment, when Michael Manley and others dreamed of using the UN to make a new kind of economic world order, had been buried. When he left office, just a little over a year after Thatcher's own long stint in power had ended, Manley would say that he now shared political perspectives 'very, very similar to those of Margaret Thatcher'.[47]

Third World Debt

From the perspective of today, the rise and fall of Michael Manley's project to change first Jamaica and then the world is a tragedy. Not only in the modern sense, with all the sadness and suffering caused by the surrounding violence, but also a tragedy in the classical sense – like the protagonist of a Greek play, Manley's Jamaica and its Third World allies carried, right from the beginning, a flaw that would ultimately prove to be their undoing – they were all in debt.

In the 1960s, Third World countries typically held small sovereign debt, on account of being relatively new sovereign countries. The little debt that they did owe was typically to other governments or to the World Bank for loans taken out to finance development projects. However, the OAPEC oil shock in 1973 meant that developing countries needed to get more money very quickly if they were going to be able to keep their lights on. A further oil shock in 1979 and the decision by the USA to increase its interest rates at the same time only exacerbated the problem for Third World governments dependent on external trade. Spying an opportunity, commercial banks stepped in to provide these countries with generous loans to meet their immediate shortfall, with substantial rates of interest for repayment attached. Each year, the debt ate up more and more of the national budget of these countries, and when they realised that they were unable to keep up with their repayments, they had no choice but to turn to the international financial institutions, the IMF and the World Bank, for help. Michael Manley's Jamaica started the trend in 1973 by signing a short agreement with the IMF for a loan that could help the island overcome its shortfall.[48] While the interest rates were not as high with the IMF, this loan was expensive in other ways. Before they would lend Jamaica the money, the IMF required that the government agree to adjust the structure of its economy by accepting big public spending cuts (the 'structural adjustment policies' discussed in Cancun). Manley despaired, but what other choice was there?[49]

Jamaica was caught in an early example of what became known as the 'Third World debt crisis'. Country after country across Latin America, Africa and Asia would soon also be trapped in this vicious cycle – the debt repayments of developing countries jumped by over 1,000 per cent between 1971 and 1982.[50] Sovereign debt had existed long before the rise of the Third World; for centuries, European monarchs would take out loans and then simply refuse to repay them – after all, who could enforce a debt against a king? The ability to use international law to keep a sovereign country tied to its debt was tested in interwar Germany, following the imposition of huge war reparations in the Treaty of Versailles. However, after the Second World War, economists realised that keeping Germany locked in a state of indebtedness had fuelled the rise of Nazism.[51] The Bretton Woods system was meant to stop nations falling too far into debt, but by the time the Third World debt crisis arose, the collapsed system wasn't an obstacle to global capital, and the IMF and World Bank no longer feared the consequences of keeping a nation state chained by international debt.

Manley decided to sever Jamaica's ties to the IMF as he was getting ready for the 1980 election, yet this only resulted in further hardship for his already impoverished people. The country was now facing economic isolation and, in Britain and the USA, it was being talked of as the new Cuba.[52] Manley was presented as an Anglophone version of Fidel Castro, despite his attempts to insist that he was not making Jamaica a communist country but a democratic socialist one. His goal was for the Third World to be a place of respect and prosperity in its own right, 'independent of the United States, of Britain, of the Soviet Union, of Cuba, of anybody', but with Jamaica presented as a tool of Soviet communism, few in the West were willing to halt its spiral into more debt, least of all its Commonwealth 'mother country' of Britain.[53] Edward Seaga was able to ride this wave of discontent to victory over Manley in the election, promising to the desperate people that he was going to make 'money jingle in yu pockets'.[54] Yet when Manley returned to office in 1989, the debt had only grown, despite Seaga having signed additional IMF structural adjustment loan agreements. Manley had little choice but to agree to a further bailout and therefore more reform conditions, including further cuts to spending on health, education and housing and more selling off of the state's assets to private companies. In 2013, when Jamaica signed its latest structural adjustment loan, its debt was still 147 per cent of the island's gross domestic product, meaning even if the country put absolutely everything into paying off the debt, a third would still be unpaid every year.[55] Austerity has become a permanent state of existence of the sovereign nation state of Jamaica; by 2019, the island had spent thirty-two of its fifty-seven years of independence tied into one IMF structural adjustment programme after another.[56]

As the Third World debt crisis spiralled out of control in the 1980s, economists like Thatcherite acolyte Professor Peter Bauer still insisted that the debt must be paid, no matter the cost. Peter Bauer was the member of the Mont Pelerin Society who perhaps paid the closet attention to the Third World, openly seeing it, rather than the West, as being the primary battlefield of economic policy. Thatcher also elevated him to the House of Lords during her first term in power, but it is his impact on the international stage that is more significant.[57] Bauer's work transformed the discipline of development economics, and helped establish a picture of what a 'good' developing economy should look like, which was increasingly embraced by international institutions. His work helped to convince the bureaucrats at the IMF, the World Bank and eventually the World Trade Organisation that attempts by sovereign countries to control their economy – fixed price controls, protectionist trade tariffs and public ownership of vital industries – actually created rather than alleviated poverty. For Bauer, what the Third World needed was to open itself up to the power of the free market. And it also needed to pay its debt.

Bauer pushed the idea that Third World countries were simply lying about not being able to pay off their debts.[58] He felt they could make their repayments if they really wanted to, but as they were not being punished for extending their loans, they saw no reason to. To raise the money, he argued, indebted nation states could always tax their working citizens more, sell off more of their state assets or even seize the assets of their citizens.[59] Instead, by letting the debt of these countries simply grow and grow, the world was showing that 'Third World governments can be expected to behave like children with no thought for the morrow'.[60] For Bauer, the answer to this problem was to insist on even more stringent methods to get the money back from indebted governments and to resist any temptation to compromise on the debt. He warned that forgiving or reducing the debt 'will give succor to those who disregard their obligations . . . and also reinforce the politicization of life in the Third World'.[61] Any contention that Bauer's sole concern was simply the reduction of poverty in the Third World can be rebutted by pointing to his stance against freely available birth control in the developing world, despite it being the most commonly held method of easily reducing poverty.[62]

Debt took away control from impoverished people, keeping them trapped in subservience, all the time insisting that it is their own fault. The 1980s was the decade when the idea that Caribbean,

Latin American and especially African countries were corrupt, incompetent and perpetually impoverished was fixed in the global imagination. In Britain, the 1980s saw the emergence of global charity as mass entertainment, with Live Aid and Comic Relief filling up television schedules with images of malnourished black children fighting for survival. These images were displayed completely detached from historical or economic factors, and were instead presented as the result of some sort of natural disaster, an unfortunate curse that had befallen these damned peoples which could only be lifted by generous donations from those more fortunate. There was certainly no suggestion that the poverty BBC news cameras was capturing in Bangladesh, Sudan or Jamaica was in any way connected to Britain's past imperial actions and its crucial role in facilitating neoliberal globalisation.

The Boomerang of Debt

Back in Britain, economic revolution was in full swing. This was the decade of 'greed is good', as Britain's state industries opened up to private finance and money was free to roam the globe in search of opportunities for even larger profits. The inequality that has become such an essential feature of the British economy of late was crystallised in this era, but those on the right side of Thatcher's divided Britain amassed great personal wealth thanks to the prime minister's policies. Thatcher even reinterpreted Jesus's parable of the good Samaritan as a story that was really about the benefits of trickle-down economics. 'No one would remember the *Good Samaritan* if he'd only had good intentions; he had money, too,' argued the prime minister as she defended the import-ance of the 'greed is good' mentality.[63] The charity of Live Aid and Comic Relief was only possible because the Britons who were fortunate enough to own property and capital as the money markets were unleashed were able to amass greater riches. Rather than the increased profits of financial and legal services being shown as a cause of poverty in the Third World, they were presented as its only hope for salvation. As a result, the long-term global consequences of what was happening in the Third World were ignored.

The 1980s Third World debt crisis was at the heart of a restructuring of the global economy that would transform life, not just in Kingston, Accra and Lagos, but in London as well.[64] With money freed from its post-war constraints by the collapse of fixed exchange rates and capital controls, the path to riches became the trading of credit and loans to people across the world, as commercial banks saw profits skyrocket through the interest gained while people struggled to pay off their debts. The Third World debt crisis accelerated the commercialisation of debt – each time a new loan was taken out, another asset was added to the international financial market to be traded across the globe. In Britain, private debt exploded. Credit cards had been a rarity before the 1980s; suddenly they were everywhere. As wages continued to flatline over the next few decades, people turned to credit in order to maintain their lifestyles.

Nowhere was this more clearly seen than with the largest debt that most people ever take on – a mortgage. Larger and larger mortgages enabled regular working people to still become home-owners even though wages had stagnated. By the turn of the millennium, 100 per cent mortgages were being sold to customers, with the banks doing less and less due diligence on the ability of the receiver to clear their loan. After all, this system of loose credit meant that house prices were skyrocketing and, as long as they kept rising, the customer had nothing to worry about. Eventually, they would just sell the house, clear the debt and get a nice profit themselves. The housing market became the main engine of economic growth in Britain as the country stopped producing goods; property ownership was the dividing line between those who were able to ride the Thatcherite wave and those who were 'left behind', with the mortgage providing the keys to the castle. Like a giant game of pass the parcel, whether you were able to attain economic security in Britain soon depended not so much on what you could do, but on your ability to take on debt and then pass it on to the next person in time.

In the winter of 2007, the music stopped. Anchoring the global economy on debt speculation turned out to be a risky idea, as first America and then Europe fell into a historic financial crash.[65] Houses were repossessed from heartbroken families behind on their loan repayments. Small businesses had to close their doors permanently when they found themselves unable to pay back their start-up loans. Governments preached the gospel of personal responsibility to those who were struggling; as Britain's soon-to-be prime minister David Cameron said at the time, 'it is time to start living within our means'. Once again, the fault was not placed on the global economic system; this time it was down to individual irresponsibility.[66]

Yet governments across the world had been overextending themselves since the money taps were opened in the 1980s. Sovereign debt proved to be a contagious disease, rising rapidly across the world in the final decades of the twentieth century, with countries in Europe and America leading the charge. When the financial crash hit in 2008, it was now the turn of European countries to find their shoulders bent under the weight of sovereign debt, most prominently Portugal, the Republic of Ireland, Greece and Spain. In Britain, while the public debt didn't spiral to levels seen in some of its European neighbours, it was still seen by politicians as enough for them to justify a stringent period of austerity in which the social capacity of the British state was cut to ribbons. In the name of debt reduction, Britons saw how policies that would otherwise be seen as extreme – the tightening of disability benefits, the closing down of libraries and cutting support to children's centres – were suddenly presented in a neutral, even moral language. Whilst the banks that had caused the crash through risky asset speculation were bailed out with public money, public services were made to pay the bill. Protest groups railed against the cuts, arguing that the public debt should be cleared by increasing taxes on the wealthy. Not only was this dismissed as the politics of envy, opponents emphasised the point that if taxes were raised then the wealthy could just flee the country with their money, thanks to worldwide relaxing of controls on the movement of money in the 1970s and 1980s. As he imposed crushing austerity policies on the country, David Cameron recalled Thatcher's old riposte to the Third World, telling a struggling Britain 'there is no alternative' to the painful cuts they would have to endure.[67]

Despite talk of sovereign debt, the deficit, austerity and public services cuts consuming political discourse in the years following the 2008 economic crash, few analysts in Britain connected their own debt crisis with the Third World crisis that had haunted much of the globe over the past few decades. Of course, significant differences separated the UK in 2008 from Jamaica in 1978 – the UK's much bigger GDP compared to the size of the debt, and a stronger currency making debt repayments easier to manage. But what the Third World debt crisis did preview was how economics was changing, particularly with regard to finance. What the UK and Europe would eventually learn after 2008 is the political power that sovereign debt carried.[68] From literature to religious mythology, we know that debt is not only an economic condition but also a metaphysical one; it requires its bearer not only to commit to repayments but to submit to the control of its creditor. The best type of debt is the one that can never be paid. This is how sovereign debt has come to function – while never being cleared, the 'project' of paying off the debt can be a useful umbrella under which to remake the economic basis of a society. The power of debt is almost transcendent – by just invoking its name, you can get people not only to agree to things that they would not normally agree to but you can even get them to see it as not just a necessity but also a welcome opportunity for purification and renewal. For the Third World in the 1980s, paying off debt became more important than providing clean water to rural villages, more important than funding medical programmes to combat infectious diseases. In Britain after the 2008 crash, debt was the ever-ready justification for cutting funding to higher education, mental health facilities and social housing.

The idea that sovereign debts must be paid, no matter the social cost, had been regularly weaponised, when politically useful. Like the relaxing of capital controls, the privatisation of public services or the commitment to low taxes, our ideas around sovereign debt may now appear as though they are irrefutable facts of nature, but they were pushed forward by intellectual endeavour. The connection Peter Bauer drew between insisting that countries keep paying their debt and stopping the 'politicization of life' provides an insight into the real power sovereign debt holds – it neutralises the unpredictability of politics. When a debt has to be paid, the ups and downs of elections, democracy and the shifting agendas of sovereign governments are all caged within the limitations of meeting repayment obligations; suddenly it is the accountants and not the politicians who are really deciding national policy. For corporations and investors looking to make money, in the right circumstances an indebted nation provides a much cleaner, much calmer atmosphere in which to trade. Passions are tempered by numbers. And governments are open to relinquishing the grip of sovereign power over their territories.

Freedom for Capital

The concept of a 'freeport', a port where trade can be allowed to flourish free from the taxes, rules and regulations usually insisted on by the sovereign authority of the land, has been around at least as long as the sea-cities of the Italian Renaissance. During the rise of European empires, the French (Marseilles), the Germans (Hamburg) and the Belgians (Antwerp) all used the freeport model at times in an attempt to gain a foothold in global trade. But Britain, despite being the largest sea trading empire of them all, did not create any freeports on the British

Isles.[69] The only places the British Empire experimented with the freeport model were in its colonial outposts, in Hong Kong, Singapore and the West Indies.[70] Until the late twentieth century, freeports were still a relatively rare phenomenon and, with decolonisation and the rise of the UN seemingly heralding the age of sovereign nation states, they might have been expected to disappear into the pages of history books. Yet the re-emergence of the freeport has been among the most significant changes that global capitalism has undertaken in the last fifty years.

When Michael Manley agreed to open the Kingston Free Zone in 1976, there were seventy-nine free-trade zones (FTZs) across twenty-five different countries. By 2006, the year before the global economy would begin to collapse, there were 3,500 FTZs spread among 130 of the world's 193 countries.[71] Where they once occupied a few coastal outposts, freeports now span the globe – not just as conventional ports but also as cities, airports and rural areas that are exempt from the taxation or customs laws that govern the rest of the country. The freeport is a character with many names. It is known as the 'export processing zone' in the Philippines, the 'special economic zone' in China or the 'foreign trade zone' in India; a network of interconnected cogs tied together to facilitate global trade outside of the prying eyes of host nation states.

In the 1970s and 1980s, when sovereign debt led to country after country agreeing to structural adjustment programmes with the IMF and World Bank in exchange for further loans, one of the policies governments would be encouraged to undertake was the creation of FTZs where exemption from local regulation could attract international corporate investment.[72] Jamaica ended up signing more structural agreement deals than almost any other country in the decade after Manley first brought in the IMF in the late 1970s.[73] Therefore, it also served as a test case for the modern freeport model, as the creation of FTZs became a key part of the IMF's demand for Jamaica to increase its non-traditional exports. The first freeport set up on the island was the Kingston Free Zone, established in 1976. The Montego Bay Free Zone followed in 1985, soon joined by the Garmex Free Zone, Hayes Free Zone and Cazoumar Free Zone. In addition to tax-free trade, companies in the FTZs also get to escape the usual licensing laws, employment regulations and controls around business practices that govern the rest of the country.

The goal of the freeports is to use these beneficial terms to entice international companies to set up factories and workshops in Jamaica, increasing overall employment opportunities. In a way, this did work, as space in the FTZs was taken up by garment-stitching factories or food-processing sites where thousands of Jamaicans, especially young women, were able to find work. But while the free zones have increased the flow of money into Jamaica, little of that has found its way into the hands of the Jamaicans who actually work at the plants, factories and warehouses on site. Pay from companies in free zones is very low compared to the cost of living on the wider island.[74] An attempt by the workers in the Kingston Free Zone to unionise in 1987 was crushed by the Seaga government, keen not to upset the corporations operating on the site.[75] Today, without strong labour laws and trade unions, working conditions remain poor on the Jamaican freeports and local people complain that they have little opportunity to advance up the career ladder within the corporations that employ them.[76] The creation of commercial spaces free from government regulation also proved to be a magnet for money-laundering and drug smuggling.

After Thatcher's privatisation of the UK's ports in the 1980s, Britain did experiment with the freeport model at a handful of locations. However, due to the country's membership of the European Union, the incentives that could be offered to attract multinational corporate investment were greatly limited. EU freeports are much narrower in scope and restrict the support that governments can offer companies to set up in them, meaning they cannot compare with the greater levels of deregulation on offer at freeports in Dubai or Jamaica. The last of Britain's free-ports closed in 2012, but Boris Johnson put forward the opportunity to set up truly free-trade freeports as among the great new opportunities the country could take up if it left the EU. As soon as the Brexit vote was successfully won by the Leave campaign, the Thatcher-created Centre for Policy Studies, in partnership with a then little-known junior MP called Rishi Sunak, published a report calling for the creation of 'free-trade zone'-style freeports in the UK.[77] In this report, Sunak, who had only just been elected to Parliament, argued that now was the time for Britain to 're-connect our economic growth with our proud maritime history' by setting up freeports across the country.[78] Sunak felt that Britain had been blocked from the opportunities of the freeports model by its membership of the EU, but now it was becoming independent again, it should take the opportunity to create FTZs at Britain's dilapidated ports.[79] Freeports were also presented as an opportunity to 'rebalance the British economy away from London towards the regions', foreshadowing a growing trend of politicians presenting greater deregulation as being the answer to Britain's persistently unequal economy, rather than being a contributor to it.[80] In February 2020, the UK government launched its plan to open ten new freeports around the country.[81] Here again, we have a further reminder that the innovations that are implemented for capitalist accumulation in the Third World tend not to stay there for ever. Their ricochets continue to remake the rest of the world, Britain included.

The Developing World and the Frontier of Capitalism

I remember that when I would return to school saying I had spent the holidays in Ghana, people would respond, 'Oh, where's that?' Not just the students, but also the teachers. Yet complete ignorance about this place, which had been a British colony but a few decades earlier, wasn't enough to discourage wild assumptions about what life must be like there. 'Is it boring spending all summer with no TV?' 'How do you get around without cars?' To show everyone pictures of myself and my family in Accra, eating cornflakes while watching the BBC, was to turn the world upside down. Rather than being a world away, life in West Africa was, in fact, over-saturated with the trinkets of Western modernity. Of course, the presence of Western consumer goods in places like Ghana is actually symbolic of the country's poverty, but a poverty that functions very differently from the vision of mud huts and open wells that my teachers had in their minds. A large part of the afterlife of empire has been the work of ensuring that the decolonised countries continued to buy huge shipments of consumer goods produced by the world's major companies. A requirement of the structural adjustment programmes that countries like Ghana entered into in the 1980s and 1990s was that they opened up to Western trade. You can't pass a traffic junction in Accra without someone offering to sell you the Disney toys that couldn't be sold in Europe or a refrigerator that was returned to the warehouse from an American supermarket. The economic realities of global trade make countries like Ghana essentially a captive market for the same products we fill our houses with in Britain.

To see overwhelming evidence of this dynamic, go to Accra's industrial area. In the shadow of the city's shiny international hotels and commercial towers lies an area called Agbogbloshie, home to what has been described as the largest electronic waste site and scrap metal yard in the world.[82] Smoke from burning cables fills the air as toxins seep into food and water here. Children climb on top of broken computers and car tyres while their parents dismantle the waste products in search of recyclable materials that they can sell on. Much of the electronic waste in Agbogbloshie is imported directly from the West, but the bulk of it, according to the UN, comes from consumer goods discarded in West Africa, an overflow of the ever-increasing supply of electronic products in the region. An avalanche of unsellable commodities, shipped in from London and Rotterdam as well as Lagos and Kumasi, piles up here, at the ultimate depository of capitalism's global supply chains. The amnesia of empire leads many in Britain to think that the problem of the Third World is that the people living there just can't get access to the by-products of Western consumer capitalism. The reality is that they can't escape them.

In 2011, as Jamaica prepared to celebrate the fifty years of independence from Britain, the country's largest newspaper found that 60 per cent of Jamaicans felt that they would be better off if the island had remained a colony.[83] Sovereignty had not delivered the desired change in peoples' day-to-day reality, as the Jamaican economy remained wholly reliant on foreign investment and tourism. Parallel lives were still being lived on the island, the inequality and injustice that Bob Marley sang about having remained ever-present. Rich white tourists could pass by a local seamstress, never considering how she was being economically excluded from the luxury hotel they were about to enjoy. The challenge of achieving economic as well as legal equality was one Michael Manley tried to meet in the 1970s, not only for the island of Jamaica but for the entirety of what was then proudly calling itself the Third World. Manley and the project of the NIEO showed the briefest glimpse of how our international economic system could have developed along a different path to the one it is on today.

However, Manley underestimated the strength of the counter-offensive that was already underway in Europe and America. Once Thatcher entered Downing Street and, shortly afterwards, was reinforced with the election of Ronald Reagan in the USA, it was clear that the international economic order was going to be remade, but not in the way that Manley and the NIEO had hoped for. Controls on money were relaxed, laws protecting property across borders were fortified and international institutions became tools through which renegade countries could be brought into line. The IMF and World Bank were redeployed from acting as guardians against speculative capitalism to becoming the enforcers of global market discipline, essentially serving as bailiffs for the world's investors to ensure that they would get their money back from governments, plus ever-increasing interest, no matter the social cost.

When we wonder how endless talk of debts, deficits and austerity became an ever-present part of our political discourse and the justification for the removal of more and more sovereignty from people, we should remember the story of a young, independent Jamaican's attempt to change the international economic system in the 1970s. This Third World insurgency was defeated in the name of freedom. Governments were not only told to cut public spending, to reduce regulation and to remove worker protections, they were told that these actions were for their own good, that this was the only pathway that would free them from the prison of debt. It didn't. As of 2021, developing-world countries are still heavily indebted and are due to face another repayment crisis as the long-term consequences of Covid-19 constrict economic activity.[84] While we still tend to see debt as a temporary condition that we should look to escape from as soon as possible, following the Third World debt crisis, contemporary finance capitalism has come to see debt as a way of creating markets, fuelling trade and keeping government policy in check. Attempts to actually pay off what is owed become a Sisyphean struggle, as more and more countries are drawn into the whirlpool of spiralling sovereign debt. Furthermore, the problem didn't stop at the borders of the Third World. The free movement of money has become a runaway train, careering across the world in search of ever-greater profits, leaving more and more people with more and more debt at every station it stops at.

The remaking of the global economy following the Third World debt crisis reinforced the power of transnational capital. Debt had proved to be effective at throwing cold water onto the potential threat of mass sovereignty that had been created by decolonisation. Debt creates a hierarchy between ostensibly equal entities and, what's more, it tells the subordinate entity that its disempowerment is its own fault. What people in the UK must ask themselves is this – why would transnational capital only use such an effective strategy against 'developing' governments? For the last twenty years, the language of debt was offered as the most useful weapon with which governments can break apart the dying remnants of Attlee's welfare state. With Covid-19 requiring the UK government to incur more debt in order to meet emergency public-spending commitments, the next few years could see a fresh insistence that 'there is no alternative', as dramatic policy decisions are rushed through under the umbrella of economic recovery. Once, it was only the 'do-gooders' who cared about the developing world who talked about public debt forgiveness. Now, those from across the spectrum in Britain are calling for a debt amnesty.[85]

The experience of Jamaica over the later decades of the twentieth century has a lot of tell us about the relationship between debt, sovereignty and capitalism in the contemporary global economy. By facilitating the spread of the modern freeport, the Third World debt crisis also offered an answer to the danger of democratic sovereignty – parts of the land would simply be taken 'offshore', and out of the scope of governmental oversight. Currently, the British government is pushing forward with its plans for low-tax freeports across the UK, despite warnings from multiple sources about the negative social and economic consequences that tend to be triggered by such sites. But it should be remembered that Britain has a long history of 'offshore' escape valves for global capitalism, one that also goes back to the moment of decolonisation.[86] In the same newspaper poll in which 60 per cent of Jamaicans declared that they wished the country had never received its sovereignty, one of the reasons offered was the different fate of the country's neighbour, the Cayman Islands, since the era of decolonisation.

Rather than seek complete independence, the Cayman Islands remained a British overseas territory, and its colonial governors used its position as an 'offshore' outpost of the UK to turn it into the world's most well-known tax haven. By the fiftieth anniversary of Jamaican independence, the GDP of the Cayman Islands was $43,800 per person, while Jamaica's was $7,500.[87] However, while its tax-haven status might have been beneficial for the living standards of some who reside in the Cayman Islands, its consequences for the global economy are beginning to boomerang back on life in Britain. Understanding contemporary political and economic trends is not possible without understanding how the fall of empire led to the rise of the 'offshore' world in what was once called the British West Indies.

5

The Tax

If British imperial rule was all about extending liberalism, democracy and fair play across the world, then somebody forgot to tell the 'Bay Street Boys' of the Bahamas.[1] As late as the 1960s, this small group of white businessmen still ran the islands as their own personal fiefdom. A few families passed lucrative contracts and key governance positions between each other, transitioning from administering the colony's original plantation economy in the eighteenth century to profiting from its twentieth-century trade in money laundering. For 300 years, England (and then the UK) had controlled this picturesque corner of the Caribbean, and generations of Bay Street Boys, who gained their collective name from the main business street in the Bahamian capital, had enjoyed much of the resulting financial benefits.

Given the Bay Street Boys' long grip on power, it is easy to see why the black politician who finally managed to break their monopoly was nicknamed 'Black Moses' by the rest of the country.[2] Lynden Pindling was a highly intelligent and charismatic lawyer, who is often compared to his childhood friend and the most famous son of the Bahamas, Academy Award-winning actor Sidney Poitier. The son of a retired policemen, Pindling grew up as a studious child, excelling at various colonial schools until he gained a university place in London, a rare achievement for a black Bahamian at the time. Like so many other independence-era leaders, it was while studying in London and later qualifying as a lawyer at Middle Temple that Pindling's ideas about challenging the British colonial order began to cohere. He returned to the

Bahamas in 1953 and joined the newly formed Progressive Liberal Party at a time when most black Bahamians didn't even have the right to vote.

On 27 April 1965, Pindling entered the House of Assembly as the parliamentary leader of the Progressive Liberal Party and produced one of the most dramatic moments in Bahamian political history. During an intense debate over electoral boundaries, he began to suspect that the ruling United Bahamian Party was trying to establish the boundaries so as to limit the democratic power of the islands' majority black population. In retaliation, Pindling leapt from his seat and grabbed the 165-year-old gold-plated speaker's mace that was the representation of the authority of the Assembly and, by extension, British colonial rule. With his fellow parliamentarians watching in shock, Pindling threw the mace out of the top window, letting the symbolic might of the British Empire clatter and crack on the ground below, as crowds of his supporters waited outside. This astonishing moment of public defiance by this energised black politician signalled to onlookers, both friend and foe, that a seizing of power by the black masses of the Bahamas was both figuratively and literally underway.[3] Two years later, Pindling was elected prime minister of the Bahamas and shortly afterwards announced the news that the Bay Street Boys feared: he intended to lead the islands towards independence from Britain. The Bahamas finally became an independent state in 1973, but by then some of the white business elite that had run the colony had already fled the country at breakneck speed (they had been doing so for a couple of years), taking with them much of the money they had hidden on the islands for decades. In a dramatic example of the capital flight that a number of decolonialising governments would come to endure for the rest of the twentieth century, Pindling found that despite his British education, charming nature and actually rather conservative political and economic worldview, his election as prime minister was enough to spook the capitalist interests invested in his country, purely because of what he appeared to represent.

While the Bahamas had been part of the British Empire, it had developed a reputation as a safe haven for ill-gotten gains, a place where bags of money could be dropped out of passing aeroplanes with no questions asked. The Bay Street Boys had cultivated a legal and financial culture that lent itself to being the preferred money-laundering spot for the world's more nefarious characters – international criminals, recently deposed autocrats etc. – but now it was independent and ruled over by a popular representative of the majority black population, could these islands still be trusted to look after the world's dark money? Where else could offer the same discreet financial-warehousing services that the Bahamas had come to specialise in? Fortunately for those who feared the era of decolonisation might lead to the end to opportunities for 'offshoring' their wealth, another set of Caribbean islands was ready to step in to fill the void. To this day in the Cayman Islands, lawyers and bankers joke that the government should build a statue to Sir Lynden Pindling of the Bahamas.[4]

Following the upheaval of Bahamian independence, the Cayman Islands was able to firmly establish itself as perhaps the leading example of a new type of state – not the old model of the tax haven as a hideout for dirty money, but the new, modern form of 'offshore financial centre', a tax haven that doesn't seek to run away from the law, but instead runs towards the law and learns how to use just enough of it to legally keep much of the wealth in the global economy marooned safely 'offshore', away from the redistributive demands of the masses. Through establishing its expertise in 'offshoring', the Cayman Islands transformed itself from a set of neglected tropical swamplands into the glistening front line of the global financial world in just a few short decades. And, crucially, it achieved this change by staying under the protective umbrella of British sovereignty rather than seeking independence, becoming the model for the growth of what the journalist Nicholas Shaxson has called 'Britain's Second Empire' – the matrix of remaining British territories across the world that continue to entrench the transnational movement of financial interests across the world, deep into the twenty-first century.[5] In the aftermath of empire, when the spread of sovereignty was supposed to make the world more equal, we have instead seen inequality in terms of wealth reach new levels. One of the key elements behind this contradiction is the rise of Britain's offshore children from the ashes of the empire and the role they have played in separating the world of wealth from the world of work.

Britain's 'Offshore' Children

In 2016, besieged British Prime Minister David Cameron was facing down a packed and raucous House of Commons during a debate on tax havens. Cameron was using his speech to declare that it was 'unfair' to place Britain's Crown Dependencies and overseas territories at 'the top of the pyramid of tax secrecy' across the world.[6] While coming up against a barrage of aggressive questions from Labour leader Jeremy Corbyn, Cameron resisted calls for the UK to blacklist tax havens, arguing that he didn't feel that would be the 'right approach' and that he was confident the British government could find a way to cooperate with the British overseas territories (BOTs) who experts identified as sitting at the heart of the global tax-avoidance network.[7]

Just the week before this parliamentary session the Panama Papers had been leaked to the press and Cameron had himself been exposed as a beneficiary of an offshore investment fund, owned by his father.[8] The leaked documents revealed that Cameron's father had kept Blairmore Holdings, an investment fund named after the family's ancestral home, registered in the Bahamas by hiring local Bahamian residents to sign the fund's paperwork.[9] When questioned about whether it was a problem for the prime minister of the United Kingdom to be personally profiting from the offshoring of family wealth at the same time that public anger was rising against tax havens, Cameron's spokesperson simply waved off the question by stating it was 'a private matter'.[10] After all, there was nothing illegal about the way Blairmore Holdings had been structured; the fact that the fund had not paid any tax in the UK for the entirety of its thirty-year history was not the fault of the fund's directors, they were simply responding to the incentives laid out by the global legal and economic system.

Blairmore Holdings wasn't a criminal enterprise, but a lawful and logical consequence of the way the financial world had been structured. Over the course of the twentieth century, a set of jurisdictions emerged throughout the globe whose *raison d'être* became to insulate wealth and capital from the burdens of popular democracy. With decolonisation bringing about the spread of sovereignty and, potentially, an increase in public accountability, with more presidents, more governments, more voters to answer to, the tax haven emerged as the defender of private wealth. It helped create a world where the billionaires who ran multinational corporations routinely paid less tax than the people that they paid to clean their offices. It also helped create a world where compan- ies could benefit from the health, education and transport infra- structure that these countries provide, yet pay little to no money back into their systems. Far from being the 'private matter' that Cameron described it as, the tax haven had become a crucial anchor for today's global networks of trade, finance and wealth.

There is no single universally agreed definition of what a tax haven is, a problem reinforced by the fact that all the places commonly understood to be tax havens are the first to insist that they are not. In many ways, the name 'tax haven' is now a misnomer. The opportunities that the twenty-first-century offshore financial centre offers to those with the resources to enjoy it go far beyond simply allowing people to escape paying tax. By the turn of the millennium, the tax haven had become the preferred vehicle through which wealthy individuals and companies could avoid the demands of corporate regulation, questions of ownership or rules of transparency in the countries in which they operated. Just as important as the low tax rates on offer are the powerful secrecy protections that the havens provide. For example, if you want to register a trust fund but keep the beneficiary of those funds secret, there are places in the world that specialise in this service.

The spread of these offshore jurisdictions over the past few decades has tilted the entire orientation of the global economy and has become one of main obstacles that economists concerned with inequality have faced. A large number of lawyers, bankers and accountants have transferred huge piles of wealth to these exclusive financial bunkers each year, resulting in as much as 10 per cent of the total output of the global economy now estimated to be hiding out in tax havens.[11] For those companies and individuals able to afford the expensive advice of these experts, tax havens have become as essential to the movement of money globally as airports are to the flow of planes. The losers in this new balance of global capitalism have been the citizens confined to the 'onshore world', who have to hear the news year after year that the money they were counting on to provide for their public resources like schools, hospitals and care services would be declining once again.

The issue of taxation brings together the distant worlds of finance and morality. It ties together notions of property, the question of what rightfully belongs to us, with notions of obligation, what we owe to the people we share the earth with. The idea of tax, while never popular for obvious reasons, has largely been accepted by most people as being the financial representation of the social contract that a society has collectively chosen to share in. If you want to live in, profit from or be part of a society, then paying your tax has come to be understood as part of your price of entry. In the age of the nation state, taxation has been understood in national terms – you pay a contribution to the nation and it is paid back to you in the form of welfare and public services. But for those with the necessary means, the tax haven has offered an invaluable get-out clause from this social contract. The flexibility of corporate property rights and the fluidity of money has meant that the very same companies and highly wealthy individuals who are able to maximise their profits by trading across the world are also able to reduce their tax burdens by moving their money to offshore hideouts, where increasing amounts of the world's wealth are being harboured. Access to these lucrative tax havens is easier if your wealth is held in assets. For the workers of the world, tax is normally paid at source; you get your monthly pay cheque and the money for tax is already gone. For salaried workers, there is no opportunity to minimise their tax exposure by shifting their profits around. However, if your income can be received through capital gains, inheritances, trust funds, stocks and shares or property sales there is more opportunity to use a variety of avoidance schemes to protect your money from tax obligations. Companies create a dizzying array of subsidiaries, holding companies, shell companies and affiliates spread across different jurisdictions in order to shift profits to where the tax burden might be lightest. In a nutshell, offshoring has helped propel wealth inequality as it is a practice that only benefits those who are already wealthy.

With the Covid-19 pandemic pushing inequality to new levels as workers were forced to stay at home while asset prices soared, the question of tax havens finally returned to the international agenda in 2021, after decades of inaction. New US president Joe Biden called for a global minimum tax rate on corporate profits at the G7 supranational forum made up of the USA, the UK, Canada, France, Germany, Italy and Japan. In the run-up to the meeting, the UK was reported to be dragging its heels to commit to the global minimum tax rate deal.[12] Former prime minister Gordon Brown admitted that the UK had become 'the biggest obstacle' to this multilateral proposal to claw back some control from the world's lucrative tax havens.[13] Eventually Britain did join the rest of the G7 in signing up to the proposal for a global minimum corporate tax rate of at least 15 per cent. By creating the framework for countries to impose this rate across the board, the global minimum tax rate is supposed to stop countries continually undercutting each other and accelerating a race to the bottom on tax. The deal signals a change in rhetoric from governments after years of shrugging their shoulders and acting as though tax havens are as inevitable as the cycle of the seasons. Regulation was always dismissed as pointless because tax havens were seen as equivalent to a game of Whac-a-Mole – if you hit one over here, then the same thing will simply pop up elsewhere. The global minimum tax rate, while far from solving the problem of offshoring, does reveal that the inevitability of tax havens has always been a lie. They exist because the world's traditional powers have allowed them to exist, with the UK playing a highly significant role in this process.

At the time of writing in June 2021, the British government was already being accused of pushing to exempt the City of London's financial services from the obligation of compliance with the agreement it had just signed.[14] The return of attention to the issue of tax havens has the potential to shine a spotlight on Britain's particular relationship with the offshore world. Even when announcing the global minimum tax rate, the British government continued to frame tax havens as being 'out there' – distant and discreet tropical lands where nefarious authorities allow the world's wealth to be buried. In some ways the mystery around tax havens is understandable. The offshore world is secretive by its very nature. It is a world of secret trust funds and corporate structures that are deliberately obtuse, wrapped in mystery and misdirection. However, the history of the offshore world helps us to unravel its enigma. The rise of the offshore world is not a foreign story to Britain. Today's offshore world was created by policy decisions made in the outposts of the British Empire during the era of decolonisation, with the tacit or sometimes explicit consent of London. It is part of this island's imperial afterlife.

BOTs are perhaps the most overt signs that the UK's decolonisation of its empire is still an incomplete project. They are composed of fourteen small pockets of land, sprinkled around the globe, allowing Britain's jurisdiction to continue to stretch from the Chagos Islands in the Indian Ocean to the Falklands Islands at the bottom corner of the South Atlantic Ocean. Where once Switzerland or Luxembourg were the popular images of a tax haven, over the latter half of the twentieth century these overseas territories have become the new faces of financial offshoring. According to a 2019 index produced by the Tax Justice Network, the world's three most corrosive corporate tax havens are all BOTs, with the British Virgin Islands topping the list, closely followed by Bermuda and the Cayman Islands.[15] We rarely see reports on these places in the news or read stories about them in the news-papers, but these tax havens are as much British territory as Sheffield or Swansea. They are all ruled by a British governor who represents the crown, carries the final say on the law and, every year on the Queen's birthday leads the island's population in a rousing rendition of 'God Save the Queen'; they serve as time capsules of the culture of the old British West Indies.

The confusion about the status of BOTs comes partly from their position as internally self-governing countries that the British government continues to hold ultimate authority over, with the Foreign Office assuming responsibility for them. The inside/outside position that they enjoy within the British state has actually proven only a benefit in making them attractive to the world's wealthy investors. By remaining under the patronage of British sovereignty, maintaining aspects like the Queen as their head of state and the Judicial Council of the Privy Council as their highest court, BOTs are able to give investors the confidence that they are putting their money into a reliable jurisdiction with a long history of English financial and legal expertise. But by also being self-governing entities that are largely autonomous from the British state in their day-to-day operations, the same territories can market themselves as free from the democratic pressures that a large, populous state like the UK might face. They offer investors the promise of protecting their money in a secluded Caribbean island, far away from the politicised struggles and strife that the 'onshore' countries of the world can be susceptible to. And by staying one step removed from each other, the UK and its overseas territories are both able to maintain some plausible deniability if one or the other gets their hands caught in the cookie jar. When faced with calls to clamp down on the role that its overseas territories play in facilitating tax avoidance, the British government has, in the past, pleaded that it cannot force these dependencies to comply with increased regulations.[16]

It is true that BOTs enjoy a great level of self-government. They have their own constitutions, their own legislative assembles and are now largely financially self-sufficient, thanks in no small part to hosting offshored riches. However, the British crown continues to hold reserve powers over all the constitutions in its overseas territories, and these powers have been exercised through the governor at times. Behind the smoke and mirrors, these offshore havens have played a key role in the political and economic make-up of Global Britain over the late twentieth and early twenty-first centuries.

The 'Offshore' Company

If our political discourse considers the question of the aftermath of empire at all, then it is often through the Commonwealth. The Commonwealth has come to be seen as the British Empire's friendly family reunion, the contemporary representation of the benevolent nature of the empire. By being a rather toothless organisational body that focuses its energies on matters of soft power – royal tours, collaborative art projects and a downgraded version of the Olympic games – the Commonwealth has contributed to the idea that Britain's imperial legacy is something that only really concerns the cultural world. However, the financial network of BOTs highlights how the remnants of the British Empire impact the world in a more material manner, determining the movement of money across the world. The seeds of the current network of British overseas tax havens were sown in the legal structure of the empire, and the uneven way that sovereignty was parcelled out across the different regions of 'Greater Britannia'. As discussed earlier in this book, the empire contained a plethora of different constitutional arrangements all governed under the ultimate authority of Westminster – crown colonies, protectorates, dominions and overseas territories. With such a multifaceted jurisdictional arrangement, the British Empire outsourced control over accounting and tax laws to local governors. Also, over the course of the nineteenth century, the British Empire needed people on the ground to populate and govern its colonies. Offering settlers a life with little to no tax was a good way to entice them onto boats to start again in distant lands. Generally, tax codes that were applied to British residents in the colonies were much lower than those they would face back at home. British colonial residents could also qualify for various exemptions from local taxes or remain confident that local authorities lacked the resources, enforcement powers or general will to chase them up.[17]

However, the generous tax rates on offer in the colonies didn't just attract adventurous settlers who wanted to carve out new lives under the sun. With the unevenness of the tax obligations across empire, British corporations also soon realised that by being flexible with their 'location' they could keep their hands on more and more of their fortunes. In 1904, a company was incorporated with the aim of collectively purchasing and profiting from land in Egypt – the Egyptian Delta Land and Investment Company. Three years later, the directors of the company took the decision to move the workings and management of the company to Cairo. All the company's directors relocated to Egypt, with all the firm's meetings, all its bank accounts and all the dividends paid out from the company registered as taking place in Egypt. However, UK company law required that if a company is incorporated in Britain, it has to have a residence in the country. So, the company appointed a London secretary, who provided them with a registered office at his address at Gresham House, Old Broad Street. The address was only a paper address – there was no actual physical office used by the company at this location. In fact, it turned out that at this business address there were more companies registered than there were rooms available in the house.

The secretary's only power was to submit the company's paperwork in London, after it had been drafted and checked in Cairo. When the time came for the Egyptian Delta Land and Investment Company to pay its income tax, the directors argued that as the company was not resident in the UK, it shouldn't be subject to British tax laws. In 1928 the case went to the highest court in the land, the House of Lords. The judges wrestled with the question of whether a company that had been incorporated in the UK, maintained a registered office in the UK, continued to lodge an annual summary with the British government and sought to abide by UK company law with its practices, could also claim to not be resident in the UK for tax purposes. In the end, they decided that it could. The Egyptian Delta Land and Investment Company was defined by the judges as a being a 'non-resident company', and therefore not bound by the usual tax-paying obligations. It could have the best of both worlds – the reputational advantages of being a British company alongside the financial opportunities opened up by being a company based in the under-regulated colonial peripheries.[18] The lucrative potential of this inside/outside tax position was now backed by the power of English common law.

Decolonisation and Capital Flight

Though the 'non-resident' status of the Egyptian Delta Land and Investment Company pioneered a new jurisdictional structure that other multinational corporations would rush to exploit, by the time the case was decided, in 1928, the sands were already shifting under the feet of British imperial companies. Within a generation, Egypt would be an independent republic under the control of a nationalist leader, Gamal Abdel Nasser, who is forever immortalised in the world's history books for seizing the property of another colonial land corporation, the Suez Canal Company, in 1956. The 1950s and 1960s saw country after country turn from imperial playground into a sovereign nation state, causing the families and companies that had enjoyed the loose tax arrangements on offer in the colonies to bolt for the exit door, en masse. As the historian Vanessa Ogle has detailed, the era of decolonisation saw the Europeans who had settled in the colonies as civil servants, educators, missionaries or financiers not only rush to leave the colonies but try to carry with them as many of the goodies that they had collected over the years as possible.[19]

The settlers had enjoyed a charmed life while living in the exclusive European neighbourhoods of Nairobi, Kenya or Kingston, Jamaica. The tax exemptions from which they benefited while living in the colonies were presented as part of the rewards they received for being willing to do the dirty work of managing the colonial project. These were the evangelicals carrying the gospel of British civilisation across the continents and they deserved to be financially compensated for it. The tax burden in the colonies was instead placed on the shoulders of the native population, who often had to pay through the nose for the privilege of being colonised. Many settler families managed to build up impressive wealth reserves while sunning themselves in the tropical promised lands. But decolonisation meant that communities who had moved to Africa and Asia to govern colonised native populations suddenly found their world turned upside down. Within a few short years, the supposedly primitive locals were now moving into presidential palaces, driving ministerial cars and sitting as judges in courts of law. This new atmosphere of 'national liberation' left settler communities feeling that perhaps their time in the tropics was coming to an end.

When settler communities left the colonies in Africa and Asia after independence, more than just people were transferred across the globe. To understand the rise of today's offshore world, it is important to appreciate that decolonisation wasn't just a process of flags being lowered and new presidents making soaring speeches; away from the cameras the businessmen, lawyers and bureaucrats of the empire were hurrying their families to pack up their belongings and wave goodbye to the household staff.[20] The period of decolonisation accelerated the world along the path of financialisation. The material assets of the colonial world – the farms, factories and mansion houses – became the financial assets – the stocks, bonds and trust funds – that would help build the offshore world.

In addition to losing their lavish lifestyles in the tropics, the colonial families faced a further problem. The economic climate back in Europe, including Britain, wasn't particularly inviting to them at that time either. High tax rates and capital controls were in the ascendency in the UK during the 1950s and 1960s, as governments sought to fund the welfare state. The post-war recovery was built on levels of taxation that we are told would be impossible today. In the era when Britain had 'never had it so good', corporation and income tax reached unprecedented levels, with the peak coming with the 95 per cent 'supertax' rate imposed by Labour Prime Minister Harold Wilson in 1966, which even inspired protest songs by The Beatles. Trapped between having to hand over huge amounts of their colonial riches to their home governments upon their return or risk having that wealth seized by the new independent governments now in power after decolonisation, the Europeans coming back from the tropical colonies were desperate for another option to present itself, an escape from the closing web of sovereignty. Fortunately for those families and companies, not all of Britain's territories were heading towards independence. While large colonies like India, Nigeria and Kenya broke away, a few small and previously insignificant outposts of the empire remained under British jurisdiction, and they reimagined their relationship to the old mother country in ways that would have significant consequences for the entire global economy.

The Cayman Islands Find Another Path

Nearly forty years prior to its unification with Scotland, the kingdom of England gained control of the Cayman Islands at the same time that it took over Jamaica, through the 1670 Treaty of Madrid with Spain. The territory consists of three islands – Cayman Brac, Little Cayman and Grand Cayman, the largest. These three islands are barely visible on a standard map of the world, hidden in between the much larger islands of Jamaica and Cuba. Yet despite being minuscule in size, the Cayman Islands are no less significant to understanding the world we live in today than their more illustrious neighbours. Under British imperial rule, the Cayman Islands were administered as part of the colony of Jamaica. Having previously served as hideouts for seventeenth- and eighteenth-century pirates, by the start of the 1950s they were largely forgotten, overshadowed by their more illustrious neighbours in the British West Indies. The economy was primarily made up of fishing, farming and the disposable income of the few sailors still passing through their shores.[21] The tourist industry consisted of a few humble hotels and there was not a single bank on any of the islands. Life on Grand Cayman, Cayman Brac and Little Cayman was very quiet, except for the constant buzz of the mosquitos that overran the place.

However, during the 1950s, the tranquillity of the Cayman Islands began to be disturbed by the impending spectre of decolonisation. It became clear that Britain's relationship with its West Indian territories was coming to a point of crisis, and when Jamaica started to move towards independence, in 1959, the Cayman Islands began to be governed as a colonial entity in their own right. The separation from Jamaica was solidified in 1962 when, as Jamaica became its own sovereign nation state, the Cayman Islands decided to stay under direct British rule. A small, remote outpost, lacking any abundant natural resources; the Cayman Islands would not have been the bookies' favourite for prosperity in the new, post-war world of nations. Yet over the following decades, alongside the other remaining British territories in the region, like Bermuda and the British Virgin Islands, the Cayman Islands morphed into the new type of hotspot of capitalist accumulation.

Today, the Cayman Islands appear, on the surface, to still be the elysian Caribbean hideouts they always were. They have a population of only 65,000, around the same as the town of Rochester in Kent.[22] But the wealth of the Cayman Islands lies not in the number of people but in the much larger number of assets that took up residence there during the age of financialisation. When looking at the movement of money across the world, we can trace how these unassuming islands came to form a key hub in the flow of global finance. In recent years, the Cayman Islands have come to be considered as one of the world's largest financial centres, alongside New York, Tokyo and London. Among the tourists who now flood the islands, you will also find scores of highly paid lawyers, bankers and accountants working for the world's largest companies, the air conditioning in their offices turned up to the maximum while they finalise contracts to protect their clients' assets.

The Cayman Islands set the standard for how peripheral jurisdictions can attract huge amounts of foreign wealth in the post-imperial era. At the height of the financial crisis, when then US President Barack Obama sought to redirect public anger that was building against the American financial system, he pointed towards the Cayman Islands. Obama spoke out against a building in the Cayman Islands where, according to official records, more than 18,000 US companies were registered as residing. 'Either this is the biggest building in the world or it is the biggest tax scam in the world,' Obama told his audience.[23] The implication of Obama's statement was that despite being the sitting head of state of the largest military, financial and political power in the world, he was still powerless to challenge the 'offshore world'. The recent global minimum tax rate agreement has exposed this cry of helplessness as an illusion. In reality, the offshore world has not emerged against the wishes of rich Western states. These states were always highly complicit in legitimising the tax haven, especially Britain, which, for decades, has cloaked its offshore overseas territories in the respectability of the English legal system.

How did the Cayman Islands turn from being a sub-region of the British colony of Jamaica to being such a powerful financial hotspot? One of the first steps was to reimagine the role of the tax haven. Rather than present themselves as the type of tropical paradise where international gangsters could deposit briefcases of cash while regulators looked the other way, the Cayman Islands gained prominence as an offshore financial centre through reassuring respectable investors that their assets would be protected by expertly crafted property and secrecy laws. Laws that were not only backed by the power of the Crown but also, thanks to the ongoing influence of English common law, would be recognised and respected across the world.

The journey towards this path began in 1960 when, as it became clear that Jamaica was moving towards independence, the Cayman Islands passed its own Companies Act.[24] This act allowed for companies to register as being resident in the Cayman Islands without having to pass through Jamaican law. The registration fees collected from the first companies that took up the offer provided funds for an extensive mosquito eradication programme, clearing the islands to make them more hospitable for the bankers, lawyers and accountants that who would soon start arriving.[25] The 1960 Companies Act was followed two years later by a new constitution for the Cayman Islands, which was implemented to coincide with its former parent colony, Jamaica, receiving its independence from Britain.[26] The old legal connections with Jamaica were terminated, and the Cayman Islands reinforced its relationship with Britain by committing to be governed by an administrator appointed directly from London.[27]

However, at the same time as tying the territory closer to Britain, the 1962 constitution also provided the Cayman Islands with the leeway it would need to present itself as an 'offshore' jurisdiction, somewhere 'independent' of the social-democratic economic model in the ascendency in Britain at that time. The British administrator retained the power to ensure the peace, order and stability of the islands, but domestic affairs, including business regulation, were placed under the control of a new, locally elected legislative assembly.[28] The Cayman Islands were now able to enjoy a degree of self-government while remaining under the umbrella of British sovereignty. With the Queen remaining head of state and the UK maintaining ultimate authority for all laws coming from the Cayman Islands, Westminster now held direct control over defence, foreign policy and security matters, while the assembly was free to decide things like tax laws, trust laws and exchange-control laws. This new structure left the Cayman Islands in the perfect position to benefit from a pool of fast money that, unbeknown to the general public, was flowing into London during the post-war era.

The Birth of Eurodollars

The growth of the financial industry in the Cayman Islands was spurred on by transactions in what became known as the 'Eurodollar market', which emerged in London during the 1950s and 1960s.[29] At first, decolonisation threatened to reduce the role of the City of London in the new world of nations. The 1947 Exchange Control Act was passed in Britain amid the global trend towards containing global currency speculation. With all the changes occurring across the world at this time – the rise of national sovereignty, the institutionalisation of international law, the growth of welfarism – for a brief moment it seemed that maybe a leash had been put on London's banking industry. However, some innovative thinking from a British bank founded in Birmingham in the middle of the nineteenth century, the now forgotten Midland Bank, would open up a new pathway for the country's financial interests that would help fuel the rise of the offshore world.

Because American financiers had been trading US dollars across the world in the interwar period, the Wall Street crash in 1929 turned into a global depression that lasted a decade. As a result, the redrawing of the international economy after the Second World War was partly motivated by a desire to restrict banks' trading in foreign currencies as well as to restrict the flow of money around the world, as discussed in Chapter 3. However, Midland Bank realised that, in the divided world that was emerging in the early stages of the Cold War, a lot of people around the world who were no longer comfortable with the US government would nevertheless want to keep their money in US dollars, which had now firmly replaced the pound sterling as the world's reserve currency. Midland quietly started letting these dollar-rich investors leave their money in British bank accounts. No one knows how long this was going on for, but in 1955 the Bank of England noticed that Midland Bank was holding large amounts of US dollars, seemingly not for the purposes of any specific transactions. This amount of transnational financial exposure was exactly the type of scenario that the restrictions on the flow of money were put in pace to minimise. By covertly accepting large sums of US dollars and offering high rates of interest on such deposits in order to attract more dollar holders, Midland Bank began to corrode the foundations of the post-war system of economic control from within.[30]

The Bank of England was faced with a dilemma: ignore Midland's actions and undermine the system of exchange controls, or discipline the bank but chase away a lucrative new source of foreign money and, perhaps more importantly, signal to the world that the curtains really were closing on the City of London's time as the centre of the international financial world. After some consideration, the Bank of England decided to go with the first option. It raised no objection to Midland holding large deposits of 'offshore' US dollars and by so doing gave implicit permission to other British banks to do the same if they wished.[31]

As other banks began copying Midland, it became common for them to hold two sets of books; one for onshore operations and another for their offshore ones.[32] By the start of the 1960s, it became clear that there was now a mountain of US dollars being held in the City of London.[33] The actions of Midland Bank were against the rules, but they had also helped the City find its way through the challenge that decolonisation presented. The Suez Crisis took place just a year after Midland Bank dollar deposits were discovered; Ghana became the first sub-Saharan African country to gain independence the year after that. The winds of change would blow apart much of the rest of the empire in a few short years, and the 1960s began with Britain's closest ally, the USA, openly saying that 'Great Britain has lost an empire and has not yet found a role'.[34] However, perhaps Dean Acheson, the US Secretary of State who came up with this line, underestimated the depth of the legal and financial roots that British capitalism had spread across the world over the previous few centuries. Midland Bank's innovative offshoring signalled a new role for Britain's financial industry to take up after the fall of empire; London no longer had to be the 'workshop of the world', it could become the conductor of global capitalism, directing and distributing wealth worldwide, helping the rich keep their money out of reach of the covetous hands of those less fortunate.

The term 'Eurodollars' emerged to describe these secretive stashes of dollars that were escaping US banking regulations. Midland Bank's practice of holding and trading offshore deposits of US dollars spread to other European countries, but the City of London always remained the epicentre of the Eurodollar market; not Amsterdam, Frankfurt or Paris. This was not just because of the historical and linguistic connections between the USA and the UK. The growth of the Eurodollar market in London was aided by the structure of English common law. As opposed to the legal systems on the European continent, which seek to specify what is permitted, English common law focuses on establishing what is prohibited, implicitly permitting anything that has not been explicitly prohibited. Furthermore, London was home to the City of London, the ideal nowhere-land for offshore trading in US dollars owing to the unique jurisdictional position it enjoys within the larger British state. When the Bretton Woods system of post-war financial controls collapsed in 1971, the *New York Times* pointed to London's Eurodollar market as being 'the villain of the crisis'.[35]

The City of London

For the uninitiated, it is important to briefly clarify the difference between London the city and the City of London. London is the capital city of the UK. Spread over 600 square miles, it encompasses everything from Alexandra Palace in the north to Crystal Palace in the south and just keeps growing. The City of London is something quite different. It is the old Roman City of Londinium, which sits within the larger modern metropolitan area of London. Better known as the 'City' or the 'Square Mile', as just over 1 square mile in area, the City serves as London's financial district. But it is something far stranger than simply London's equivalent of Wall Street. It reflects the boundaries of the old City of London that defied William the Conqueror when he established monarchical control over England, and the legacy of this defiance is still carried over into the autonomy that the City is granted today.

The City of London enjoys its own independent police force, its own unique local authority – the City of London Corporation – and its own unique system of elections; most of its voters are not everyday people, but representatives of the companies who are located within the City. When the ruling British monarch visits the City, they will stop at the boundary and wait for the head of the City of London Corporation, known as the Lord Mayor, to present the City's Pearl Sword to the monarch in deference. Convention holds that the monarch simply touches the sword in acknowledgement, before allowing the Lord Mayor to retain it. This ceremony exemplifies the City of London's arm's length relationship to the Crown and, by extension, the British state.[36] Its powers are ancient, predating not only the modern state of Britain but even the emergence of England as we know it today. This long history of being not just a financial district but one blessed with its own powers of self-government, made the City of London fertile ground in which the new offshore market in US dollars could grow. The City of London was already an offshore island buried in the middle of a sprawling metropolitan city. For those who feared that the growing importance of sovereignty in the mid-twentieth century was placing their fortunes at risk, the City's historical and jurisdictional semi-autonomy from the British government provided reassurance that their money would be safer passing through its doors.

The City of London remains, in many ways, its own city-state within the wider British nation state. It continues to share many of the characteristics of Britain's overseas territories; a semi-feudal political arrangement which corporate interests use to dampen expressions of mass democracy. And, in addition to being medieval, it is also home to a hyper-modern, highly digitised financial industry that continues to drive much of the global capitalism in the twenty-first century. England's old pipe-and-slippers gentlemen imperialists have morphed into sharp-suited, cut-throat international traders over the past hundred years, feeding the need of the globe's richest people to move their money across jurisdictions as quickly as possible. When decolonisation threatened to ground the flight of money around the globe, the City of London was able to help take this money offshore.

A New Role for Offshore Britain

The Eurodollar market was a godsend for the Cayman Islands. The islands were ideally located close to the USA, just a stone's throw from Miami, but resided under Britain's jurisdiction, while also having the freedom to develop their own business regulations and take the City of London's autonomy many steps further. The Cayman Islands began to promote its own fledgling financial industry as the ideal final resting place for the Eurodollars that were hiding out in the City of London's banks. This strategy worked. By 1980, the Cayman Islands was home to around 30 billion Eurodollars.[37] The forgotten Caribbean colony had been in the right place at the right time to take advantage of the changing dynamics of global capitalism. The Cayman Islands declared themselves open for business just at the moment when those with wealth were looking for new sanctuaries. Thanks to persistent, darker ideas about which racial groups were suitable to be trusted with global finance and which ones were not, decolonisation and the rise of black majority rule turned other Caribbean islands like Jamaica, Barbados or Guyana into places that European investors feared were too volatile and unpredictable to leave your money in. It is more than symbolic that the legal instrument the Cayman Islands came to particularly specialise in is the trust – a vehicle for holding assets for a period of protection in order to pass them on to a specific beneficiary. Presenting themselves as the Caribbean hideout that global capital could trust was key to the success of the islands – here there would be no rabble-rousing Michael Manleys or Lynden Pindlings suddenly seizing power and turning their backs on the 'British' way of doing business. Therefore, the number of companies registered in the Cayman Islands increased by nearly 400 per cent between 1970 and 1976.[38] Once the Bretton Woods system fell apart in 1971 and exchange controls began to fall around the world, the money that was flowing towards the Cayman Islands would become a tsunami.

The Cayman business model has been replicated across many of Britain's current and former colonial territories, leading to offshore Britain coexisting with standard territorial Britain. This global network has given the UK a unique role within the structure of twenty-first-century capitalism, with the legacy of the old British Empire being mobilised to turn the quasi-autonomous City of London into the financial sun around which a solar system of offshore tax havens orbits, including Jersey, Bermuda and the Cayman Islands. Lucrative deals are concluded in London but then registered offshore, thanks to the ease of connection. Furthermore, companies can be confident that should their deals fall apart, they can call on the English legal system to resolve their conflicts. For generations, Westminster politicians have claimed there is nothing they can do about companies that have hidden their profits in places like the Cayman Islands, but a study of the legal structure of these offshore financial centres clearly shows that the money isn't buried in some magical nowhere-land – it resides in a British overseas territory that is still under the jurisdiction of the government that the British people elect. It is an institution residing on Britain's mainland that these offshore jurisdictions still ultimately turn to in order to decide their laws.

The Common Law and the Offshore Territories

Perhaps the most shadowy body within Britain's complex constitutional network, more so than even the House of Lords, is the Privy Council; an inconspicuous institution that is home to the formal advisers to the monarch of the United Kingdom. It is one of the last routes through which the power of Britain's ruling king or queen can still be exercised. One of the Privy Council's roles is to hear legal cases from an array of overseas territories and Commonwealth countries through the Judicial Committee of the Privy Council (JCPC), which was once the final court of appeal of the British Empire.

The JCPC was created by an 1833 Act of Parliament, and was the place where legal issues that arose in the British colonies came to be resolved. This meant that, in theory, all subjects from every corner of the British Empire had the right to appeal directly to the reigning British monarch. In the early twentieth century, around the same time that proposals for the imperial federation were gathering support, there were also moves to try and combine the highest court of the English legal system, then the House of Lords, with the highest court of the empire, the Privy Council, to create a single 'Imperial Court of Final Appeal'.[39] While a full union between the Privy Council and the House of Lords wasn't realised, the former did enjoy the final say over not only colonial territories but also over a small number of domestic issues in the UK, and still does today. Until the 2009 foundation of the UK Supreme Court, the JCPC was even the final authority on 'devolution issues' regarding Scotland, Wales and Northern Ireland. The court was created to aid the coherence of laws throughout the empire; if colonial legislators or governors passed laws that were contrary to English law, they were made invalid by the Privy Council.

After decolonisation, many independent countries kept the Queen as their head of state and the Privy Council as their highest court. Over the years, this tension between national liberation movements and this constitutional legacy of British rule resulted in most former British colonies eventually removing the Queen as head of state and becoming republics. Ghana took this step in 1960, three years after independence. Nigeria followed in 1963, Kenya in 1964, Trinidad and Tobago in 1976.[40] At the same time as becoming republics, these countries usually abolished the Privy Council's role as being their highest court of appeal, but other countries, especially in the Caribbean, retained the monarchy and the old colonial court system, even after independence. The Privy Council is still the final court of appeal for British overseas territories like the Cayman Islands and Bermuda, Crown Dependencies like Jersey and even some independent Commonwealth nation states like the Bahamas and Grenada. In theory, it is supposed to provide essential, international protection for ethnic or religious minorities in the new independent states, who may believe they struggle to gain justice within their own country. In practice, the process of appealing to the Privy Council is incredibly expensive and favours the wealthy across these societies, especially if they can sustain the case over the lengthy period of time it often takes to be heard.

The role of the Privy Council in deciding legal cases that emerge from offshore Britain is just another example of the authority that Britain still wields over jurisdictions like Bermuda, the British Virgin Islands and the Cayman Islands, despite protestations to the contrary, like those offered by the Cameron government after the leak of the Panama Papers. The British government was happy to use their powers of direct rule over BOTs to forcibly expel the Chagos Islanders from their lands in the late 1960s, in order to make way for a US military base. As recently as 2009, Britain imposed direct rule on another of its overseas territories in the Caribbean, the Turks and Caicos Islands – suspending the local government after allegations of corruption.[41] At that same time, in the aftermath of the financial crisis, there was a great deal of fear in the Cayman Islands that Prime Minister Gordon Brown might use the UK's ultimate authority over its overseas territories to reform their financial services industry, in order to calm public anger at home.[42] Fortunately for the Caymans, Brown would lose the general election in Britain the following year to a direct beneficiary of offshore Britain, David Cameron.

The Cayman Islands remain very much British, having rejected the possibility of independence on multiple occasions. In 2003, at a UN meeting looking at the last few places still not to have gone through decolonisation, the representative of the Cayman Islands stressed that the territory 'did not want independence'.[43] Admitting that the UK Treasury continues to interfere in economic matters in the Cayman Islands, the representative argued that any constitutional review that was going to happen in the UK should consider more protections for the Cayman Islands, especially as, at that time, Britain's seemingly inevitable deeper absorption into the EU threatened the Caymans' economic privileges.[44]

Indeed, the EU eventually put the Cayman Islands on a black-list in February 2020, thereby allowing member states to apply more controls on payments going to this jurisdiction. It was the only BOT that was singled out on this list, released a month after the UK had officially left the EU. The Cayman Islands' premier immediately travelled to London to seek help in addressing the EU's blacklisting.[45] In October, the EU removed the Cayman Islands from its blacklist, much to the anger of tax reform organisations like the Tax Justice Network, who argued, 'This is an extraordinary decision, and hard to know whether it's testament to the lobbying efforts of the world's worst financial secrecy jurisdiction, Cayman, or the sheer methodological ineptitude of the EU blacklist.'[46]

The Tax Justice Network calculated that around $70 billion worth of tax filtered out from other countries to the Cayman Islands, through corporate tax abuse and private tax evasion. This money would be enough to cover the salaries of over 5 million NHS nurses.[47] Far from being an abstract, distant problem, the rise of the Cayman Islands and the rest of the offshore world is intimately connected to the wealth inequality and economic challenges of the UK today.

The Boomerang of the Offshore World

Prior to 2008, the offshore world rarely flickered on the radar of politics in Britain. Tax havens were an issue of concern for mafiosos and money-grabbing dictators, not civilised democracies. But in the aftermath of the financial crisis, the offshore world has been dragged into the politics of street protest across Britain. The crash led to a programme of austerity being imposed by the government to cut down on public spending; a programme which hit Britain's poorest and most vulnerable communities the hardest.

With the country looking around for people to blame for its financial problems, community groups pointed to systems of offshoring and tax avoidance as some of the key culprits. They argued that if the government was short on money, then surely it should be closing tax loopholes before closing youth centres or libraries. In city centres across the country, high-street companies accused of indulging in tax-avoiding offshoring practices – including Vodafone and Topshop – suddenly found their stores being picketed by furious protesters. In the midst of the remorseless cuts being imposed on social programmes in the name of balancing the budget, anti-austerity campaigns, most prominently UK Uncut, sprang up to channel public anger towards the multinational companies that had enriched themselves during the boom times, and then skipped out of paying their tax bills when the country needed money.

Suddenly, the offshore world was receiving the only type of currency it didn't like: attention. The protests made the issue of transnational tax avoidance front-page news. Furthermore, by discussing the role of tax havens in the global economy in the context of the austerity being implemented at home in Britain, the efforts of groups like UK Uncut made explicit the connection between vital services that were being closed across the country and the ability of multinational corporations to hide their profits offshore.

Soon, UK Uncut moved their attention from the shops to the banks, targeting the financial institutions that had caused the crash but that seemed to have escaped its consequences. In the middle of the working day, bank branches were be invaded by protesters, who would then proceed to turn what had been an HSBC or a NatWest into a food bank, where protesters could hand out meals to families who had been evicted from their homes or lost access to support payments. The contrast between the world of financial banks, where life had returned to business as usual, and the world of the food bank, where the crash had upturned whole communities, was stark. Eventually, the protesters realised that, as powerful as the financial institutions of the Square Mile were, they were only able to take advantage of the opportunities that the offshore world afforded them because of the complicity and inaction of the British state. Without forcing the government to take a more aggressive stance against the offshore world, any attempts made to hold these companies accountable would prove futile.

In 2013, UK Uncut dragged Her Majesty's Revenue and Customs (HMRC), the tax-collecting arm of the UK government, into court over a deal it had struck with Goldman Sachs.[48] Along with a set of fellow investment banks and other financial firms, Goldman Sachs had been caught using offshore subsidiaries to pay their bankers their bonuses, so that they could avoid paying taxes in the UK. While the other firms held their hands up and paid the taxes they owed, Goldman refused to back down, and instead used its financial might to bring the British government to the negotiating table. In 2010, at the height of the government's austerity programme, while elderly widows were being hit with a bedroom tax for the audacity of having spare rooms in their house, and disabled mothers were having their benefits cut and being told to find non-existent jobs, a backroom deal was struck between the government and Goldman. This 'sweetheart deal' allowed the financial firm to escape some of the tax liabilities it had built up through its offshore bonus payments, particularly the interest that had accrued over the years, worth up to £10 million. Instead, they were allowed to clear their debt by paying a lower amount. This deal was uncovered by UK Uncut in the midst of their campaign against tax avoidance and became their flagship example of how the British government remained complicit in the offshoring practices of the world's financial juggernauts.

However, almost a century after the Egyptian Delta Land and Investment Company decision, UK Uncut would find that the English courtroom continued to prove to be barren terrain for challenging the offshore world. Despite accepting that the deal agreed with Goldman was against the government's own stated policies, which committed it to not agreeing to 'package deals' or undercharging tax and interest debts in order to gain easy settlements, the courts decided that the 2010 'sweetheart deal' was legal, overall. The judge presiding over the case admitted that the 'settlement with Goldman Sachs was not a glorious episode in the history of the Revenue', and highlighted errors that government officials made when negotiating with Goldman Sachs, but accepted that, ultimately, this kind of 'sweetheart deal' was allowed to stand.[49] Following the decision, the energy behind UK Uncut and similar protest groups dissipated. As the austerity years continued, the question of corporate tax avoidance moved from the front pages of the newspapers to being buried in the financial section, and the media and politicians began to shift the blame for Britain's ills on to their favoured easy targets – immigrants, the EU and benefits claimants.

The anti-austerity movement that sprang up in Britain following the 2008 crash made substantial progress in revealing how the dismantling of Britain's welfare state was intimately related to global systems of tax avoidance. UK Uncut and others showed how offshoring undermined the social safety net that so many of Britain's most vulnerable communities relied upon. Inequality was not just a fact of nature, it was being actively created by policy choices. It was the result of a government choosing to cut the budget for public services while turning a blind eye to the offshoring practices of the world's richest companies; it was the result of a government interrogating disabled benefit claimants harder than it interrogated its own overseas territories, which were insulating huge amounts of financial reserves. When the government introduced further welfare cuts in subsequent years, anti-austerity protesters were quick to point to sweetheart deals like the one HMRC had agreed with Goldman Sachs, or the deal that a whistle-blower reported it had agreed with telecommunications company Vodafone, which is estimated to have cost the public upwards of £6 billion.[50]

Yet what was missing from the anti-austerity movement's analysis of tax avoidance was an exposure of the connection between the offshoring practices of wealthy companies that help produce inequality and Britain's colonial history. The inertia that settled over movements to challenge corporate tax avoidance at that time partly came from a feeling that, no matter how angry people were about the system, there was nothing that they could really do about it – the offshore world seemed too nebulous, and trying to control it would be like trying to catch smoke with your hands. However, reframing the growth of the tax haven as part of the afterlife of the British Empire brings the issue back into the jurisdiction of the British public. This money doesn't just magically disappear overseas; it moves through British hands and British institutions, and often into a British overseas territory. By emphasising how most of the world's leading tax havens are either current BOTs or former British territories that remain agreeable members of the Commonwealth, global tax reform can go beyond the global minimum tax rate to be seen as a major domestic issue as well as an international one.

Today, offshoring is an essential element of global capitalism; it isn't the secretive dark side of the system, in many ways *it is the system*. The global shift towards the power of sovereignty – that looked, for a moment, to be heralded by decolonisation – wilted in the face of innovative legal structures and techniques which allowed corporations to disappear into a jurisdictional escape pod. For sovereign states to capture global capital flows now, they must try and track not just the movements of shell companies (companies which only exist on paper with no employees or offices), but mailbox offices (where a company's physical location is just a mailbox), flags of convenience (shipping companies that are able to buy the right to register in different countries to avoid regulation) and asset-holding companies (companies that don't conduct their own operations, but hoard assets for investing purposes) as they all hop from one jurisdiction to another. This system of profit shifting is not going to disappear overnight with the global minimum tax rate. It will need further aggressive reform aimed at dismantling the inequality in the global economy that has calcified over the past few decades. A two-tiered world has begun to emerge, resembling the dystopian future of a small community of leisured elites shadowed by the toiling, downtrodden masses depicted in H. G. Wells's *The Time Machine*. Those who are tied to territory are subject to all the laws and controls of the sovereign state, while companies and individuals who can access the offshore world find themselves enjoying the freedom of the globe.

The companies that fill up our high streets, from BP to Tesco, now have registrations in the Cayman Islands. In both Britain and the Caribbean, many in positions of power have viewed this state of affairs as mutually beneficial. The Cayman Islands' position as a BOT makes it more attractive to hedge funds than low-tax nation states like Belize or Panama, and successive British governments have been happy to see the Cayman Islands transition into one of the world's major offshore financial centres.

It is perhaps unsurprising, therefore, that the UK has often been accused of frustrating attempts at global tax reform in the twenty-first century. In 2015, when some of the world's 'developing' countries tried to use the UN as a way for them to exert more influence over global tax policies, it was the lobbying actions of the wealthiest countries, including the UK, that blocked them.[51] In an inversion of the language of decolonisation, whenever tentative steps have been made to limit Britain's overseas territories' offshoring role, like the recent drive to make public who was registered as owning or benefiting from the accounts registered in these jurisdictions, the leaders of these territories denounce such moves as 'modern-day colonialism'.[52]

In reality, it is the protections that tax havens provide to transnational capital that are the real continuation of empire's dynamics of extraction and exploitation. In country after country, despite the appearance that decisions are being made by elected politicians, the network of tax havens weakens the ability of democratic actors to take any decisions that would harm the financial markets. There is always the threat that the rich will take their money and run to the Cayman Islands.

Tracing the genealogy of the offshore world reminds us that these places are not distant from life in Britain, but are part of the afterlife of the British Empire in the Caribbean. Growing out of the history of sugar plantations and slave revolts comes the contemporary world of hedge funds, secret trusts and shell companies registered offshore. The decisions made in the Cayman Islands in the 1960s have ricocheted back in the motherland, and help to determine how lives are lived in twenty-first-century Britain. The changes in the global economy the spread of tax havens ushered in have helped to further sever the links between the sphere of wealth and the lives of workers. Britain's role in propelling the offshore economy into existence is almost never mentioned when politicians and media figures are debating the legacy of empire; they choose to focus instead on whether we should change the names of honours like the MBE (Member of the Order of the British Empire). Britain's intimate history with the offshore world reminds us that the afterlife of empire extends beyond symbolic honours and helps to explain the legal and economic traditions that continue to materially benefit some people at the expense of others.

Taking the story of the aftermath of empire in Britain from the symbolic discussion of flags and statues towards material issues like offshoring wealth troubles the presumption that true patriots defend the legacy of empire while those who 'hate Britain' are the ones who want to challenge it. In early September 2020, for instance, the UK's headlines had been captured by a manufactured controversy over whether the BBC Singers would perform 'Rule, Britannia!' or 'Land of Hope and Glory' at the annual Last Night of the Proms concert. The *Sunday Times* reported that a decision had been made not to sing the lyrics of these songs in response to the summer's Black Lives Matter protests since both songs carry links with slavery and colonialism.[53] The BBC explained that the decision was due to the restrictions of the Covid-19 pandemic regarding singing and reminded the press that instrumental versions of the songs had been performed at the Last Night of the Proms before. This explanation fell on deaf ears, however. By linking to a broader cultural war over the legacy of empire, politicians were able to whip up large public outrage at the BBC, forcing them eventually to reverse the decision and allow the songs to be sung by a small choir. To celebrate the victory, Conservative politician Jacob Rees-Mogg stood up in the House of Commons and played a recording of 'Rule, Britannia!' into the Speaker's microphone. Presenting the legacy of empire as just another battleground in an ongoing culture war allowed him to play the role of patriotic defender of the people. This stance is harder for him to maintain if the topic moves from the cultural legacy of empire to its material legacy: from 'Should we play "Rule, Britannia!"?' to issues like 'Should we confront the offshoring of wealth in Britain's remaining overseas territories?' The investment management firm that Rees-Mogg co-founded, Somerset Capital, has launched subsidiaries in the Cayman Islands and Singapore, both key sites in Britain's spider's web of tax havens.[54] Following the leaking of the Paradise Papers, a collection of investment documents that fell into the hands of the world's newspapers in 2017, Rees-Mogg was cited as being one of a number of flag-waving Brexiteers who tend to keep their own money safely locked away offshore.[55]

While promoting British nationalism, the campaign for Brexit was supported by a number of rich individuals who take great efforts to ensure that, when it comes to their tax status, they protect their wealth outside Britain. Wealthy people can benefit from being registered as 'non-dom' (i.e. non-domiciled) taxpayers in the UK, meaning they only pay tax on their UK income. All the money they make abroad remains theirs. For almost every other nation-state, if you are resident in that jurisdiction then you pay tax there for all of your global income. Yet the UK's non-dom rule is another part of the legacy of empire, which emerged during Britain's imperial heyday to allow those who owned lands or businesses in the colonies to still live in the UK but avoid paying tax on the wealth they possessed overseas.[56] This rule has survived into the twenty-first century and is no longer accessible just to rich 'citizens of the empire' but to the global 1 per cent, making the UK an attractive location for everyone from Russian oligarchs to Nigerian billionaires to Saudi princes to take up residence, driving up house prices and the general cost of living while they escape paying tax on all the assets they own across the world. It also allows wealthy British billionaires to keep their income abroad away from the taxman if they are able to gain 'non-dom' status through their overseas connections.

The refusal to confront how the legacy of the British Empire contributes to financial offshoring has hampered our ability to see how issues of wealth inequality, not only globally but in Britain as well, are linked to issues of race and empire. The UK's history has played a pivotal role in the current architecture of multi-national capitalism, and any reform of the global system will eventually require a reckoning with this legacy. A British government looking to confront the material aspects could close tax loopholes in its overseas territories, restrict offshore ownership of UK state assets, abolish the non-dom rule or tax capital flows to and from tax havens. The decoupling of British state support from these jurisdictions would also play an enormous role in damaging their global appeal.

Yet, British politics appears to be moving in the opposite direction. As the state becomes more explicit about the active role it takes in propping up a floundering free market, the language of the culture war has become an increasingly essential distraction from an unequal, hyper-financialised economic model with roots stretching back to the days of empire.

6

The City

On 27 October 1986, Prime Minister Margaret Thatcher changed the rules governing financial trading in the City of London to allow larger and riskier trades.[1] The deregulation, known as the 'Big Bang', was the culmination of Britain's decade-long drift towards financialisation. With the Bretton Woods system now torn apart, exchange controls removed and the offshore world firmly established, the Big Bang allowed London's banks to exploit looser trading rules, old international connections and new electronic technologies to become the epicentre of the new, fast-paced, financialised world. But this was not a return to the genteel world of nineteenth-century bankers with bowler hats and cigars. The quintessential image of this new glorious age of financialisation became the crowded trading floor. The world became familiar with the scene of frantic, sharp-suited stockbrokers waving their hands and screaming at each other in a desperate attempt to secure that all-important trade. The accelerated volatility that had been unleashed through this new age of financialisation was starkly highlighted by the collapse of Britain's oldest merchant bank, an institution that was the embodiment of the old gentlemen imperialists.

Three years after the Big Bang, the same year that the Berlin Wall fell and history was supposed to have officially ended, Nicholas Leeson joined Barings Bank as a back-office clerk. Raised on a working-class council estate in Watford, the bespectacled, inconspicuous Leeson became the manifestation of the Thatcherite 'greed is good' mantra. He rose through the ranks of this most establishment of British financial institutions and, by his mid-twenties, was being viewed by the directors at Barings as a potential trading 'whizz-kid'. But the Securities and Futures Authority in the UK had notified Barings it would not allow Leeson to trade in the City of London – he had failed to disclose that he had once received a county court judgement against him for a debt he owed to NatWest bank.[2]

However, in 1992, Barings appointed Leeson to be the general manager of a new trading office they were opening in Singapore, using its international structure to sidestep the regulatory oversight of the Securities and Futures Authority. Initially, Leeson's magic touch appeared to follow him to Asia. The year after he arrived, Leeson's trading on the futures market of the Singapore International Monetary Exchange (SIMEX) earned £10 million profit – 10 per cent of the bank's total profits for the year.[3] In September 1994, SIMEX celebrated its tenth anniversary, and while all of the black-tied attendees were toasting champagne and celebrating themselves in the luxurious surroundings of the Raffles ballroom, there was one table on which the glory shone brighter than the rest. Leeson and the Barings Bank team were receiving a shower of praise and multiple awards for the success they had enjoyed in this exciting 'emerging market' stock exchange. Singapore's founding prime minister, Lee Kuan Yew, addressed the audience, announcing an exciting set of sweeping new measures to further liberalise investment trading in Singapore.[4] Investment banks from across the world looked to follow Barings and ride to further profits on the backs of what were being called Asia's new tiger economies.

However, on the night that should have been his crowning glory, Leeson refused to go on stage to collect the awards that Barings were receiving. Beneath his success lay a grave secret. Early in his time in Singapore, when an inexperienced member of his team had made a mistake that led to a £20,000 loss, Leeson had created a secret account to hide this loss from his superiors in London. Once this secret account had been set up, Leeson began to use it time and time again to cover up all the losses that he was accumulating in Singapore. Every time he made a loss on a trade, he would bet double his loss on the next trade. Trapped inside the high-speed roller coaster that international financial trading had become since the Big Bang, Leeson's losses quickly snowballed. Yet he was able balance the books on his bad trades by successfully requesting more and more additional funds from London, which were duly transferred across the world without any questions being asked.[5] Eventually, in February 1995, having amassed losses totalling over £800 million, twenty-eight-year-old Leeson left a note on his desk simply reading 'I'm sorry', and fled Singapore with his wife Lisa, sparking an international manhunt. Three days later, Barings Bank, Britain's oldest investment bank and the second oldest investment bank in the world, was declared insolvent.

Leeson was eventually caught in Frankfurt and dragged back to Singapore to answer for his crimes. He would be convicted on charges of fraud and sentenced to six years in prison. Immediately, a comfortable narrative around Leeson and the sinking of Barings Bank began to cohere in the general public discourse: Leeson was simply a 'rogue trader', a scoundrel whose individual deviousness and depravity were beyond anyone's ability to predict. This banking collapse, that had not only taken down one of Britain's most famous banks but had also wiped out the investments of charities and pension funds across the country, did not provoke any great reflection on the British or global financial systems. Kenneth Clarke, the Conservative Chancellor of the Exchequer at the time, was quick to reassure the public that 'this failure . . . appears to be a specific incident unique to Barings, centred on one rogue trader in Singapore'.[6] This had nothing to do with the new ease of moving money across borders, the relentless drive for accelerating profits brought about by financialisation or the autonomy that banks had gained through deregulation. In Singapore, the country's finance minister, Richard Hu, downplayed any accusations of failure of oversight being levelled at SIMEX, arguing that regulators had trusted the judgement of Britain's oldest investment bank when it let Leeson undertake riskier and riskier trades.[7] They had assumed that, this being Barings, it must know what it was doing. But even this banking titan of the eighteenth and nineteenth centuries was unable to navigate its way through the post-imperial enhancement of financial markets.

In a few years, the drama surrounding Nicholas Leeson's risky trades was largely forgotten, and the financialisation of the world economy carried on at an ever-more frantic pace. There was little examination of the historical and economic forces that had drawn Barings, the classic top-hat-and-tails banking dynasty of the age of the British Empire, into opening up a trading department in the city-state of Singapore just as the age of globalisation was entering full swing. Yet both the location of this dramatic event and the speed with which Leeson was able to build up such big losses pointed to more than an isolated act of fraud. At the very same moment when advocates of the 'end of history' thesis were prophesying the stable progress of permanent capitalist globalisation, the collapse of Barings suggested that the future might be much more turbulent than expected.

Singapore-on-Thames

The financial transfers between the City of London and the city-state of Singapore that brought down Barings Bank highlighted a new geography of the world economy in the era of globalisation. During the second half of the twentieth century, Singapore came to capture the imagination of international capitalism as the model global city, an ideal terrain for the flourishing of the free market. And today, Singapore's financialised model of growth is celebrated perhaps loudest of all in its former motherland of Britain. Politicians and commentators who elsewhere might be found downplaying the significance of empire break character for Singapore, and enthusiastically point to it as proof of the civilising legacy of imperialism. In the UK's corridors of power, Singapore has come to be looked upon as the child that made it, the one Third World colony that adopted the Anglo-Saxon values of respect for property and free trade and has duly been rewarded.[8] When liberal theories of development are challenged by critics who point out that the same countries considered 'poor and developing' fifty years ago are still considered 'poor and developing' today, defenders are quick to turn to Singapore as the exception that proves the rule. The city-state is pushed forward as evidence that the system works, there is no great legacy of empire that still hangs over former colonies; if they would simply follow Britain's example then it is possible to move through the stages of history. The story of Singapore has become story of the little engine that could. Here is the proof that it is possible to move from Third World to the First World, in the words of founding Prime Minister Lee Kuan Yew.[9] And recently, in the context of the Brexit debates, Singapore even came to be heralded by some as a potential model for Britain's own future.

In August 2019, the Adam Smith Centre held an event in Singapore to commemorate the 200th anniversary of British rule over the city-state. Among the speakers at the event was the politician, writer and key Brexit ideologue Daniel Hannan. In his speech, Hannan declared that 'in some former British colonies, it would be completely taboo to mark the moment of the British arrival', but this was possible at this event because 'Singapore has now plainly surpassed the old colonial power in almost any metric of standards of living or economics.'[10] While post-war Britain had fallen into the temptations of welfarism, Singapore had remembered what the old mother country had forgotten, that 'the role of government is to create a system' where the 'ingenuity' of the free market is given free reign.[11] Crucially, while Hannan cited the influence of Britain's century of rule over Singapore for embedding norms of property rights, respect for contracts and free trade in the city-state, he saw the real catalyst for the country's economic triumph as being what he called 'Singapore's hard Brexit in 1965', its own 'ill-tempered split with a large federation', in this case

Malaysia. Comparing 'the clever-dick opinion of the world' at the time of Singapore's independence with the similar proclamations of doom that were being made over Britain's 2016 decision to leave the European Union, Hannan found inspiration in this example of how a small, resource-poor country might be able to brand itself as an open house for international financial transactions.

Hannan was far from the only British politician to publicly fantasise about turning an 'independent' Britain into a 'Singapore-on-Thames', a vision of Britain as a low-tax, lightly regulated 'offshore' island on the edge of the EU.[12] It was an idea that caught the imagination of MPs, think tanks and newspapers across the country, all of whom publicly called for the government to embrace the project.[13] In their eyes, no longer would it just be British overseas territories operating as 'offshore' enclaves; the same principles could be applied to the mainland as well. One after another, influential MPs lined up to declare that 'the Singapore model is our Brexit opportunity'.[14]

It is not just politicians who wish to push forward Singapore as the ideal model for an independent Britain's future. The idealised image of the city-states' economic success story has also attracted admiring glances from Britain's business elite. Sir Martin Sorrell, the founder of the world's largest advertising company, has called for Britain to become 'Singapore on steroids'.[15] John Longworth, the former director-general of the British Chambers of Commerce, has declared that 'Singapore offers a shining vision of how Britain will thrive on its own'.[16] Peter Hargreaves, the billionaire stockbroker who poured his wealth into supporting the Brexit campaign, celebrated Singapore as the example of what a Britain free from the EU could become: 'It was a mosquito-infested swamp with no natural resources,' he stated. 'All they had were people with brains and hands and they turned it into the greatest economy in the world. I believe that will happen to us, too.'[17] Unlike many of the politicians who argued for Brexit, Hargreaves did admit that leaving the European Union would create a great deal of economic insecurity for people living in

Britain, but he welcomed this scenario, arguing that 'we will be become incredibly successful because we will be insecure again. And insecurity is fantastic.'[18] Of course, an obvious rebuttal would be that insecurity means different things to a nurse or a school-teacher than it does to a billionaire. Yet for all the romanticising of Singapore's free-market credentials that you find in contemporary British political discourse, a closer inspection of the city-state points to its story being more complicated than the low-tax, financial Wild West image that is often painted.

When the idea of Singapore-on-Thames is raised, it is often used to refer to an economic model where the lack of taxation or regulatory obligations liberates the market to work its own magic. In the Western imagination, the story of Singapore after independence has become the favourite example to illustrate the miracle of the free market; a once Third World country raised into prosperity by embracing libertarian values. The only problem is that this isn't actually how Singapore functions. Far from being a jurisdiction where the state has retreated to grant the market free reign, Singapore's economic model is reliant on a highly interventionist state to cushion the risks of capitalist trade by prioritising the freedom of asset holders over the freedom of everyday citizens. A review of Singapore's post-colonial history illuminates how it didn't simply become a hotspot for international capital through deregulation and low taxes. Its success has been the result of recognising that you have to actively create the conditions for the market to prosper, even if the means of doing so are authoritarian. If Singapore really is the post-colonial story that will boomerang into Britain's future, then it is worth appreciating the moral: perhaps free markets work best in unfree societies.

Britain and the Lion City

Britain's rule over Singapore came about as the result of the actions of another 'rogue trader' back in the early nineteenth century. Similar to Nicholas Leeson, Stamford Raffles also began his working life as a clerk, in his case, for the infamous East India Company, and he was also posted to East Asia to help open up an expanding market in the region. Raffles worked first in the colony of Malay before helping to coordinate the British invasion of Java (now part of Indonesia), illustrating through his own career the interconnectedness of state, military and corporate power in the British imperial project.

In 1818, Raffles aimed to realise his ambition of establishing a new British base on the trade route that flowed from British India to China, despite that route being dominated by Dutch colonial interests at the time. In January the following year, he travelled to the island located at the southernmost point of the Malay peninsula, known to the people who lived there as Singapura, 'lion city'. Upon arriving on the island, Raffles ran into an obstacle when he encountered the sultan and found that he had already established friendly relationships with the Dutch.

Illustrating the sleight of hand that characterised so much of empire building, Raffles sidestepped this problem by simply recognising the sultan's long-embittered older brother as the rightful sovereign of the territory, before signing a treaty with him granting the East India Company exclusive rights of trade over the island. The company and Raffles decided to allow ships passing through the Singapore Strait to enjoy free passage, essentially setting up the island as not just a maritime trading post but also a freeport.

Singapore became a key staging post for Britain's military and commercial interests in Asia over the next century, with the population of the island swelling with labour brought in from Malaya, British India, and especially China.[19] However, British control over Singapore was forever fractured by the Second World War. The fall of Singapore in 1942 to the Japanese Empire constituted the largest surrender in British military history. The island returned to British rule after the end of the war, but the myth of British colonial protection had now been exposed. Politicians and activists were able to marshal the deep resentment many people felt towards the colonial motherland for having abandoned them into a campaign for independence. The figure best able to capture this energy was Lee Kuan Yew.

In 1966, one month before he would be unceremoniously deposed from power, Kwame Nkrumah welcomed his friend Lee Kuan Yew to Ghana. As two leaders of newly independent countries both struggling to escape from the structural dependency of colonialism, Nkrumah and Lee shared a political problem as well as a personal affinity for each other. During his tour of the first black African nation to have escaped colonialism, Lee dined with Nkrumah and a select group of his senior ministers. The atmosphere was thick with suspicion and distress. Three days after he arrived in Accra, the Ghanaians told Lee that a bloody coup had just happened in neighbouring Nigeria. The Nigerian prime minister had been assassinated and the country was descending into infighting over who would control the massive oil resources that had just been discovered there. Everybody feared the same thing could happen in Ghana. While Lee admired the man he called 'Osagyefo' (Redeemer), Nkrumah's inner circle left him far from impressed. Speaking to them as they travelled through the tropical rivers and waterfalls of the country's picturesque Volta region, Lee got the impression that Nkrumah's ministers had already given up on the dream of a sovereign Ghana and were now only in government to see what they could get for themselves. He flew out of Accra with a sense of despair about Ghana's future, and wasn't surprised when he learned a coup had taken place in the country shortly after he left.[20]

At the time, the fate of Singapore looked just as stark as the scenario Lee had seen in Ghana. In addition to being a small city-state, Singapore also had to wrestle with the challenge of having emerged as a multiracial society during the colonial era, with cultural and sometimes political divisions emerging between the island's Chinese-speaking and English-speaking populations. Lee Kuan Yew carried the promise of transcending these divides, being a Singaporean of Chinese ancestry with an English education. Known as Harry in his family, Lee was educated at Raffles College in Singapore before attending the University of Cambridge, followed by barrister training at Middle Temple in London.[21] Yet despite his elite education, he was drawn into radical politics in his youth and was even suspected by the authorities of being a communist. He had been a defender of labour rights as a lawyer and was connected to both trade unionists and some of the radical student leaders who had been arrested as part of the Malayan Emergency – the guerrilla war that had been fought between the British Empire and the Malayan National Liberation Army during the 1950s. Following this, Lee became a key figure in the People's Action Party (PAP), founded in 1954. In the PAP, Lee would be supported by allies like the economist Goh Keng Swee, the physiologist Toh Chin Chye and perhaps the key intellectual architect of this vision of a new Singapore, the journalist Sinnathamby Rajaratnam.[22]

With the support of its left-wing allies in the organised labour movement, the PAP helped to pressurise Britain into granting Singapore greater powers of self-government, gaining a new constitution in 1958. The next year, the party won the first fully contested Singaporean general election under the leadership of Lee Kuan Yew, making him the first prime minister of Singapore. But Lee's hold over his party still appeared tenuous at that stage. He and his inner circle formed an English-educated elite sitting at the top of a largely Chinese-speaking party of trade unionists and radical students. However, the PAP's leadership were able to play off the British colonialists and the more radical elements of their own party against each other, reminding each of them that there was a far greater threat facing them if they did not stick to the plan. New laws were passed to tame the militancy of the trade unions. But soon Lee and the PAP had even bigger challenges to wrestle with.

As Britain became swept up by the 'winds of change' and decolonisation emerged as the accepted order of the day, Singapore began to plan for life outside the British Empire. Initially, it appeared that the logical path forward for the island would be to join the newly independent Federation of Malaya. After a referendum in 1962, Singapore joined the Federation of Malaya, North Borneo and Sarawak to create the new union called Malaysia.[23] However, Singapore's time in the union would be short-lived. With neighbouring Indonesia openly hostile to this new union and political tensions between Singapore and the other members emerging, on 9 August 1965 the parliament of Malaysia voted to expel Singapore. For a tiny island nation with few resources to trade, surrounded by much larger, hostile neighbours in the Muslim superstates of Indonesia and Malaysia, the prospects for an independent Singapore appeared stark. But only if you looked at the world in terms of traditional nation state politics; prioritising territorial scope and military power. If you adjusted the lens to see the world in terms of the global movement of money, then Singapore was in prime position to launch itself as the type of global city that would come to dominate the planet.

The Global City

On 21 September 1965, a delegation of PAP politicians travelled to New York City to accept the United Nations' admission of Singapore as a sovereign nation state. In the grand surroundings of the UN General Assembly Hall, surrounded by dignitaries and heads of state from every country, one of Lee Kuan Yew's key lieutenants delivered a statement that would point towards the unique path that Singapore sought to plot in this new world of nations. Sinnathamby Rajaratnam was a testament to the multiracial romance story of the new Singapore. Born to a Tamil family in Sri Lanka, Rajaratnam had moved to Singapore as a child before, as was common with future independence-era leaders, moving to Britain for his university and political education, studying law at Kings College London. However, unlike Lee, Rajaratnam was not drawn into legal practice. Instead, he was destined for more artistic endeavours, becoming a celebrated journalist and fiction writer. His short stories were published in anthologies alongside the likes of James Joyce, Ernest Hemingway and William Faulkner.[24] Through his writing, Rajaratnam expressed the beauty and tragedy of rural life across Asia. But the political upheavals occurring in his country drew him out of the arts and into politics. Once Singapore was expelled from Malaysia in 1965, Rajaratnam was appointed as the new country's foreign minister and dispatched to the UN to stake Singapore's claim in the new world of nations.

In New York, Rajaratnam announced to the rest of the globe that 'Singapore is essentially a trading community'.[25] It wanted no part of the rising military tensions that stalked the First, Second and Third World structure of the Cold War. Rajaratnam stated that in the new Singapore 'almost all our energies, resources and talents are devoted to developing our trade and industries. We have no military, aircrafts and no tanks.'[26] In an age when it appeared sovereignty was in the ascendency, with country after country celebrating its new-found powers of state, Rajaratnam warned countries not to embrace 'the dangerous myth of absolute sovereignty'.[27] Understanding the tensions that existed between rising nation statehood and transnational capitalism, Singapore was committed to becoming a new type of state, one that would survive by pleasing the market.

In 1972, Rajaratnam decided to brand Singapore as something he called a 'global city'.[28] The global city was a response to the world of nations, a reimagining of the spatial order of the world as a collection of dispersed centres of capital connected by trade. Today, to be labelled a global city has become the must-have status for any self-respecting mega-metropolis. New York, Paris, Hong Kong, Shanghai, Singapore, Johannesburg, Mumbai and, of course, London can all be considered worthy carriers of that label. On every continent, rural and industrial communities have been gradually left behind as the global-city network produced a new map of accelerated production and consumption. Rajaratnam foresaw that in a world of hyper-mobile capital and property rights, what mattered more than countries were the sprinkling of commercial centres that wealth moved between.

Britain had already used Singapore's geographic location between the Indian Ocean and the South China Sea to establish it as a hub in the global shipping routes. However, rather than merely allow the goods to flow through its ports, Singapore also sought to capture the commercial profits generated by this trade by constructing a thriving banking, insurance and financial services industry around it. For Rajaratnam, 'the strongest evidence of Singapore's absorption into the emerging system of Global Cities is its link-up, more and more, with international and multi-national corporations'.[29] Singapore also invested in its aviation industry to establish its airport as a key transit hub for those flying into and out of Asia. Appreciating the transformative impact of commercial air travel, Rajaratnam gambled that by becoming one of the select group of locations through which air traffic is directed, 'global cities' like Singapore, London and New York would be closer to each other than to other cities and towns in their own countries.

The government passed a wave of legislation to turn Singapore into a global city that would be attractive to foreign investors. Lee would later say, 'far from limiting the entry of foreign managers, engineers, and bankers, we encouraged them to come'.[30] The Economic Expansion Incentives Act 1967 reduced the tax burden that was being placed on multinational companies. The Employment Act and the Industrial Relations (Amendment) Act of 1968 restricted the negotiating power of workers. To suppress dissent against these changes, an old British colonial law, the Internal Securities Act, was resurrected, enabling the government to arbitrarily detain large numbers of political rivals who they branded communists or racial agitators. Then, in 1972, the National Wage Council was established to further tighten the government's hold over labour issues at a time when the rising wage expectations of Singapore's workers threatened to discourage further foreign investment. Union leaders who had once been political allies found themselves imprisoned without trial. The anti-capitalist rhetoric that had carried former labour rights lawyer Lee Kuan Yew to power had been wholly abandoned by his government.

This transformation into a global city saw Singapore drift away from the rest of the Third World in ideological as well as economic terms. In 1970, Rajaratnam secured Singapore's membership of the non-aligned movement and over the rest of the decade showed some sympathies with the Third World project being led by Jamaica's Michael Manley and others. However, Singapore's commitment to building an economy based on the ability to attract multinational corporate investment ensured that the country always remained an outlier within the movement. Eventually, at a 1983 meeting of the non-aligned movement in New Dehli, Rajaratnam, by then Singapore's deputy prime minister, took to the stage to castigate the other speakers, telling the audience that the people 'will view this summit as merely a foregathering of leaders whose pronouncements and rhetoric will not put one extra grain of rice into their near-empty rice bowls or a roof over their heads.'[31]

Undoubtedly, the approach taken by Lee and Rajaratnam at this time was successful in attracting international foreign invest-ment. In the thirty years between Singapore becoming independent and the collapse of Barings Bank, the economic growth of the city-state was exceptional. GDP in Singapore rose by an average of over 7 per cent each year during that period.[32] By opening itself up to international finance, Singapore was able to weather the oil price spikes and debt crises that ruined so many of its former Third World allies. Even the fall of Britain's oldest invest-ment bank into insolvency on the Singapore International Monetary Exchange did little to dampen the country's appeal in the eyes of global capital. In 2019, Singapore was crowned the world's leading hotspot for maritime trade for the fourth time in a row.[33] In 2020, the list of the world's leading free-market coun-tries compiled by the American think tank the Heritage Foundation named Singapore as 'the world's most free economy' for the first time, firmly establishing the city-state at the very forefront of global capitalism.[34]

However, the story of Singapore after empire isn't the vindication of free-market economics that today's Brexiteers seek to present it as. It did not follow the gospel of development that was being sold to the post-colonial world, of privatising public services, shrinking the government and implanting a liberal system of rule of law. Singapore's economic success did not come about as a result of the state stepping back and allowing the market to work its magic; the island was able to win the confidence of transnational asset owners the world over by showing itself to be a one-party state where the government was committed to stepping in to protect them when necessary. Far from being a testament to the brilliance of deregulation and laissez-faire economics, it is this interventionist streak that has given Singapore the edge over its competitors.[35] Furthermore, the PAP developed a method of using the state as a corporation itself. The government operates its own commercial companies and investment agencies, such as the Government of Singapore Investment Corporation, which are able to prop up major national industries. The government of Singapore remains the majority shareholder of the companies that provide the country's major infrastructural needs, such as transport and telecommunications. Singapore's sovereign wealth fund has served as a cushion for capitalists across the world, not only those invested in the island city-state. When Western banks find themselves short on capital, one of the first phone calls they make will be to the sovereign wealth funds of countries like Singapore, as well as other former British territories like Qatar or Kuwait. The Singapore Land Authority owns the majority of the island, allowing it to intervene to curb property speculation where necessary. Rather than showing privatisation to be an all-encompassing good, Singapore's economic success exposes how much the market relies on the power of sovereignty to be deployed in its service in order to find its ideal conditions.

There is also a more punitive side to the Singaporean miracle. During the summer of 2020, Ye Yuen Ming, a thirty-one-year-old British man from London, was stripped naked, tied to a frame and whipped in Singapore's Changi prison. After his torture, he continued his twenty-year sentence for the crime of supplying drugs to some of his friends.[36] In the context of Singapore's draconian drugs laws, Ming might count himself lucky. If the quantity of drugs he had been caught supplying had been higher, the court would have applied the death penalty – Singapore remains one of only a handful of countries in the world that carries out executions for drugs offences.[37]

Petty drugs dealers are not the only people who can be whipped for their crimes – those convicted of vandalism or inciting rioting can also face the same humiliating punishment. Homosexuality remains against the law and there are heavy restrictions placed on freedom of speech, the press and rights of association. Even gum chewing, dropping litter or crossing the road at an undesignated road junction are criminal offences. This authoritarianism is useful for maintaining discipline amid the inequality that has grown alongside Singapore's GDP. In the midst of the Brexit debates, politicians and business moguls tried to fit an imaginary version of Singapore into their grand narrative of linear progress, tied to the embrace of British values of property, liberalism, democracy and the rule of law. But underneath this rhetoric bubbled admiration, or even envy, for the way draconian state power has been wielded by the city-state in the interests of asset owners. Far from seeing the market as this force of nature that would operate perfectly if only governments stopped getting in its way, the laws and policies of the state are essential to maintaining and protecting capitalism from the dangers of democracy. In Britain, the more interventionist stance that the government has adopted in response to the Covid-19 pandemic has led to the talk of the post-Brexit, Singapore-on-Thames idea falling away. But a more interventionist government, especially when accompanied by draconian policies such as the criminalisation of protest or the restriction of teaching about racism in schools, is not necessarily a break away from the market. What the market likes more than anything is legal certainty, and the pandemic has shown the importance of an interventionist state in protecting capitalism from the shocks of the world. Perhaps an authoritarian state intervening in the market and disciplining the population may reflect the history of Singapore more than the no tax, no regulation free-for-all that politicians usually envisage when they refer to the city-state.

The Boomerang of the Global City

Singapore is, of course, a one-city state, and in many ways, Britain has become the same. Since the post-war decline of the industrial cities that grew so rich during the age of empire, one city has come to function as the political, cultural, legal, technological and financial capital of the country. London's significance for the UK is truly remarkable; it is the equivalent of Washington DC, New York, San Francisco and Los Angeles all wrapped up in a single city. This allows London to draw talent and wealth from the rest of the country and, in terms of financial services, from much of the world as well. Across the planet, it is recognised that if you want to do currency and commodities trading, you go to the City of London. Despite the emergence of other financial centres, like New York, Frankfurt and Tokyo, the City of London is still global capitalism's preferred location for banking, commercial insurance and legal services. Its unique history helps it to function as the mediator in financial transactions that connect every corner of the globe. In the decades following the Big Bang, a second 'City' has sprouted up at the old docklands area of Canary Wharf, a perfect metaphor for the demise of old industrial, workshop Britain at the hands of the resurgent financial industries.

Just as the transition to 'global city' status transformed the island of Singapore, so the capital city of its former imperial motherland has been through its own metamorphosis over recent decades. The past forty years have seen London being reshaped by the forces of globalisation, although if you just walk through the cobbled backstreets of the UK's capital, the mountain of wealth that has taken up residence in the city is not always easy to spot. The number of skyscrapers in the Square Mile has multiplied since the NatWest Tower was built in 1980, but in general London has avoided the ostentatious displays of opulence you might find in Dubai or Doha. Even the rich parts of the city are still composed of the same terraced homes and drab pubs that have been around since the Georgian age. But even if its true scale is hard to see, the wealth is there, hidden in plain sight. In 2021, the annual study of the world's wealthiest people by the commercial property consultants Knight Frank named London as home to the highest number of millionaires in the world.[38]

London's emergence as arguably the world's premier 'global city' since Margaret Thatcher's revolution has remade the space of the city, which is now home to a web of private gated communities, private car parks and private members' clubs that conceal their wealth from the view of most people. London is Europe's busiest city for private jets, as the world's frequent-flyer class float in and out of the UK.[39] Luxury air travel into the city doesn't only pass through Heathrow and Gatwick, but through an array of small private airports like Stapleford, Farnborough and Biggin Hill, littered across London and its surrounding counties. Free-flowing money allows the wealthy to move in to, out of and around London in a way that insulates them from the city that is actually lived in by the majority of people.

For while the wealth buried in London often likes to keep hidden, the poverty it coexists with can be all too visible when walking through the city. In 2010, analysis by geography professor Danny Dorling found London to be the most unequal city in the developed world.[40] The landscape of the city is still marked by the high-rise public housing that was put up during the post-war era of social welfarism, but these tower blocks are now in desperate need of refurbishment. All the money in the city has been poured into developing luxury properties, driving house prices beyond the reach of most workers, no matter how much they save.[41] Even people in traditional, professional middle-class jobs are pleading poverty in twenty-first-century London, with doctors and teachers finding out that all their degrees are no defence against the mushrooming wealth of financiers, property speculators and hedge-fund managers.

Instead of the wealth trickling down, unaffordable living costs have crept up on people who might once have assumed that they wouldn't ever have to live from pay cheque to pay cheque. As a result, while being home to the most millionaires in the world, London also has the highest rate of child poverty of anywhere in the country, with an estimated 37 per cent of all children in London living in relative poverty once housing costs are taken into account.[42] Too often, political discourse in the UK assumes that all of London is spectacularly rich and knows nothing of the problems communities face in other regions of the UK. In reality, there is not just drastic inequality to be seen between London and the rest of the country, but within London as well, which has become a two-track city, dividing those whose entrenched wealth increases with spiralling asset values from those struggling every month to make ends meet. As with all global cities, the gulf between rich and poor in London has brought with it the gentrification of neighbourhoods, the spread of casualised, insecure service work and the intensification of policing and surveillance tactics.

Brexit and State Capture

In many ways, the Brexit vote tapped into the resentment towards London felt in much of the rest of the country. For years, Britain's (almost wholly London-based) media has presented London as too rich, too cosmopolitan, too removed from the country that it is located within. It had become a cypher for all the forces of globalisation, and then the EU referendum arrived, presented by some of its advocates as a referendum on globalisation. In truth, many of Brexit's architects always saw it as an opportunity to accelerate globalisation – only this time with their own hands more firmly placed on the levers. Their promise that Brexit would allow Britain to 'take back control' was one they were making not to voters but to themselves.

In 1989, Margaret Thatcher advanced the conservative Eurosceptic movement by announcing, 'We have not successfully rolled back the frontiers of the state in Britain, only to see them reimposed at a European level with a European super-state exercising a new dominance from Brussels.'[43] This speech, made in the Belgian city of Bruges, gave birth to the Bruges Group – the anti-EU lobbying group that would eventually give rise to the Brexit movement in the early twenty-first century. However, rather than rolling back the state, Brexit now looks more like a vehicle to mobilise the power of the British state at the service of international capital, much as Singapore did after independence. One thing that separates Thatcher from her current inheritors is that today, few still honestly believe that the free market is a self-sufficient, miraculous system, always self-correcting if only government would get out of the way and stop meddling. Nowadays, there is greater recognition that government needs to take an active role in defending the market, craft laws and regulations that will protect asset owners.

Similarly, for many champions of the Leave vote, the afterlife of the British Empire in countries like Singapore provides an example of a legal order through which capitalist wealth can be entrenched and protected. Capital will find better shelter and more freedom in the English legal system than any other. Whereas the first generation of neoliberals feared the masses and their ability to threaten the interests of capital through unpredictable weaponisations of democracy, their successors today are confident in their ability to use nationalism and xenophobia to redirect the will of the people into reinforcing authoritarian protection of the market.

Sir James Dyson, Britain's richest person according to the 2020 *Sunday Times* Rich List, was a vocal advocate for Brexit. Then, in 2019, as the details of Britain's withdrawal from the EU were being finalised, Dyson announced that he was relocating his company headquarters to Singapore.[44] This move hardly inspired confidence in the Brexit project, with one of its biggest industrial backers seeming to move to insulate his company from any economic fallout that was to follow. Dyson's chief executive insisted that the move had nothing to do with Brexit or tax obligations.[45] Dyson already held a Singapore office; the only change was that office would now be where the company itself would be registered. But the *Financial Times* argued that 'The change of HQ would subject Dyson to less rigorous financial disclosure'.[46] Rather than a rejection of Brexit, Dyson's relocation offered further confirmation that those who championed it see Singapore as the ideal environment for business.

Brexiteer admiration for Singapore is a further example of how the areas of the map once considered the peripheries now sit at the vanguard of capital, in many ways. For all the challenges that result from trying to hold together a city like London, a grossly unequal metropolis of over 9 million people, it is important to remember that London is not even in the top twenty largest cities in the world. Cities like Dhaka, Lagos, Karachi and Cairo have long overtaken the population of their former imperial centre, and will continue to grow rapidly over the coming decades. For the architects of Brexit, the inequality that comes with the global city model is a price worth paying for increased wealth. They know that the armies of low-paid workers who are needed to prop up the lifestyles of high-flying insurance brokers and investment bankers in this type of economy will include many of their own voters.

For all their glitz and glamour, global cities simply cannot function without the people who maintain the foundations upon which their globalised economies rest. London, as much as Singapore, needs an extensive precarious workforce of both domestic and immigrant labourers to look after the wealthy – cleaners, cooks, drivers and providers of childcare services. In an ideal neoliberal world, in order to help this workforce better meet the needs of their employers, they will have little to no control over their lives – no bargaining power, no security of contract, no right to demand improved working conditions, their working day governed by sophisticated methods of high-tech surveillance to track, monitor and record their activities. The division between the haves and have-nots in the global city emphasises how those who have been 'left behind' by globalisation do not need to take back control from the EU or immigrants or the cultural elite – but from those with capital.

Despite his embrace of financialised capitalism, Lee Kuan Yew's writings display a certain romantic sympathy for the Third Worldist movement that is unlikely to be shared by many of the British conservatives currently championing his example. When Kwame Nkrumah was removed from office in a coup, Lee wrote him a letter deploring the turn of the events. In a tone of comradely solidarity rather than ideological enmity, Lee concluded his letter by writing 'may what you stand for, a united Africa and a great Ghana, triumph and flourish'.[47] Had the historical context in the mid- to late-twentieth century been different, or if Singapore had carried large reserves of in-demand resources like oil, gold or Bauxite in the way Iran, Ghana and Jamaica did respectively, then the city-state might have trodden the same path of many other former British colonies.

Its deviation from that path and its alignment with financial services is not, contrary to some racist ideas, the result of certain populations or races being more suited to capitalism. It is the result of necessity. In the words of Deputy Prime Minister Wong Kan Seng in 2011, 'For Singapore, becoming a global city is not merely an aspiration, it is a pre-requisite for our survival . . . Closing our doors will turn us into an island of no consequence.'[48] Singapore did not have the choice or ability to confront the power of global capital. Britain has both. What is presented as admiration for Singapore by leading Brexiteers is actually just an admiration for themselves, the assumption that any progress made in Singapore is the result of Britain's legacy. The only parts of the city-state they want to boomerang back to the old motherland are the draconian legal system and highly financialised economy. They do not discuss how the state invests in social housing and cheap and efficient public transportation. They do not explore how the state could intervene in more than just asset protection. It could invest in all levels of education, including university, and better social security protections. A 'Singapore-on-Thames' would be a choice rather than a necessary response. A choice driven by nationalists who seek to write a new unifying story while maintaining and protecting the infrastructure that has driven Britain's wealth divergence over recent decades. True sovereignty would be empowering working people to challenge the interests of global capital. It would also require confronting the aftermath of empire, and asking how the UK could limit the spaces capital has used to accelerate inequality all over the world in recent decades.

Conclusion: There is an Alternative

In 2007, the first signs that the world was moving into a new stage of history started to appear. The promise of the 'end of history' thesis of the 1990s was that there would be no more dramatic events in the age of financialised globalisation. We had seen the 'end of boom and bust', Gordon Brown said. But the unwavering confidence in the global capitalist system that had shone over the West since the end of the Cold War finally began to falter as an unprecedented economic crisis loomed. In Britain, this was the year that panic started to spread as the realisation slowly dawned that the property wealth that had powered growing inequality across the country over recent decades had been built upon the slippery sand of financial speculation.

By the end of the year, the waves were crashing in. Hundreds of customers could be seen jostling with each other outside branches of Northern Rock, one of the main banks that had overindulged in the buffet of cheap credit that had been on offer since Thatcher's 'Big Bang', and was now collapsing. Suddenly, our TV screens were full of emergency bulletins where nervous government ministers and central bankers talked of the need for drastic action to stop our entire economic system from disintegrating.

Meanwhile, across the ocean in Ghana, 2007 was a year of national celebration. Fifty years of independence was being commemorated, a full half a century since Kwame Nkrumah announced the birth of 'a new African nation'. While Britain was bracing itself for the coming financial crash, in the place it once called the colony of the Gold Coast, the only explosions to be seen were the fireworks being used to mark a pivotal anniversary of the first black African country to claim its sovereignty. When I arrived in Accra that summer, the city was a sea of red, gold and green, the national flag plastered over palm trees, lamp posts, billboards, church walls and seemingly any other available surface. Highlife songs of freedom from the 1950s echoed across the city's streets from passing taxi radios while children walking to school clapped and sang along. At almost every traffic crossing or road-side junction I would have to fend off the vendors trying to sell me another 'Ghana at 50' commemorative T-shirt.

The only person who didn't seem particularly excited by Ghana's golden jubilee was my grandfather, now nearing what we soon learned would be the end of his long life. Every day, I would try to cajole him into the party spirit; smiling, he would simply whisper, 'Ah, but when I was born, there was no Ghana.' In the midst of an atmosphere of intense national fervour, he was reminding me of the inherent fiction of any nation state. My grandfather was almost into middle age by the time that the Gold Coast was combined with Britain's Ashanti crown colony, the protectorates of the northern territories and British Togoland to form the sovereign nation state of Ghana. He had always been a great believer in Ghana; however the promise of an independent nation state that had brought him back from London in the 1950s was not the symbolic promise of flags, anthems, ceremonies and anniversaries but the belief that this change might help usher into existence a fairer, more equitable world. At the time of independence, everyone from Richard Nixon to Martin Luther King and Coretta Scott King followed the same journey that my grand-father took to Accra in order to see the birth of this first sovereign black African state. 'An old order is passing away and a new order is coming into being,' were the thoughts of Martin Luther King as he sat among rapturous crowds on the night of independence.[1] When a floodlit Nkrumah started dancing as the Union Jack was lowered and the new Black Star of Ghana began to rise, hope spread among the poorer people of the world. Like my grandfather and millions of other men, women and children across the colonies, King believed that the independence of Ghana would forever mark a new morning for the world. The sovereign African state had entered the international stage and the calendar would surely show that this was the day that the four-hundred-year history of extraction and exploitation, of slavery and colonialism, was confined to the dustbin. Now, in the world after empire, human beings of all races and cultures could finally be equal and enjoy exercising control over their own lives.

That promise has never arrived. Even after the demise of empire, the financial tentacles it had grown over the centuries still managed to eventually tie the hands of the new states in debt, privatisation and corporatisation, ensuring there was no great redistribution of wealth at either the global or local level. The power of sovereignty was watered down as soon as the people of the colonies had been able to get their hands on it. Sovereignty brought with it new national icons, myths and conceptual framings, through which people could understand themselves collectively, but tangible, material self-determination was to be hidden away. At the time of its fiftieth anniversary, an independent Ghana was still being celebrated as the democratic example that all of Africa should follow. Every four years the country hosted elections regularly praised by the Western media as being the most peaceful on the continent. Presidents would abide by the democratic process, the two-term limit would be respected and the transition of power would proceed relatively smoothly.

Yet nothing would ever really change for the woman who sold groundnuts at Kaneshi market. Or for the mother in Kumasi who had to decide which one of her three children she should pay to send to school. The country was still helpless to stop its gold and cocoa and timber and oil from being extracted and traded on the global markets at terms many felt were unfair. The citizens of Ghana appeared to get very little out of the state whose birthday they were celebrating. Their care had been largely outsourced, their safety net non-existent. NGOs had placed sticking plasters over the wounds opened up by the dismantling of public services in the service of the structural adjustment gods. Now hospitals were run by development agencies; schools run by international churches or private entrepreneurs. Only when it was time to discipline the people did the state suddenly make its presence felt, again. On the roads named after the famous independence leaders, police officers set up checkpoints at will, intimidating informal traders and squeezing money from any unlucky taxi drivers who might pass by. Access to Accra's airport, gated communities, five-star hotels and luxury shopping malls was tightly controlled. For the masses of the country, the democratic potential of decolonisation had been strangled at birth. I sensed my grandfather found something lamentable about celebrating an anniversary of national sovereignty where a great deal of nationalism was on display but little in the way of sovereignty. Ghana and many of the other newly independent states that followed it had been hamstrung shortly after they came into being in order to deliver the liberation of financial markets. The same forces of free-flowing capitalism that, by 2007, were crashing banks and overturning the economy in the old imperial mother country, had already swept through the decolonised world decades earlier.

I couldn't help but recall my grandfather's indifference to Ghana's golden jubilee when Britain celebrated its own 'independence' after leaving the European Union in 2020. Across the country, people were celebrating what Jacob Rees-Mogg described as the dawn of 'a golden age for the United Kingdom when we are free of the heavy yoke of the European Union, which has bowed us down for generations.'[2] For the country that had always been a land without a birthday, here at last was its own 'independence day'. On the night the UK finally left the EU, Boris Johnson declared that this was a moment of 'recaptured sovereignty', Britain could thrive now that we were once again 'making our laws and rules for the benefit of the people of this country'.[3] He had fulfilled his predecessor Theresa May's promise to make Britain 'a fully independent, sovereign country'.[4] Among the crowds that celebrated with Johnson and his team, Brexit may have been the cause that had brought them all together, but this was clearly not just about Brexit any more. Brexit was a signifier for something much bigger, the arrival of a new era of aggressive nationalism that promised to overturn all the systems and structures that many communities across the country felt were eroding any control they once held over their own lives.

Where had this control gone? Had it just been the European Union all along? How was it possible that people in the UK, once the heart of empire, were now themselves searching for independence, sovereignty and control? The EU was by no objective measure exercising 'imperialism' over Britain, but you wouldn't have known that from some of the hyperbolic rhetoric that politicians were drawing upon. The same figures who would be the first to defend the legacy of the British Empire were quick to caricature the uniquely privileged position that the UK had carved out for itself within the EU as equivalent to colonial subjugation. Jacob Rees-Mogg, who had gone on record describing the 'good bits' of the British Empire as 'really wonderful', called the UK leaving the EU an end to the 'colonial effect' that Europe had on the British economy.[5] Boris Johnson argued that unless Britain got full regulatory freedom from the EU, it was heading for 'the status of colony'.[6] This moment wasn't about evidence. It was about emotions. A new narrative was being used to explain away the instability, insecurity and inequality that so many people in Britain had been living with for so long. They lived in Britain, an advanced nation, a democratic nation. So why did everyone feel unable to do anything about the direction of their lives? Now, here was a moment that promised a great return of national sovereignty. But among the bluster of nationalism, how much sovereignty was actually being delivered?

Through the metaphor of the boomerang, Aime Césaire exploded the European myth that history moves only in one direction.[7] He was writing to everyone who still assumed that events outside Europe's borders had no relevance to understanding the dynamics at play within them. This forewarning has been completely disregarded in the mainstream political debate in Britain where the silence around the topic of empire pushes some of the most significant events of recent decades outside the purview of legitimate analysis. Government minister Kemi Badenoch described the growing calls for decolonisation in universities, schools and cultural institutions as a 'recent fad' that is 'not just misguided but actively opposed to the fundamental purpose of education'.[8] Illustrating how common it is to assume that a nearly four-hundred-year-old empire had no impact on Britain, Badenoch insisted that 'our curriculum does not need to be decolonised, for the simple reason that it is not colonised'. She even affirmed that the government considers the teaching of topics of race and empire in schools in an unbalanced manner to be 'breaking the law'.[9] Obviously, following a warning like this from a minister of state, any teacher would be best served to avoid the topics of empire and decolonisation all together. But then how are we to think through problems like the rise of corporatisation without asking where the commercial corporation came from? Or about the disappearance of factories without asking where the factories went to? British children cannot hope to understand the country that they live in if they have to ignore the centuries of empire that actually brought it into existence. They cannot expect to understand why the classroom includes children named Fatima or Ifeoma or Ramesh without learning about the many ways that empire and its afterlife continue to mediate Britain's relationship with the rest of the world. The omission of empire from our education is the product of a worldview that has long been myopic, but that is now also beginning to look increasingly masochistic. The myth of national exceptionalism is now actively harming the UK's ability to interpret and respond to the global dynamics that are impacting upon it. Despite romantic ideas of standing alone, Britain is not insulated from what is happening across the rest of the world.

Underlying Health Problems

In March 2020, as the coronavirus pandemic began to sweep across the globe, the World Health Organisation (WHO) warned that to contain the virus, countries must start comprehensively testing and tracing their citizens. The WHO pointed to the success of places like South Korea in responding to Covid-19, making it clear that 'countries simply have to have in place a system to detect, isolate, contact trace and quarantine contacts' in order to avoid a public health emergency.[10] In Britain, at the start of March, the impact of the virus was not yet as severe as in China or Italy, but the infection numbers were beginning to rise. Yet, despite the obvious warning signs being displayed across the globe, the government decided it did not need any lessons in infection control from the WHO or the likes of South Korea; Britain would follow its own idiosyncratic path in order to contain the disease. The UK's Deputy Chief Medical Officer, Dr Jenny Harries, made the government's position on this clear when she dismissed the WHO's guidance for mass testing, arguing 'the clue for WHO is in its title. It is a World Health Organisation and it is addressing all countries across the world . . . including low- and middle-income countries'. Harries explained that Britain would exempt itself from this advice as 'we have an extremely well-developed public health system in this country and in fact our public health teams actually train others abroad'.[11] It was assumed that Covid-19 would recognise the accepted line of history and impact the poorest, developing nations worst of all, while advanced countries like Britain and the USA were already prepared to stave it off.

The crisis that followed over the next few months highlighted some of the dangers of Britain clinging to old ideas of national exceptionalism. Prime Minister Johnson continued to thumb his nose at the international advice and told the country to continue 'going about our business as usual', even bragging about going into hospital with coronavirus patients and shaking hands.[12] At the same time that other countries were closing down their economies and going into lockdown, Johnson was calling for Britain to 'take off its Clark Kent spectacles' and become 'the superman of global free trade'.[13] It played well to his audience, but Johnson's bluster in the face of the pandemic almost had fatal consequences. By April, not only had he contracted coronavirus himself but he had to be admitted to intensive care as his condition was critical.

Yet Johnson did not let a mere personal brush with death nor the high number of coronavirus victims across the nation shake him out of his belief in British exceptionalism. When the UK eventually did embark on testing a few months later, the change of policy was filtered through the same old lens, with Johnson declaring that 'we will have a test and trace system that will be world-beating'.[14] Towards the end of the year and into 2021, the success of Britain's vaccine development and rollout programme was not credited to the remarkable work of the country's scientists and healthcare professionals, but to the spirit of Brexit. The blame for any future waves of the infection were squarely pinned on other countries who 'have healthcare systems which are ill-prepared to manage this pandemic'.[15] All this despite the UK having registered one of the worst death rates in world in 2020.[16] Prior to the vaccine rollout, other countries had been using Britain as an example of what *not* to do when they were outlining their plans to control the spread of Covid-19.[17] But by the end of year, any idea that the challenges of the pandemic might lead the country's leaders to re-evaluate their presumptions of Britain's relationship to the rest of the world disappeared under an avalanche of vaccine nationalism.

In the midst of the pandemic, former prime minister John Major provoked a national furore by daring to suggest that perhaps the UK was 'no longer a great power' and 'will never be so again'.[18] This led to a flutter of articles and TV talk shows asking if he was correct. And, if he was, then where is Britain placed? In the top four? Top ten? Witnessing so many of the country's politicians and public intellectuals choosing to argue about where Britain ranked in the world during a pandemic that was killing people by the thousands and bringing the entire global economy to its knees was like watching two men standing on the deck of the *Titanic* arguing about which one of them was taller, as the water rose up towards their noses.

The Boomerang of the Promise of Nationalism

This book was contracted at the start of 2020 and so its lifespan has spread across an unprecedented global pandemic. As it was being written, it seemed as if many of its themes were beginning to bleed into the surrounding world. The book was planned before the Covid-19 crisis, the lockdowns, the Black Lives Matter Protests and the resurgent interest in questions of empire. As I was writing, I could see the themes that I was exploring – Britain's imperial legacy and the entrenched inequality of Britain's economy – consistently appearing in the headlines. But always at different times, never discussed or analysed together. The debate around decolonisation in Britain today was presented as creating division in an otherwise harmonious society. Then, in the very next story there would be a discussion about how Covid-19 and the resultant shutdown of the economy was exposing just how divided our society had really become. The pandemic forced many of us to confront a simple but stark question – do you have to go to work to survive? The virus shut down places of work, leaving so many people who were unable to work from home stuck at home, reliant on state support. Small businesses had to close their shutters and families faced eviction because they couldn't afford the rent, despite government attempts to intervene. Meanwhile, asset prices soared to new heights. People kept paying their debts and even took on new ones. Less money was being spent on disposable goods and more was being poured into investments. The value of the stock markets and property portfolios continued to inflate even as the rest of the world suffered through a public health and economic disaster.

When it arrived, the pandemic was seen as being 'the great leveller'; this was a crisis that threatened everyone equally no matter your race, gender, nationality or bank balance. Yet in reality, Covid-19 only accelerated those inequalities we were already wrestling with. Racial inequalities were highlighted as the impact of the virus fell disproportionately on the black and ethnic-minority communities who had long taken up many of the front-line caring roles in our society. Gender inequalities were exposed as mothers across the country bore the brunt of balancing the new demands of both working from home and home-schooling children. But perhaps the starkest division that the pandemic exposed was the disconnection that had been growing for decades between the world of assets and the world of living, breathing human beings. Perhaps the perfect metaphor for how the world has moved steadily towards more freedom for property than for human beings was the 'Stanley Johnson loophole' in Britain's rules restricting travel during Covid-19. This was a clause named after the prime minister's father that allowed people to override the regulations if they were preparing property overseas for sale or rent.[19] People could not cross borders to see their children or to say goodbye to dying elderly relatives, but in the service of facilitating the movement of property, then exceptions could be made. Even in countries like Britain that sit at the heart of the global capitalist system, the pandemic reminded us just how different the interests of capital had become from the interests of people.

The pandemic has been a blessing for private and public debt. In order to purchase the resources required to fight the virus and support the economy through lockdowns, the UK has built up its highest levels of national debt since the 1960s.[20] For the first time in generations, public debt has risen to beyond 100 per cent of GDP.[21] The weaponisation of debt is now once again a tool in the political arsenal of those leaders who might need it. The pandemic proved to be a blessing for many enterprising private companies. The UK's inbuilt orientation towards outsourcing went into overdrive. Companies were quick to lobby friends and former colleagues in government in order to win contracts to supply personal protective equipment and medical resources to the country, even if they had no previous experience in this field. The newspapers cried out that the British state had been seized by a 'chumocracy' or 'cronyism', a rather quixotic description for a problem that, had it occurred in one of the post-colonial countries in Africa or Asia, would have been called out as corruption.[22] Furthermore, this corruption would be implicitly or explicitly racialised, highlighted as an example of these developing peoples' persisting backwardness and inherent inability to assimilate the norms of civilised, liberal democracy.

In 2016, Prime Minister David Cameron was recorded describing Nigeria and Afghanistan as 'fantastically corrupt' countries while in a conversation with the Queen.[23] By 2021, he was facing his own accusations of corruption. The revelation of Cameron's efforts during the pandemic to lobby his former colleagues in government for a loan on behalf of Greensill (a company for which he was a paid adviser and shareholder) caused a national scandal. To see the problems of the developing world as corruption and the current problems in Britain as just chumocracy is a shallow way of looking at the global dynamics at play. This corporatisation of all aspects of public life, with more and more control going to big companies, is not just the failing of a few amoral politicians or opportunistic entrepreneurs – there is a longer history of the power of the state being mutated by capital across the world which is informing our current age of cronyism.

The trend towards privatisation, deregulation and corporatisation that, in the West, we came to know as neoliberalism, began in the post-colonies after the end of empire. After independence, decolonised governments' ability to interrupt the flow of global capital was quickly removed and the purpose of state office was limited to serving the appetite of the market. Politics became the process of negotiating between the global multinational corporations and the local labour and material resources they coveted. Nationalist authoritarianism spread across the African, Asian and Latin American continents not because of some innate cultural or racial failure within the populations, but because this political model had become the most effective method for managing the inequality and insecurity that resulted from being held hostage to the fluctuations of the market.

The consequences of using financial markets to weaken democracy in decolonised countries after empire are now haunting the West. Following the 2008 financial crash, states across Europe saw their own turns towards nativism, with the successes of Matteo Salvini and the Northern League in Italy, Marine Le Pen and the National Front in France, Andrzej Duda in Poland and Viktor Orbán in Hungary. The remarkable one-term presidency of Donald Trump in the USA also reflects this so-called return to 'national sovereignty' in the West. Even countries that encouraged the shift towards financialisaton are now realising that unfettered finance capitalism will kill its own host, if allowed. The boomerangs of market forces and nationalism now hurtling back towards Britain are at the sharp end of this trend. In the UK, as elsewhere, nativist government is not challenging global capitalism, but is using the power of the state to protect asset holders while redirecting anger for the economic inequality and social ills it produces on to minorities and 'enemies within'. Hence the framing of empire as an issue of petty resentments, as though the dynamics that produce entrenched inequality in Britain suddenly stop at the white cliffs of Dover.

At many points in this book, I returned to Enoch Powell's vision of the world after empire, specifically how he felt that Britain could preserve its pre-eminence. Powell's new world would be one in which turbo-charged free-market capitalism could move freely across bounded, ethnically homogeneous nation states. In each country, the 'nation' would take precedent over the 'state', as governments created the ideal conditions for market prosperity by focusing on protecting borders and property. Internationally, there would be no need for institutions like the United Nations or the World Health Organisation, which might impinge on national sovereignty; the Commonwealth could be dispensed with along with all other memories of the imperial age; and European integration, despite its explicit capitalist orientation, should be resisted at all costs. For Powell, the sphere of the international should remain narrow, and follow in the footsteps of private English common law. It should prioritise the rights of capital asset owners across borders above all else, especially by protecting those assets from the grasping hands of ungrateful Third World governments.

This vision holds more than a passing resemblance to the nativist resurgence which has spread across Britain and much of the world over the past decade. Border walls are getting harsher, international collaboration is getting weaker as private accumulation continues at pace. Turning every political problem into a nationalistic culture war has become the default tactic that politicians employ to cover up the deep structural issues within Britain's economic model. Government reports insist that working-class schoolchildren are being left behind, not due to cuts to youth services, school funding or welfare provisions but because there is too much talk about 'divisive terms' like white privilege and others matters concerned with race.[24] At the time of writing Baroness Dido Harding, the woman who oversaw the UK's unsuccessful, outsourced test and trace system, is looking to become the next chief executive of NHS England. She generated headlines when she promised that, if she was appointed to this role, she would end the NHS's reliance on foreign doctors and nurses.[25] Her first priority was not to commit to more government support of the underfunded health system or to provide the NHS staff with much deserved payrises in recognition of the enormous sacrifices they had made over the course of the coronavirus pandemic, it was to appeal to nationalism and xenophobia to mask the structural deficiencies in Britain's public health service.

With confidence in the inevitable progress of humanity declining, many people are being seduced by this turn to nationalist politics, in the hope that it might at least offer a lifeboat – if the ship is sinking, focus on saving yourself. Secure your assets; sever the links between work and individual rising living standards; don't waste time or resources trying to imagine a world other than the one we already have. Life is so daunting and insecure that conversations around the legacy of empire can appear as a luxury that regular people just don't have time for. But the afterlife of empire is deeply connected to that insecurity that many people are feeling. It isn't just about whether people should or shouldn't defend a statue of Churchill, but about how the ability of ordinary people to exert pressure on transnational capital is controlled. The politics of nationalism in the age of hyper-capitalism offers little to those communities who have been left behind by the financialisation of the world over the past few decades. Politicians with offshore accounts and corporate interests spread across the globe are preaching the gospel of national unity to people for whom in-work poverty has become a fact of life. They can't rescue everyone, but they'll make enough room on the lifeboat for just a few more, as long as you turn against each other and fight it out for the space.

The truth is that this ship sailed a long time ago. The politicians seated in Westminster are aware of the deep structural transformations that would be required to deliver rising wages for the working people of Britain, greater welfare provisions for our most vulnerable communities and renewed prosperity for deindustrialised towns. Inequality in Britain has hardened to the extent that the Office of National Statistics has stated that the ratio of the income share received by the richest 10 per cent of households is now equal to that of the poorest 40 per cent of households.[26] Racial minorities, single mothers, carers and the disabled are at the sharp end of this division but are too often presented as being the enemies of the good, honest 'left behind' communities of Britain. Yet, underneath vague promises of levelling up, few politicians will commit to transforming welfare provisions, collective labour rights or implementing policies that help drive the redistribution of wealth. Instead, politicians from both the Conservative and the Labour parties are using the Union Jack as a shield against difficult questions. In a world of economic stagnation, unrestrained global capital movement, data hoarding by big tech and increasingly precarious work conditions for the masses, if you are being told by those you are asking to help you to simply wave a flag, it is because they have already abandoned you, leaving you stranded in the wreckage while they sail away.

Confronting the Aftermath of Empire

In recent years, there has been an attempt to draw a stark line between people who care about race and empire and people who care about the communities that have been economically 'left behind' in Britain over the last few decades. At times, those in favour of paying more attention to the legacy of empire have contributed to this false impression by making a moral issue of it: you learn about empire if you are a good person, if you are kind and concerned with righting the wrongs of the past. In response, their opponents have pretended that all this talk about empire and decolonisation is just part of metropolitan identity politics: real people don't have time for such moralising nonsense. The overall effect is to reinforce a real desire in the UK to forget all about it. Let's just move on, shall we? It is more than just lethargy; discussions of empire and its legacy can provoke an almost audible collective groan when raised. Empire is bracketed off into debates about race, as though conversations around its legacy are essentially the concern of bitter racial minorities inflicting their frustrations on everybody else. But this is an old trick. For centuries, the discourse of race has always been used to cleave an artificial division between human factions. It lulls the dominant group into believing that the violence they saw being done to others has no possibility of befalling them too. This was always a lie. Violence never stays neatly within its prescribed borders. Race just allows particularly vulnerable populations to serve as target practise. Sooner or later, the weapon always turns towards other bystanders.

So much of the economic violence covered in this book has been absent from political, economic and social discourse in Britain over the years due to the residual belief that black lives do not matter, even if they were British until very recently. When sovereign debt crippled the island of Jamaica, the accompanying images of impoverished black fishermen only reinforced prevailing ideas of the natural order of the world. When structural adjustment programmes left millions of children across Africa and Asia living hand to mouth this was received as further evidence of old, unspoken ideas about a hierarchy among the world's people. When nation after nation in the Third World buckled under the pressure of globalised capitalism following decolonisation, this was viewed by many in Britain as a problem with *them*, not a problem with *our* global system. A new myth of cultural or even racial inferiority was whispered through corridors of power – *See, here is the evidence that these people were always too backwards, too greedy, too inherently unintelligent to handle the complex pressures of sovereignty.*

But recently, there has been a glimmer of hope that more and more people, especially the younger generation, are starting to appreciate the importance of countries like Britain reckoning with their colonial pasts, not just for the good of others but also for the good of ourselves.[27] In the midst of the coronavirus pandemic, the decades-long suppression of any serious conversation about race and imperialism exploded onto the streets across the country. The Black Lives Matter protests in the summer of 2020 were the largest anti-racism protests in British history, and sparked the closest thing to a public conversation about Britain's colonial legacy that this country has ever seen.

Significantly, protesters poured onto the streets not only in the UK's main multicultural centres of London, Manchester and

Birmingham, but also in rural, primarily white areas like Buckinghamshire, Cornwall and the Shetland Islands.[28] Witnessing this while writing this book was a revelation. Clearly there were more people than I had thought with an appetite for these kinds of conversations; people who suspected that in the history of empire and its afterlife they might find answers to some of their questions about how the imbalanced world that they live in came to be. Despite a barrage of government figures condemning the protest movement, by the end of 2020, over half of the British public supported the Black Lives Matter movement, with that number rising to seven in ten for young people.[29]

The interest that the younger generation showed in the issue of empire seemed to catch political observers across the country by surprise. Newspapers have been jammed full of articles despairing that the nation's youth was being 'brainwashed' into challenging the legacy of the British Empire by teachers, the media, pop stars, footballers or an ever-changing line-up of public enemies.[30] Statistics do point to a sharp change in ideas about empire among younger Brits, with only 18 per cent of eighteen- to twenty-four-year-olds now seeing empire as something to be proud of, compared to 43 per cent of those older than sixty-five.[31] But while this shift in attitude has generated a great deal of anger towards ungrateful, unpatriotic millennials, rarely is the question asked: why are the young, from all racial backgrounds, so receptive to conversations around decolonisation at the moment? Is it really mass generational brainwashing? The naivety of youth? Or is it grounded in a suspicion that for young people the systems that may have enriched their forebears are no longer serving them?

En masse, young people in Britain are witnessing the lives they envisaged for themselves now slipping out of view, the lives that they were told – as members of an advanced nation – they had a right to expect if they worked hard and played by the rules. Many have done just that but now recognise that they may never own property, they may never be able to afford to raise children, they may never have secure work and, in all likelihood, they could still be paying off their student debt when they are preparing to receive their pensions. The bank of mum and dad has become many people's only hope for salvation, leaving those without rich parents trapped. This isn't just the case for teenagers. The students who graduated in the financial crisis of 2008 were approaching forty years old by the time the coronavirus pandemic descended. Many of them were still concussed from the first event when this further economic sledgehammer hit them. Now they fear their lives will once again be left at sea while the corporate world is rescued. Disaster after disaster has struck them and yet asset prices continue to soar uninterrupted, houses are more expensive, jobs are more insecure, their options get more and more restrained. Can they really be expected to maintain their faith in a system even as it cuts them adrift?

When faced with a choice between honouring or rejecting a figure such as Edward Colston, not just a slave trader but the director of the type of colonial company that built the modern world, is it so surprising that many of this generation lined up behind those who were dumping Colston's statue into Bristol harbour? This isn't just a moral stance, it's a wholesale disassociation with the liberal promise of inevitable progress that tells us that racism is a personal prejudice, only held by ignorant people. They know that racism isn't just a matter of politeness but about how ideas and institutions reproduce power, and that this won't simply disappear if we all just promise to never, ever mention it again. The rejection of the Colston statue revealed a growing recognition that empire was not just about identity and race but also about poverty and wealth, democracy and control. While government ministers seek to paint conversations about decolonisation as being as silly as they are dangerous, people on the streets are increasingly recognising that empire is, quite simply, at the root of this country's political and economic system. You cannot hope to change the system significantly without grappling with its aftermath.

However, this movement cannot stop with the toppling of statues if it really wants to create a fairer world. Speaking about culture and symbolism are powerful ways to describe how people experience the hangover of empire in contemporary Britain, but there must also be a reckoning with the primary reason why empire was created in the first place: to materially enrich some people at the expense of others. Challenging the aftermath of empire in Britain means reinterpreting the British state and its constitution in light of its development through empire, under-standing the role that English conceptions of property play in reinforcing global corporate power, placing the never-ending immigration debate in the context of Britain's global legacy, looking at the role that the City of London and Britain's overseas territories play in financial globalisation, and asking how many of the problems that Britain itself is now facing are themselves a consequence of the afterlife of empire. In order to deal with its own spiralling wealth inequality, Britain needs to deal with the afterlife of its empire, both at home and abroad. Though the government is still invested in the idea that racism is a personal prejudice rather than a system maintained by institutions of law and economics, the global project of empire tells us something different. Racism did not spread because of an inherent fear and hatred of people of different appearance, but because there was a need to gain more resources and wealth, and that required making others disposable, particularly those who inconveniently lived on the lands where those resources were located. Those who currently shout 'Black Lives Matter' in the streets of Liverpool, London and Manchester must recognise not just the value of the black lives next door but the value of those in Accra, Nairobi and Kingston. This version of Black Lives Matter may prove a little harder for global corporations to support via a well-placed social media post or celebrity endorsement deal. But it will help us to identify some of the economic transformations that would be necessary to make the changes being called for by the movement.

It is possible that, one day, telling the story of the twentieth century without reference to decolonisation will look as ridiculous as trying to explain the global changes of the eighteenth century without mentioning the French or American revolutions. The idea that the process through which three-quarters of the world's people freed themselves from legal subjugation is just a niche interest at best, should, rightfully, look bizarre to future generations. The figures who drove the period of decolonisation after the Second World War were asking many of the same questions which we are all wrestling with today. What does sovereignty mean? How can we exercise control of the market? How can we share resources across the world equitably? The characters we have encountered in this book certainly did not have all the answers, and made many mistakes of their own. They were as convinced by the industrialised ideal of development as everybody else. They remained largely a boys' club, ignoring the concerns of the women who had done so much to drive their successful national liberation campaigns. They indulged in autocracy and let themselves believe that whipping up the nationalism of their population would be enough to overcome the deep political and economic challenges they faced. Once they got their hands onto instruments of state sovereignty, they often found it easier to wield its power against their own people than against the multinational corporations profiting from their lands.

But in the rubble of their struggle and defeat, we find the building blocks of our own unequal world. Today, there is renewed value in reading Nkrumah on the limits of national sovereignty, or Manley on the regulation of corporations. For too long, the conversation around economic inequality has been conducted as though it comes from a different solar system to the conversation around the legacy of empire. Over the space of a few chapters, I have sought to upend this assumption by offering a snapshot of just a few significant scenes in the break-up of the British Empire, criss-crossing the oceans to take in moments of economic struggle from the Caribbean to West Africa, from Singapore to the City of London, in order to show the connections between then and now. In just these few episodes, we can start to see how attempts to maintain the machinery of empire in the decades after its fall, combined with the erasure of all memory of decolonisation, has contributed to the unleashing of grim spectres that now haunt this island.

There is little point trying to reform the tax system in Britain if we don't address how Britain's overseas territories have been turned into offshore boltholes for tax avoiders. It is very difficult to be able to hold corporations to employment or environmental regulations in Britain unless countries across Asia, Africa and Latin America are empowered to do the same thing. Whether facing systems of unaccountable corporate power, offshoring, bordering or debt, we can't explain what we now call neoliberalism and all its accompanying inequalities and insecurities, without confronting the aftermath of empire.

There is an Alternative

The topic of empire is likely to remain a controversial one for the foreseeable future. I only need to open my email inbox the day after I have written a newspaper article or made a TV appearance to see how quickly the politeness of the Great British public can evaporate if you make slightest mention of the legacy of empire. In some ways this anger is understandable. People across Britain are angry and they are being told to direct that anger towards the institutions, 'experts' and academics who speak of empire. Members of Parliament have called for the government to instruct 'a team of ministers to wage war' on academics pushing the decolonial agenda.[32] Institutions once beloved by the establishment, like the BBC or the National Trust, are now castigated and threatened by high-profile public figures for making the smallest attempt to reckon with Britain's colonial legacy.

But the call for decolonisation must be about mapping out the future, not just looking back. If it is to have any substance whatsoever, then the idea of decolonisation will have to confront the entrenched interests that continue to disempower us. The UK is already far more reliant on foreign investment than other 'developed' countries. The offshore secrecy trusts, investor-state dispute resolution tribunals and all the other legal protections that emerged to shield the interests of multinational capital against the new sovereign states after decolonisation, can and will be deployed against Britain itself in the twenty-first century. It was a mistake, in the aftermath of empire, to presume that Britain's financial and legal networks could be used to empower the international capitalist class to dismantle the sovereign power of 'developing' nations without them, one day, looking to do the same back at home.

There are, however, more sustainable and equitable visions of human life than the one that currently governs the world. The laws of our political and economic systems are not carved into stone tablets by the hand of God. In some ways, the focus on winning the culture war has been understandable because, for so long, it seemed like the only thing we could affect. The global economy was like the weather, something beyond all control. However, for all the suffering it brought, the year 2020 showed this myth up as the fallacy it always was. Fiscal conservatism could be abandoned, global trade could be interrupted. But will this lead to better lives for working people? There may be more money for green technologies and less concern for austerity, but will organised labour be strengthened? Will the overheated asset market be curtailed?

This book has sought to move the subject of empire beyond the never-ending culture war. The aftermath of empire isn't just about race, identity and memory, and neither is it 'dead' history: in fact, it explains the economics and the material conditions that structure our lives. And the UK can still help mark out a different path. Privileges such as the residual strength of Britain's currency or the sheer size of its economy mean that, as a state, Britain is in a better position than most other countries to confront the insulated, international capitalist system of extraction that governs our world. 'We built the railways' is often the most common defence of the empire raised, but perhaps it's the empire's legal and economic train tracks that have had the more long-lasting impact. It is along the tracks that were laid by the British Empire and, crucially, preserved through the process of decolonisation, that much of this system continues to run.

In confronting the aftermath of empire, the UK could begin to intervene in the use of its overseas territories as offshore economies and secrecy jurisdictions. It could tighten laws on foreign trade disputes in London's commercial court, or use its outsized position in the IMF to encourage greater debt restructuring or cancellation policies. If British politicians were really committed to improving the salaries that are received by the country's working classes, they could push for the country to use its global influence to campaign for a global minimum wage. With the fossil fuel companies that continue to mine the earth passing their profits through the City and its satellites, reforming Britain's role in the global financial system is one of the biggest things that this country could do to contribute to the campaign against climate change.

To pretend that empire is all about identity politics is to protect its economic legacy of a few winners and far more losers. Conversations around empire are stifled, in my eyes, not because of a fear that they create division, but because they have the potential to unify public anger, and in so doing redirect it away from the usual targets – the poor, the vulnerable, racial minorities and those who appear different at first glance. Secrecy jurisdictions are not popular. In a 2020 poll, 82 per cent of Britons agreed that companies registered in offshore tax havens should be excluded from any potential government bailouts after the coronavirus crisis.[33] Outsourcing is not popular. When polled, 64 per cent of the British public stated that they distrust private outsourcing companies taking over public services, and this was even before the bungled handling of the Covid-19 response.[34] And a 2019 British Social Attitudes survey found that 78 per cent of people asked felt that the gap between those on high and low incomes is too large.[35] People are well aware of the entrenched divisions that mark our society in terms of income, wealth and opportunities.

Brexiteers present leaving the EU as a moment of independence for Britain, the taking back of control, the recovery of an essential sovereignty, but they rarely if ever offer it as a chance to restrain the runaway power of corporations, ground financial speculation or reduce the commercialisation of all aspects of social life. If anything, Brexit is accelerating these trends. The level of inequality in Britain today is not accidental. It is the beating heart of a world-spanning empire comprised of a multitude of jurisdictional and economic arrangements which require the rights of capital to take precedent over the rights of people.

Properly framed, conversations about empire in the UK can help drive a commitment to remaking the global order. Ambitions of 'levelling up' or rescuing the 'left behind' cannot be realised without addressing the ways in which the afterlife of empire continues to drive the machinery of the world. If we really want to confront the ways in which capitalism has led us to a new age of great divergence, we need to dismantle the protective casing in which the global financial system was placed to protect it from popular democracy after decolonisation. And we must dare to imagine a world where the security of human life is valued above the securities traded by creditors across the globe.

As insurmountable as the challenges laid out in this book may seem now, we may soon be living in a world where the task of changing our tax structures, border regimes, property laws and systems of debt looks minor compared to the apocalyptic problems we could be facing. For many, Covid-19 has reframed what an existential crisis might look like. Beyond the avalanche of terrifying reports telling us of rising infection rates and death tolls, for 'developed' countries like Britain, the pandemic provided the first glimpse in living memory of what the institutional failure of our systems of care and sustenance might look like. We saw hospital wards unable to cope with the onslaught of critical patients. We walked through supermarkets with empty shelves, stripped bare by a rush to hoard goods while external supply chains began to break down. These are not scenes that people in the 'advanced' world are meant to experience. The Covid-19 crisis has redefined our ideas of what constitutes a global problem. We are not isolated within our own little national silos; we don't just live somewhere, we also live everywhere.

The challenges we will face over the course of the twenty-first century, from climate change to demographic ageing, from the automation of work to perhaps other, more deadly pandemics, are going to be global problems that will require an international, as well as national, vision of politics. Over the coming decades, Global Britain will need more ambitious ideas than blue passports and encouraging everyone to proudly sing 'Land of Hope and Glory'. Our attitude towards climate change cannot be that we will deal with it when it becomes a crisis; if we look around the world rather than within our own borders, we will realise that the crisis is already here. Britain can still do so much to slow down the relentlessness of modern capitalism and forge a different relationship with our planet – not just as a matter of conscience but as a tool for survival. Legal systems, economic institutions and even national mythologies are much easier to change and control than the environment or epidemics. The choice we face becomes starker with each passing day.

Acknowledgements

Every book is a collective conversation, with a number of participants moving in and out of the frame during the course of its creation. I would like to thank the many people who sit behind my writing. This book gave me the privilege of working with Joe Zigmond. Your insightful and patient editing carried the text across the line. My thanks to Joe, as well as Caroline Westmore, Yassine Belkacemi and the whole team at John Murray. The support you gave to a first-time author, even in the midst of a pandemic, was impeccable.

To the many co-conspirators who took the time to read drafts of the manuscript, your critiques, challenges, excitement and encouragements were invaluable. My deepest gratitude to Michael Amaning, Nana Adu Ampofo, Justin Baidoo, Tanzil Chowdury, Alex Cobham, Luke Cooper, Oscar Guardiola-Rivera, Niamh Hayes, Frankie Mace, Kerem Nişancıoğlu, Rhodine Orleans-Lindsay, Tom Peters, Michael Pope, Robbie Shilliam, Quinn Slobodian, Bianca Talbot and Musab Younis. Any errors are mine alone, but any valuable insight that this book offers is thanks to all of you. My thinking also owes a great deal to the intellectual communities that have been kind enough to embrace me over the past few years: Birkbeck School of Law, the Caribbean Philosophical Association, the 'RICE' family and the Critical Legal Thinking team. I always felt the presence of my doctoral co-supervisor Peter Fitzpatrick during the writing process, although I shudder to imagine what his red pen would have done to my drafts.

Snapshots of the ideas that would eventually mature into this book were published in the *Guardian*, the *New Statesman*, *Dissent* and *Novara*. I'm indebted to the various editors who commissioned these articles: Hettie O'Brien, Natasha Lewis and Beth Perkin. I am also grateful to my agent Matthew Turner at RCW for consistent support of my writing.

On a personal note, my thanks to Kwadwo Okwaning Koram, Alberta Koram, Nana Afua Yirenkyi, Okwaning Yirenkyi and Kim Simpson. Finally, this book was conceived in the early days of new fatherhood. To Yaara, whenever I read it in future, each page of this book will be accompanied by the background music of your first words, first steps and first laughs. At the heart of this project were always my thoughts about the type of world you will have to navigate growing up. Now you are a little person. It's my honour to watch you on your journey.

Notes

Introduction: Seeing the Boomerang

1. The 'end of history' thesis was popularised after the publication of Francis Fukuyama, *The End of History and the Last Man* (New York: Free Press, 1992).
2. Karl Marx, *Capital*, vol.1, (London: Penguin, 1990), Preface. Friedrich Hayek, *The Constitution of Liberty* (London: Routledge 2006) pp-142–154.
3. The Organisation for Economic Co-operation and Development, 'Inequality and Income Data', based on Gini coefficient ratio 2017, available at http://www.oecd.org/social/inequality.htm (accessed 14 March 2021).
4. Adam Corlett, Arun Advani and Andy Summers, *Who Gains? The Importance of Accounting for Capital Gains* (London: Resolution Foundation, May 2020).
5. Rowena Crawford, Dave Innes and Cormac O'Dea, 'Household Wealth in Great Britain: Distribution, Composition and Changes 2006–12', *Fiscal Studies*, vol. 37 (2016), pp. 35–54, 'net income is distributed substantially more equally than wealth. The overall Gini coefficient for net income is 0.34, while that for total wealth is 0.64'.
6. Credit Suisse Research Institute, *Global Wealth Report 2014*, pp. 33, 119.
7. Arun Advani, George Bangham and Jack Leslie, *The UK's Wealth Distrubution and Characteristics of High-Wealth Households*, Wealth Tax Commission Evidence Paper no. 1 (London: Wealth Tax Commission, 2021), p. 5.
8. Richard Joyce and Xiaowei Xu, *Inequalities in the Twenty-First Century: Introducing the IFS Deaton Review* (London: Institute of Fiscal Studies, 2019), p. 4.

9. Philip Inman, 'Number of Europe's Poorest Regions in UK "More Than Doubles"', *Guardian*, 10 December 2019, https://www.theguardian.com/business/2019/dec/10/number-of-europes-poorest-regions-in-uk-more-than-doubles (accessed 16 December 2020).

10. Aimé Césaire, *Discourse on Colonialism* (New York: NYU Press, Monthly Review Press, 2000), p. 41. See also Michel Foucault, *Society Must Be Defended: Lectures at the Collège de France, 1975–1976* (London: Picador, 2003), and Hannah Arendt, *The Origins of Totalitarianism* (New York: Harcourt, Brace Jovanovich 1973).

11. Books on inequality include Branko Milanović, *Global Inequality: A New Approach for the Age of Globalization* (Cambridge, MA: Harvard University Press, 2016); Thomas Piketty, *Capital in the Twenty-First Century* (Cambridge, MA: Harvard University Press, 2014); Gabriel Zucman, *The Hidden Wealth of Nations: The Scourge of Tax Havens* (Chicago, IL: University of Chicago Press, 2016); Grace Blakely, *Stolen: How to Save the World from Financialisation* (London: Repeater, 2019).

12. This point has been explored at length in Oscar Guardiola-Rivera, *What If Latin America Ruled the World? How the South Will Take the North into the 22nd Century* (London: Bloomsbury, 2010); Jean and John Comaroff, *Theory from the South: Or, How Euro-America Is Evolving Toward Africa* (London: Routledge, 2012); Achille Mbembe, *Out of the Dark Night: Essays on Decolonization* (New York: Columbia University Press, 2021).

13. Comoroff and Comoroff, *Theory from the South*, p. 6.

14. Tony Blair, *A Journey* (London: Hutchinson, 2010), p. 126.

15. Ibid.

16. For more on the importance of the Opium Wars to modern China, see Julia Lovell, *The Opium War: Drugs, Dreams and the Making of China* (London: Picador, 2012).

17. 'Boris Johnson Likens Irish Border Challenge to Congestion Charge', *BBC News*, 27 February 2018, https://www.bbc.co.uk/news/uk-politics-43210156 (accessed 15 August 2020).

18. 'Boris Johnson Reciting Kipling in Myanmar Temple "Not Appropriate"', *BBC News*, 30 September 2017, https://www.bbc.co.uk/news/av/uk-politics-41453375 (accessed 15 August 2020).

19. Boris Johnson, 'Africa is a Mess but We Can't Blame Colonialism', *The Spectator*, 2 February 2002, https://www.spectator.co.uk/article/

the-boris-archive-africa-is-a-mess-but-we-can-t-blame-colonialism
(accessed 9 August 2020).

20. Boris Johnson, 'Britain Must Become the Superman of Global Free
Trade', *The Spectator*, 3 February 2020, https://www.spectator.co.uk/
article/boris-johnson-britain-must-become-the-superman-of-
global-free-trade; Sam Coates, 'Ministers Aim to Build "Empire 2.0"
with African Commonwealth', *The Times*, 6 March 2017, https://
www.thetimes.co.uk/article/ministers-aim-to-build-empire-2-0-
with-african-commonwealth-after-brexit-v9bs6f6z9 (both accessed
12 January 2021).

21. David Butterfield, 'What Would it Mean to "Decolonise" the
Classics?', *The Spectator*, 18 July 2020, https://www.spectator.co.uk/
article/what-would-it-mean-to-decolonise-the-Classics; Robert
Tombs, 'In Defence of the British Empire', *The Spectator*, 8 May
2020, https://www.spectator.co.uk/article/In-defence-of-the-
British-Empire (both accessed 9 August 2020).

22. Peter Stubley, 'Universities Minister Compares "Decolonisation"
of History to "Soviet Union-Style" Censorship', *Independent*, 28
February 2021, https://www.independent.co.uk/news/education/
education-news/history-curriculum-university-michelle-donelan-
culture-war-b1808601.html (accessed 20 March 2021).

23. Kumail Jaffer, 'Kew Gardens is Growing Woke! Famed Attraction
Will Have "Decolonised" Labelling Showing Visitors How Plants
Played a Part in the Slave Trade', *Daily Mail*, 12 March 2021,
https://www.dailymail.co.uk/news/article-9353241/Kew-Gardens-
growing-woke-Famed-attraction-decolonised-labelling.html
(accessed 28 June 2021).

24. Iain Martin, 'Talk of "White Privilege" is Divisive Drivel', *The
Times*, 15 October 2020, https://www.thetimes.co.uk/article/talk-
of-white-privilege-is-divisive-drivel-t7vmc0pnd (accessed 14 March
2021).

25. Matthew Goodwin, '*The Madness of Crowds* by Douglas Murray
Review – Identity Politics Attacked', *Sunday Times*, 22 September
2019, https://www.thetimes.co.uk/article/the-madness-of-crowds-
by-douglas-murray-review-identity-politics-attacked-j6n0p38xr
(accessed 3 November 2020).

26. Janice Kew, 'Accra Seen Adding Millionaires Faster than Any Other
Africa City', *Bloomberg*, 2 September 2015, https://www.bloomberg.

com/news/articles/2015-09-02/accra-seen-adding-millionaires-faster-than-any-other-africa-city (accessed 5 October 2020).

27. John Nijiraini, 'Is Africa the New Face of Rising Wealth and Opulence?', *Africa Renewal*, United Nations, April 2015, https://www.un.org/africarenewal/magazine/april-2015/africa-new-face-rising-wealth-and-opulence; Kingsley Ighobor, 'Closing Africa's Wealth Gap', *Africa Renewal*, United Nations, December 2017–March 2018, https://www.un.org/africarenewal/magazine/december-2017-march-2018/closing-africa's-wealth-gap (both accessed 17 October 2020).

28. Favour Nunoo, '29 Million Ghanaians Dey Share 55 Ambulances', *BBC News Pidgin*, https://www.bbc.com/pidgin/tori-44030411; Abigail Annoh, 'Ghana: New Ambulances Are of Acceptable Standard', *Ghanaian Times*, 18 September 2019, https://allafrica.com/stories/201909180581.html (both accessed 14 December 2020).

29. See for example 'How to Fix a "Third World" NHS Service', *The Week*, 3 January 2018, https://www.theweek.co.uk/90698/how-can-we-fix-the-creaking-nhs; Marco Rubio, 'There is nothing patriotic about what is occurring on Capitol Hill. This is 3rd world style anti-American anarchy', *Twitter*, 6 January 2021, 8.01 p.m., https://twitter.com/marcorubio/status/1346909901478522880; Michael Nedelman, '"That's When All Hell Broke Loose": Coronavirus Patients Start to Overwhelm US Hospitals', *CNN*, 25 March 2020, https://edition.cnn.com/2020/03/25/health/coronavirus-covid-hospitals/index.html (all accessed 22 February 2021).

30. Euan Cameron, 'How Will Automation Impact Jobs?', PwC analysis, https://www.pwc.co.uk/services/economics/insights/the-impact-of-automation-on-jobs.html; Mathew Lawrence, Carys Roberts and Loren King, 'Managing Automation: Employment, Inequality and Ethics in the Digital Age', IPPR, Commission on Economic Justice, discussion paper, https://www.ippr.org/files/2018-01/cej-managing-automation-december2017.pdf (both accessed 23 November 2020).

31. Michael Gove, 'All Pupils Will Learn Our Island Story', speech, 5 October 2010, Conservative Party Speeches, https://conservative-speeches.sayit.mysociety.org/speech/601441 (accessed 22 June 2021). The phrase likely echoes the children's book by Henrietta Elizabeth Marshall, *Our Island Story: A History of England for Boys and Girls* (London: Civitas, 2007).

32. Philip Alston, *Report of the Special Rapporteur on Extreme Poverty*

and Human Rights, UN General Assembly, Human Rights Council Forty-First Session, 23 April 2019, p. 1, https://undocs.org/ pdf?symbol=en/A/HRC/41/39/Add.1 (accessed 22 March 2020).

33. Akala, *Natives: Race and Class in the Ruins of Empire* (London: Two Roads, 2018); Priyamvada Gopal, *Insurgent Empire: Anticolonial Resistance and Britsih Dissent* (London: Verso, 2019); Danny Dorling and Sally Tomlinson, *Rule Britannia: Brexit and the End of Empire* (London: Biteback, 2019); Sathnam Sanghera, *Empireland: How Imperialism Has Shaped Modern Britain* (London: Viking, 2021); Kehinde Andrews, *The New Age of Empire* (London: Allen Lane, 2021).

34. Office for National Statistics, *Household Wealth by Ethnicity, Great Britain: April 2016 to March 2018*, 23 November 2020, https://www.ons.gov.uk/peoplepopulationandcommunity/ personalandhouseholdfinances/incomeandwealth/articles/ householdwealthbyethnicitygreatbritain/april2016tomarch2018 (accessed 17 June 2021).

35. See Quinn Slobodian, *Globalists: The End of Empire and the Birth of Neoliberalism* (Cambridge, MA: Harvard University Press, 2018) or Ellen Meiksins Wood, *Empire of Capital* (London: Verso, 2003).

36. Cecil Rhodes speaking to Lord Grey as referenced in Lewis Mitchell, *The Life and Times of the Right Honourable Cecil John Rhodes 1853–1902*, vol. 2 (Charleston: Nabu Press, 2014).

37. See Ashley Jackson, *The British Empire: A Very Short Introduction* (Oxford: Oxford University Press, 2013), pp. 4–5.

38. 'Scots "More Optimistic about Future" According to BBC Survey', *BBC News*, Scotland, 6 June 2018, https://www.bbc.co.uk/news/ uk-scotland-44301827 (accessed 1 May 2020).

Chapter 1: The State

1. G. I. C. Eluwa, 'The National Congress of British West Africa: A Study in African Nationalism', *Présence Africaine: Revue culturelle du monde noir Présence Africaine*, n.s., vol.77 (1971), pp. 131–49, pp. 141–2.

2. Ibid., p. 142.

3. Ibid., p. 143.

4. Ibid., p. 144.

5. See either Allan I. Macinnes, *Union and Empire: The Making of the*

United Kingdom in 1707 (Cambridge: Cambridge University Press, 2007) or John Robertson (ed.), *A Union for Empire: Political Thought and the British Union of 1707* (Cambridge: Cambridge University Press 1995).

6. David Edgerton, *The Rise and Fall of the British Nation: A Twentieth-Century History* (London: Allen Lane, 2018), p. 26.

7. Winston Churchill, *Great Contemporaries* (London: Macmillan, 1942), p. 76.

8. Lewis Goodhall, 'Who Was Theresa May's Political Hero? Joseph Chamberlain', *BBC News*, 15 August 2016, https://www.bbc.co.uk/news/uk-politics-37053114 (accessed 25 February 2021).

9. J. A. Froude, *Oceana, or, England and Her Colonies* (Cambridge: Cambridge University Press, 2011); John Robert Seeley, *The Expansion of England* (Cambridge: Cambridge University Press, 2010).

10. Charles Wentworth Dilke, *Greater Britain: A Record of Travel in English-Speaking Countries during 1866 and 1867* (New York: Harper & Brothers, 1869).

11. Seeley, *The Expansion of England*, pp. 8–9

12. A. V. Dicey, 'Will the Form of Parliamentary Government be Permanent?', *Harvard Law Review*, vol. 13 (1899), pp. 67–8.

13. Stephen B. Stanton, 'Is the British Empire Constitutionally a Nation?', *Michigan Law Review*, vol. 2, no. 6 (1904), pp. 429–45, p. 431.

14. Edward Ellis Morris, *Imperial Federation: A Lecture for the Victorian Branch of the Imperial Federation League* (Melbourne: Victorian Review, 1885).

15. Thomas Mohr, 'The United Kingdom and Imperial Federation, 1900–1939: A Precedent for British Legal Relations with the European Union?', *Comparative Legal History*, vol. 4, no. 2 (2016), pp. 131–61, p. 137.

16. Ferdinand Mount, 'Wedded to the Absolute', *London Review of Books*, vol. 41, no. 8, 26 September 2019, https://lrb.co.uk/the-paper/v41/n18/ferdinand-mount/wedded-to-the-absolute (accessed 11 March 2021).

17. Enoch Powell obituary, *Daily Telegraph*, 9 February 1998, https://www.telegraph.co.uk/news/obituaries/5899345/Enoch-Powell.html (accessed 19 February 2021).

18. Simon Heffer, *Like the Roman: The Life of Enoch Powell* (London: Faber, 2014), p. 450.

19. Mount, 'Wedded to the Absolute'.

20. Enoch Powell, *A Nation Not Afraid: The Thinking of Enoch Powell* (ed. John Wood) (London: Batsford, 1965), p. 137.
21. Ibid., p. 139.
22. Ibid., p. 138.
23. Enoch Powell, speech on the Royal Tiles Bill, 3 March 1953, Enoch Powell: Life and Views, https://www.enochpowell.net/fr-74.html (accessed 20 March 2021).
24. Powell, *A Nation Not Afraid*, p. 144.
25. Ibid., p. 139.
26. Ibid., p. 145.
27. Liam Fox, Keynote Speech at the Conservative Spring Forum, 17 May 2017, https://www.liamfox.co.uk/news/dr-liam-fox-mp-keynote-speech-conservative-spring-forum (accessed 14 February 2020).
28. Tony Blair, Leader's speech, Brighton 1997, http://www.britishpoliticalspeech.org/speech-archive.htm?speech=203 (accessed 8 February 2021).
29. Powell, *A Nation Not Afraid*, p. 145.
30. Christina Pagel and Christabel Cooper, YouGov survey, 'People vs Parliament: On the Question of Are You Worried about the State of Democracy in the UK, 84% of Remainers and 66% of Leavers Said Yes', September 2019, https://ucl-brexit.blog/2019/09/16/polling-people-vs-parliament-what-a-new-survey-says-about-our-constitutional-mess/ (accessed 10 February 2021).
31. 'Enemies of the People', headline, *Daily Mail*, 4 November 2016, https://www.dailymail.co.uk/news/article-3903436/Enemies-people-Fury-touch-judges-defied-17-4m-Brexit-voters-trigger-constitutional-crisis.html (accessed 21 February 2021).
32. Haley Mortimer, 'Cheltenham Festival "May Have Accelerated" Spread', *BBC News*, 30 April 2020, https://www.bbc.co.uk/news/uk-england-gloucestershire-52485584; Will Humphries, 'Fears that Cheltenham Festival May Have Spread Coronavirus Throughout Country', *The Times*, 3 April 2020, https://www.thetimes.co.uk/article/cheltenham-festival-spread-coronavirus-across-country-vbzmn5p9q (both accessed 18 December 2020).
33. Mark Sweney, 'TalkTalk Chief Executive Dido Harding to Step Down', *Guardian*, 1 February 2017, https://www.theguardian.com/business/2017/feb/01/talktalk-chief-executive-dido-harding-cyber-attack (accessed 18 December 2020).

34. Serco, 'Shaping UK Public Services', https://www.serco.com/about/our-strategy/shaping-uk-public-services (accessed 18 December 2020).

35. John Harris, 'Serco: The Company that is Running Britain', *Guardian*, 29 July 2013, https://www.theguardian.com/business/2013/jul/29/serco-biggest-company-never-heard-of (accessed 9 December 2020).

36. Women Against Rape and Black Women's Rape Action Project, *Rape and Sexual Abuse in Yarl's Wood Immigration Removal Centre 2005–2015*, http://againstrape.net/wp-content/uploads/2017/06/Report2015.pdf (accessed 18 November 2020).

37. Rashida Manjoo, *Report of the Special Rapporteur on Violence against Women, Its Causes and Consequences, on Her Mission to the United Kingdom of Great Britain and Northern Ireland (31 March–15 April 2014)*, United Nations Human Rights Council, 29th session, 19 May 2015, A/HRC/29/27, https://www.ohchr.org/Documents/Issues/Women/SR/A.HRC.29.27.Add.2.pdf; Mark Townsend, 'Yarl's Wood: UN Special Rapporteur to Censure UK Government', *Guardian* 3 January 2015, https://www.theguardian.com/uk-news/2015/jan/03/yarls-wood-un-special-rapporteur-censure (both accessed 18 November 2020).

38. Jamie Grierson, 'Serco Given £200m Contract to Run Two More Immigration Removal Centres', *Guardian*, 20 February 2020, https://www.theguardian.com/uk-news/2020/feb/20/serco-given-200m-contract-to-run-two-more-immigration-removal-centres (accessed 18 November 2020).

39. National Audit Office, *The Government's Approach to Test and Trace in England – Interim Report*, 11 December 2020, https://www.nao.org.uk/wp-content/uploads/2020/12/The-governments-approach-to-test-and-trace-in-England-interim-report.pdf (accessed 23 December 2020).

40. Ibid.

41. Ibid., p. 8.

42. 'Test-and-Trace: Higher Profits Expected by Serco', *BBC News*, 16 October 2020, https://www.bbc.co.uk/news/uk-politics-54569842 (accessed 18 November 2020).

43. Nicholas Ridley, *The Local Right: Enabling not Providing*, Policy Study no. 92 (Mitcham: Centre for Policy Studies 1988).

44. Institute for Government, *Government Procurement: The Scale and Nature of Contracting in the UK*, December 2018, https://www.

instituteforgovernment.org.uk/sites/default/files/publications/IfG_
procurement_WEB_4.pdf (accessed 28 January 2021).

45. Gill Pilmmer, 'UK Outsourcing Spend Doubles to £88bn under
Coalition', *Financial Times*, 6 July 2014, https://www.ft.com/content/
c9330150-0364-11e4-9195-00144feab7de (accessed 18 October 2020).

46. See Patrick Butler,'A History of Outsourcing', *Guardian*, 14 April 2003,
https://www.theguardian.com/society/microsite/outsourcing_
/story/0,,933818,00.html (accessed 18 October 2020).

47. The use of privateer partnership was also explored by Iberian and
Islamic explorers. See Jairus Banaji, 'Islam, the Mediterranean and
the Rise of Capitalism', *Historical Materialism*, vol. 15, no. 1 (March
2007), pp. 47–74.

48. Katharina Pistor, *The Code of Capital: How the Law Creates Wealth
and Inequality* (Princeton: Princeton University Press, 2019), p. 168.

49. Owen Bowcott,'Number of Solicitors Triples in 30 Years', *Guardian*, 4
April 2011, https://www.theguardian.com/law/2011/apr/04/number-
of-solicitors-uk (accessed 12 December 2020); Law Society, *Annual
Statistics Report 2019*, https://www.lawsociety.org.uk/topics/research/
annual-statistics-report-2019 (accessed 12 December 2020); Office
for National Statistics, 'Overview of the UK Population: January
2021', https://www.ons.gov.uk/peoplepopulationandcommunity/
populationandmigration/populationestimates/articles/
overviewoftheukpopulation/january2021 (accessed 22 July 2021).

50. Prem Sikka, 'A Nation of Accountants', *Guardian*, 13 June 2009,
https://www.theguardian.com/commentisfree/2009/jun/13/
accountants-audit-corruption-fraud (accessed 12 December 2020).

51. See 'Foreign Litigants Dominate Commercial Case Load', *The Times*,
28 February 2019, https://www.thetimes.co.uk/article/foreign-
litigants-dominate-commercial-court-caseload-v0kbl2nzr (accessed
15 December 2020).

52. Powell, *A Nation Not Afraid*, p.144.

53. See YouGov poll for *Sunday Times*, 6 September 2014, https://
yougov.co.uk/topics/politics/articles-reports/2014/09/06/latest-
scottish-referendum-poll-yes-lead (accessed 28 April 2021).

54. For this argument in full, see Thomas Nairn, *The Break-Up of Britain:
Crisis and Neo-Nationalism* (London: Verso 1981).

55. Heffer, *Like the Roman*, ebook location 1950.

56. Ibid., p. 459.

57. Lord Ashcroft, 'My Northern Ireland Survey Finds the Union on a Knife Edge', Lord Ashcroft Polls, 11 September 2019, https://lordashcroftpolls.com/2019/09/my-northern-ireland-survey-finds-the-union-on-a-knife-edge/ (accessed 8 April 2021).

58. YouGov report, 22 April 2020, https://yougov.co.uk/topics/politics/articles-reports/2020/04/22/brits-increasingly-dont-care-whether-northern-irel (accessed 17 February 2021).

59. Joseph Chamberlain, speech at Birmingham, 12 May 1904, in *Oxford Essential Quotations* (ed. Susan Ratcliffe), 6th edn (Oxford: Oxford University Press, 2018), DOI: 10.1093/acref/9780191866692.001.0001.

60. Niall Ferguson, *The Pity of War: Explaining World War One* (New York: Basic Books, 2000).

61. Holger Weiss, *Framing a Radical African Atlantic* (Leiden: Brill, 2014), pp. 87–8.

62. Kwame Nkrumah, *Ghana: The Autobiography of Kwame Nkrumah* (New York: International Publishers, 2001), pp. 48–9.

63. Ibid.

Chapter 2: The Company

1. Karl E. Meyer and Shareen Blair Brysac, 'How British (Really) is BP', *New York Times*, 17 June 2016, https://www.nytimes.com/2010/06/17/opinion/17iht-edmeyer.html (accessed 25 February 2021). The Shah also received some small shares in D'Arcy's company as a result of the initial contract.

2. Ibid.

3. For a review of medieval corporations see Samuel F. Mansell and Alejo Jose G. Sison, 'Medieval Corporations, Membership and the Common Good: Rethinking the Critique of Shareholder Primacy', *Journal of Institutional Economics*, vol. 16, no. 5 (2020), DOI: 10.1017/s1744137419000146. Merchant guilds also existed as an early form of the commercial company that would later emerge in the age of empires. For more on their role in pushing the commercial form of the corporation see Sheilagh Ogilvie, *Institutions and European Trade: Merchant Guilds, 1000–1800* (Cambridge: Cambridge University Press, 2012).

4. Leonardo Davoudi, Christopher McKenna and Rowena Olegario,

'The Historical Role of the Corporation in Society', *Journal of the British Academy*, 6(s1), (2018) pp. 17–47, p. 30.

5. See Countering Colston, 'Who Was Colston?', https://counteringcolston.wordpress.com/who-was-edward-colston-2/ (accessed 28 July 2020).

6. W. A. Pettigrew and A. L. Brock, 'Leadership and the Social Agendas of the Seventeenth-Century English Trading Corporation', in W. Pettigrew and D. Smith (eds), *A History of Socially Responsible Business, c.1600–1950* (London: Palgrave Macmillan, 2017), pp. 33–63.

7. Text of the Hudson Bay Company's Royal Charter, 2 May 1670, https://www.hbcheritage.ca/things/artifacts/the-charter-and-text. For further information on the Hudson Bay Company's philanthropy see either Richard I. Ruggles, 'Hospital Boys of the Bay', *The Beaver*, vol. 308, no. 3 (1977), pp. 4–11, or David Hope, 'Britain and the Fur Trade: Commerce and Consumers in the North-Atlantic World, 1783–1821', PhD thesis submitted to the University of Northumbria at Newcastle, 2016.

8. Bryan Duignan, '5 Fast Facts about the East India Company', *Encyclopedia Britannica* online, https://www.britannica.com/story/5-fast-facts-about-the-east-india-company (accessed 18 January 2021).

9. For further reading, see Philip J. Stern, *The Company-State: Corporate Sovereignty and the Early Modern Foundations of the British Empire in India* (Oxford: Oxford University Press, 2011).

10. For further on the ability of colonial corporations to wield sovereignty, see ibid.

11. 'Charter of the Royal Niger Company', 10 July 1886, in Fredrick Madden and David Fieldhouse (eds), *Select Documents on the Constitutional History of the British Empire and Commonwealth: The Empire of the Bretaignes, 1175–1688*, vol. 1 (Westport, CT: Greenwood, 1985), p. 448.

12. The 1901 agreement that D'Arcy had negotiated had been replaced by a new concession in 1933 that gave Iran better terms but left the Anglo-Iranian Oil Company with full control of Iranian oil. See Nicholas J. White, 'The Business and the Politics of Decolonization: The British Experience in the Twentieth Century', *Economic History Review*, n.s. vol. 53, no. 3 (August 2000), pp. 544–64.

13. Mark Curtis, *Ambiguities of Power: British Foreign Policy since 1945* (London: Zed Books, 1995), p. 88.

14. See Peter J. Beck, *Using History, Making British Policy* (London: Palgrave Macmillan, 2006), pp. 193–210.

15. Yuen-li Liang, 'The Question of Domestic Jurisdiction in the Anglo-Iranian Oil Dispute before the Security Council', *American Journal of International Law*, vol. 46, no. 2 (April 1952), pp. 272–82, p. 278.

16. Stephen Kinzer, *All the Shah's Men: An American Coup and the Roots of Middle East Terror* (Hoboken, NJ: Wiley, 2003).

17. US State Department, Memorandum of Conversation, Byroade to Matthews, 'Proposal to Organize a Coup d'état in Iran', 26 November 1952, National Archives, General Records of the Department of State 1950–54, Central Decimal File 788.00/11–2652, https://nsarchive.gwu.edu/document/15497-01-state-department-memorandum-conversation (accessed 15 May 2021).

18. For further analysis on this, see Sundhya Pahuja and Cait Storr, 'Rethinking Iran and International Law: The Anglo-Iranian Oil Company Case Revisited' in James Crawford, Abdul Koroma, Said Mahmoudi and Alain Pellet (eds), *The International Legal Order: Current Needs and Possible Responses: Essays in Honour of Djamchid Momtaz* (London: Brill, 2017), pp. 53–74.

19. Lord Ashcroft, 'How the United Kingdom Voted on Thursday . . . And Why', Lord Ashcroft Polls, 24 June 2016, http://lordashcroftpolls.com/2016/06/how-the-united-kingdom-voted-and-why/ (accessed 20 August 2020).

20. UN Charter, Chapter 1, Article 2 (1), The Organization is based on the principle of the sovereign equality of all its Members, https://www.un.org/en/about-us/un-charter/chapter-1. The Atlantic Charter, North Atlantic Treaty Organization, 14 August 1941, https://www.nato.int/cps/en/natohq/official_texts_16912.htm.

21. 'Mohammed Mossadegh: Man of the Year', *Time*, vol. 59, no. 1, 7 January 1952, http://content.time.com/time/covers/0,16641, 19520107,00.html (accessed 28 August 2020).

22. Ernst Kantorowicz, *The King's Two Bodies: A Study in Medieval Political Theology* (Princeton: Princeton University Press, 1998).

23. Mark Mazower, *Governing the World: The History of an Idea* (London: Penguin, 2013), p. 346.

24. Ibid., p. 344.

25. 'The Churchill You Didn't Know', *Guardian*, 28 November

2002, https://www.theguardian.com/theguardian/2002/nov/28/features11.g21 (accessed 30 August 2020).

26. Eden to Eisenhower, 5 November 1956, quoted in Peter G. Boyle (ed.), *The Eden–Eisenhower Correspondence, 1955–1957* (Chapel Hill, NC: University of North Carolina Press, 2006), p. 183.

27. Heffer, *Like the Roman*, pp. 188–92.

28. C. L. R. James, *Nkrumah and the Ghana Revolution* (London: Allison & Busby, 1977), p. 131.

29. See Fred Cooper, *Decolonization and African Society: The Labor Question in French and British Africa* (Cambridge: Cambridge University Press, 1996).

30. Colin Baker, 'Macmillan's "Wind of Change" Tour, 1960', *South African Historical Journal*, vol. 38, no. 1 (1998), p. 181.

31. 'On This Day', *BBC News*, 3 February 2005, http://news.bbc.co.uk/onthisday/hi/dates/stories/february/3/newsid_2714000/2714525.stm (accessed 10 February 2021).

32. Transcript of Nkrumah speech, 'Visions of Independence, Then and Now', *Africa Renewal*, August 2010, https://www.un.org/africarenewal/magazine/august-2010/visions-independence-then-and-now; for video of Nkrumah's speech at the UN, https://www.unmultimedia.org/avlibrary/search/search.jsp?sort=cdate_desc&ptag=KWAME+NKRUMAH&&start=10

33. Kwame Nkrumah, *I Speak of Freedom: A Statement of African Ideology* (Bedford: Panaf Books, 2009), p. 203.

34. For a video of Nkrumah's speech at the UN see https://www.unmultimedia.org/avlibrary/search/search.jsp?sort=cdate_desc&ptag=KWAME+NKRUMAH&&start=10 (accessed 15 May 2021); transcript of Nkrumah speech, *Africa Renewal*, August 2010.

35. Video of Nkrumah's speech at the UN.

36. White, 'Business and the Politics of Decolonization', p. 560.

37. Piers Brendon, *The Decline and Fall of the British Empire 1781–1997* (New York: Alfred Knopf, 2008), p. 1429.

38. Peter Brooke, *Duncan Sandys and the Informal Politics of Britain's Late Decolonisation* (London: Palgrave Macmillan, 2018), p. 45.

39. Ayowa Afrifa Taylor, 'An Economic History of the Ashanti Goldfields Corporation, 1895–2004: Land, Labour, Capital and Enterprise', PhD thesis submitted to University of London, 2005, p. 120.

40. Ibid., p.112.

41. 'Portrait of Nkrumah as Dictator', *New York Times*, 3 May 1964, https://www.nytimes.com/1964/05/03/archives/portrait-of-nkrumah-as-dictator.html (accessed 12 January 2021).

42. Taylor, 'Economic History of the Ashanti Goldfields Corporation', p. 114.

43. Ibid.

44. Kwame Nkrumah, *Neo-Colonialism: The Last Stage of Imperialism* (London: Thames & Nelson, 1965) pp. 1–5.

45. For further details on Locke's theory of property see John Locke, *Second Treatise of Government* (1690) (New York: Barnes & Noble, 2004).

46. See Thomas Piketty, *Capital in the Twenty-First Century* (Cambridge, MA: Harvard University Press, 2014).

47. See Katharina Pistor, *The Code of Capital: How the Law Creates Wealth and Inequality* (Princeton, NJ: Princeton University Press, 2019).

48. Daniel Hannan, *Inventing Freedom: How the English-Speaking Peoples Made the Modern World* (London: HarperCollins, 2013), pp. 406–8. Hannan credits the East India Company for giving India the benefit of respect for property rights in a way their neighbours didn't enjoy.

49. For more on the violence of the British tradition of property and the erasure of other native forms, see either Brenna Bhandar, *Colonial Lives of Property: Law, Land, and Racial Regimes of Ownership* (Durham, NC: Duke University Press, 2018) or Allan Greer, *Property and Dispossession: Natives, Empires and Land in Early Modern North America* (Cambridge: Cambridge University Press, 2017).

50. Ludwig von Mises, *Money, Method and the Market Process*, (Norwell, MA: Auburn, AL: Ludwig von Mises Institute and Norwell, MA: Kluwer Academic, 1990), p. 386, https://mises.org/library/money-method-and-market-process/html.

51. Meyer and Brysac, 'How British (Really) is BP'.

52. Aloysius Atkinson, 'Britain's Worst Tax Scrooges Revealed: Almost 1 in 5 of Biggest Firms Paid Nothing Last Year – and Some Even Got a Handout from the Taxman', *Mail on Sunday*, 22 December 2018, https://www.thisismoney.co.uk/money/news/article-6522913/Almost-1-5-biggest-firms-paid-year-5-got-handout-taxman.html (accessed 18 November 2020).

53. The Rt Hon Lord Maude of Horsham, 'Lord Browne Appointed to Key Whitehall Role', Cabinet Office press release, 30 June 2010,

https://www.gov.uk/government/news/lord-browne-appointed-to-key-whitehall-role (accessed 21 November 2020).

54. Ibid.

55. See either the report from the Center for Progressive Reform, *Regulatory Blowout: How Regulatory Failures Made the BP Disaster Possible, and How the System Can Be Fixed to Avoid a Recurrence*, October 2010, https://scholarship.law.gwu.edu/cgi/viewcontent.cgi?article=1648&context=faculty_publications, or the report from the Committee for the Analysis of Causes of the Deepwater Horizon Explosion, Fire, and Oil Spill to Identify Measures to Prevent Similar Accidents in the Future, *Interim Report on Causes of the Deepwater Horizon Oil Rig Blowout and Ways to Prevent Such Events*, 16 November 2010, https://www.nationalacademies.org/includes/DH_Interim_Report_final.pdf (both accessed 18 May 2021).

56. 'Boris Johnson Attacks America's "Anti British Rhetoric" Aimed at BP', *The Times*, 10 June 2010, https://www.thetimes.co.uk/article/boris-johnson-attacks-americas-anti-british-rhetoric-aimed-at-bp-b8hx2slpckl (accessed 27 November 2020).

57. Polly Curtis and Terry Macalister, 'Former BP Chief John Browne Gets Whitehall Role', *Guardian*, 30 June 2010, https://www.theguardian.com/politics/2010/jun/30/john-browne-conservatives-whitehall (accessed 27 November 2020).

58. Arthur Neslen, 'EU Dropped Climate Policies after BP Threat of Oil Industry "Exodus"', *Guardian*, 20 April 2016, https://www.theguardian.com/environment/2016/apr/20/eu-dropped-climate-policies-after-bp-threat-oil-industry-exodus; Jillian Ambrose, 'Trump Weakened Environmental Laws After BP Lobbying', *Guardian*, 23 January 2020, https://www.theguardian.com/business/2020/jan/23/trump-weakened-environmental-laws-after-bp-lobbying (both accessed 27 November 2020).

59. For a critical engagement with this phenomenon see Sarah Bentley, 'Top Global Brands Accused over Controversial "Painted Home" Adverts in Africa', *Ecologist*, 25 April 2012, https://theecologist.org/2012/apr/25/top-global-brands-accused-over-controversial-painted-home-adverts-africa (accessed 14 November 2020).

60. Frank Pasquale, 'From Territorial to Functional Sovereignty: The Case of Amazon', Law and Political Economy Project blog, 6 December 2017, https://lpeblog.org/2017/12/06/from-territorial-

to-functional-sovereignty-the-case-of-amazon/ (accessed 10 May 2021).

61. Ibid.

62. For Airbnb urban planning, see https://www.fastcompany.com/3062246/an-exclusive-look-at-airbnbs-first-foray-into-urban-planning. (accessed 22 May 2021).

63. For Amazon dispute resolution schemes see Rory Van Loo, 'The Corporation as Courthouse', *Yale Journal on Regulation*, vol. 33, no. 547 (2016), pp. 547–602.

64. For Ireland and Google see Eoin Burke-Kennedy, 'Explainer: Google and Its Double Irish Tax Scheme', *Irish Times*, 2 January 2020, https://www.irishtimes.com/business/economy/explainer-google-and-its-double-irish-tax-scheme-1.4128929 (accessed 27 June 2021); and for the Netherlands see Danny Hakim, 'Europe Takes Aim at Deals Created to Escape Taxes', 15 November 2014, https://www.nytimes.com/2014/11/15/business/international/the-tax-attraction-between-starbucks-and-the-netherlands.html. (accessed 12 September 2020).

Chapter 3: The Border

1. Indian Independence Bill HLRO Parliamentary Debates, House of Commons, 5th series vol. 439, cols. 2441–6, 10 July 1947, http://www.nationalarchives.gov.uk/pathways/citizenship/brave_new_world/transcripts/indian_independence_bill.htm.

2. Ibid.

3. Hugh Dalton, *High Tide and After: Memoirs, 1945–60* (London: Muller, 1962), p. 211.

4. Indian Independence Bill.

5. Kwasi Kwarteng, Dominic Raab, Priti Patel, Liz Truss and Chris Skidmore, *Britannia Unchained: Global Lessons for Growth and Prosperity* (London: Palgrave Macmillan, 2012).

6. Ibid., p. 49.

7. Ibid., p. 66.

8. Ibid., p. 46.

9. Ibid., p. 44.

10. Ibid., p. 55.

11. Ibid., p. 77.

12. Dominic Raab, 'Global Britain is Leading the World as a Force for Good', Torbay Conservatives, news article, 23 September 2019, https://www.torbayconservatives.com/news/global-britain-leading-world-force-good-dominic-raab; Elizabeth Truss, 'Speech Given by Secretary of State for International Trade to the WTO General Council', 3 March 2020, https://www.gov.uk/government/speeches/elizabeth-truss-outlines-bold-new-era-for-trade (both accessed 20 September 2020).

13. Edgerton, *Rise and Fall of the British Nation*, p. 49; see also George Boyer, *The Winding Road to the Welfare State* (Princeton, NJ: Princeton University Press, 2019).

14. Edgerton, *Rise and Fall of the British Nation*, pp. 217–22.

15. Labour manifesto 1945, https://history.hanover.edu/courses/excerpts/111lab.html (accessed 19 June 2021).

16. *The Spirit of '45*, film directed by Ken Loach, produced by Sixteen Films and Fly Film, 2013.

17. Heffer, *Like the Roman*, p. 112.

18. Ibid., p. 228.

19. J. Enoch Powell, MP, 'Britain's Military Role in the 1970s', John Enoch Powell Speech Archive, http://enochpowell.info/wp-content/uploads/Speeches/June-Oct%201968.pdf (accessed 30 July 2020).

20. Heffer, *Like the Roman*, p. 293.

21. Ibid., p. 317.

22. Linda McDowell, 'How Caribbean Migrants Helped to Rebuild Britain', in British Library, Windrush stories, https://www.bl.uk/windrush/articles/how-caribbean-migrants-rebuilt-britain (accessed 10 August 2020).

23. Clair Wills, *Lovers and Strangers: An Immigrant History of Post-War Britain* (London: Penguin, 2018), p. 257.

24. Ibid.

25. See Matthew Young, 'Racism, Tolerance and Identity: Responses to Black and Asian Migration into Britain in the National and Local Press, 1948–72', PhD thesis submitted to the University of Liverpool, 2012.

26. Stuart Jeffries, 'Britain's Most Racist Election: The Story of Smethwick, 50 Years On', *Guardian*, 15 October 2014, https://www.theguardian.com/world/2014/oct/15/britains-most-racist-election-smethwick-50-years-on (accessed 17 August 2020).

27. See the full text of Enoch Powell's 'River of Blood' speech, reproduced in the *Daily Telegraph*, 6 November 2007, https://www.telegraph.co.uk/comment/3643823/Enoch-Powells-Rivers-of-Blood-speech.html (accessed 7 August 2020).

28. Ibid.

29. For further reading on the links between anti-racist struggle in Britain and anti-colonial resistance in the colonies, see Adam Elliot-Cooper, *Black Resistance to British Policing* (Manchester: Manchester University Press, 2021).

30. Powell, *A Nation Not Afraid*, p. 138.

31. Extract from 'Speech by the Rt. Hon. J. Enoch Powell, M.P. at the Annual Dinner of Walsall South Conservative Association', 9 February 1968, John Enoch Powell Speech Archive, http://enochpowell.info/wp-content/uploads/Speeches/Oct%201967-Feb%201968.pdf (accessed 30 July 2020).

32. See the full text of Enoch Powell's 'Rivers of Blood' speech.

33. Amy Whipple, 'Revisiting the "Rivers of Blood" Controversy: Letters to Enoch Powell', *Journal of British Studies*, vol. 48, no. 3 (July 2009), pp. 717–35, p. 718.

34. For discussions on the role that borders played in Britain after empire, see Nadine El-Enany, *(B)ordering Britain: Race, Law and Empire* (Manchester: Manchester University Press, 2020), and Leah Cowan, *Border Nation: A Story of Migration* (London: Pluto Press, 2021).

35. David Olusoga, 'Windrush: Archived Documents Show the Long Betrayal', *Guardian*, 16 June 2019, https://www.theguardian.com/uk-news/2019/jun/16/windrush-scandal-the-long-betrayal-archived-documents-david-olusoga (accessed 30 July 2020).

36. Mark Chi-kwan, 'Decolonising Britishness? The 1981 British Nationality Act and the Identity Crisis of Hong Kong Elites', *Journal of Imperial and Commonwealth History*, vol. 48, no. 3 (2020), pp. 565–90.

37. Heffer, *Like the Roman*, p. 547.

38. See the full text of Enoch Powell's 'River of Blood' speech.

39. For a rare comprehensive analysis of this element of Powell's thinking, see Robbie Shilliam, 'Enoch Powell: Britain's First Neoliberal Politician', *New Political Economy*, vol. 26, no. 2 (2021), pp. 239–49.

40. Brad Lips, Introduction to *Freedom Champions: Stories from the Front*

Lines in the War of Ideas, Colleen Dyble (ed.) (Washington, DC: Atlas Economic Research Foundation, 2011), p. 5.

41. Gerald Frost, *Antony Fisher: Champion of Liberty*, condensed by David Moller (London: Institute of Economic Affairs, 2008), pp. 11–12.

42. Powell, *A Nation Not Afraid*, pp. 27, 11, 25.

43. Enoch Powell, *Saving in a Free Society* (London: Institute of Economic Affairs; 2nd revised edition, 1966).

44. Sir Keith Joseph, 'Speech by the Rt. Hon. Sir Keith Joseph Bt MP (Leeds NE) Conservative Spokesman on Home Affairs, Speaking at the Grand Hotel, Birmingham on Saturday 19 October 1974', Margaret Thatcher Foundation, https://www.margaretthatcher.org/document/101830 (accessed 11 June 2021).

45. Margaret Thatcher, 'The Sharp Shock of Truth', *The Times*, 6 September 1974, Margaret Thatcher Foundation, https://www.margaretthatcher.org/document/111966 (accessed 9 August 2020).

46. Hon. J. Enoch Powell, MP, 'The Fixed Exchange Rate and Dirigisme', John Enoch Powell Speech Archive, http://enochpowell.info/wp-content/uploads/Speeches/June-Oct%201968.pdf (accessed 4 August 2020).

47. Matthias Schmelzer, 'What Comes after Bretton Woods? Neoliberals Debate and Fight for a Future Monetary Order', in Philip Mirowski, Dieter Plehwe and Quinn Slobodian (eds), *Nine Lives of Neoliberalism* (London: Verso, 2020) pp. 197–219.

48. Heffer, *Like the Roman*, p. 950.

49. Ibid, ebook location 1128.

50. Schmelzer, 'What Comes after Bretton Woods?', p. 212.

51. See J. Enoch Powell, *Exchange Rates and Liquidity: An Essay on the Relationship of International Trade and Liquidity to Fixed Exchange Rates and the Price of Gold* (London: Institute of Economic Affairs, 1967).

52. Powell, 'Fixed Exchange and Dirigisme'.

53. Ibid.

54. Ibid.

55. Arthur Seldon, 'Obituary: Gottfried Haberler', *Independent*, 16 May 1995, https://www.independent.co.uk/news/people/obituarygottfried-haberler-1619722.html (accessed 5 August 2020).

56. Hansard, House of Commons debates, 5th series, vol. 972, co. 173, 23 October 1979, https://api.parliament.uk/historic-hansard/commons/1979/oct/23/exchange-controls (accessed 12 September 2020).

57. 'How London Grew into a Financial Powerhouse', *Financial Times*, 15 December 2020, https://ig.ft.com/mapping-london-financial-centre/ (accessed 21 December 2020).

58. Margaret Thatcher, TV interview for Granada, *World in Action*, 27 January 1978, Margaret Thatcher Foundation, https://www.margaretthatcher.org/document/103485 (accessed 23 December 2020).

59. Paul Waugh, 'Asylum "Flood" May Bring Back Fascists, Says Hague', *Independent*, 16 August 2013, https://www.independent.co.uk/news/uk/this-britain/asylum-flood-may-bring-back-fascists-says-hague-278828.html (accessed 18 May 2020).

60. Andrew Green, 'Hold Back the Immigrant Flood', *Sunday Times*, 4 November 2007, https://www.thetimes.co.uk/article/hold-back-the-immigrant-flood-x8ck99m036d (accessed 7 May 2019).

61. Helen Barnett, 'Mediterranean Boats Will Bring 500,000 Islamic State Terrorists to Europe, Blasts Farage', *Express*, 29 April 2015, https://www.express.co.uk/news/politics/573764/Nigel-Farage-Boat-people-will-bring-half-a-million-ISIS-terrorists-to-Europe (accessed 22 May 2020).

62. YouGov poll, 'Europeans Think UK is Toughest on Immigration', 30 August 2015, https://yougov.co.uk/topics/politics/articles-reports/2015/08/30/immigration-policy-perception (accessed 23 June 2021).

63. 'Jimmy Mubenga: Deportee Heard Screaming "I Can't Breathe"', *BBC News*, 11 November 2014, https://www.bbc.co.uk/news/uk-england-london-29998050 (accessed 15 August 2020).

64. 'Report by the Assistant Deputy Coroner Karon Monaghan QC, Inquest into the Death of Jimmy Kelenda Mubenga, Independent Advisory Panel on Deaths in Custody, 31 July 2013', http://iapdeathsincustody.independent.gov.uk/wp-content/uploads/2013/12/Rule-43-Report-Jimmy-Mubenga.pdf (accessed 18 August 2020).

65. 'Angolan Capital "Most Expensive City for Expats"', *BBC News*, 21 June 2017, https://www.bbc.co.uk/news/business-40346559 (accessed 20 August 2020).

66. 'Life in Luanda: The World's Most Expensive City, Divided by Oil', *Guardian*, 7 July 2017, https://www.theguardian.com/cities/gallery/2017/jul/07/luanda-angola-expensive-city-divided-oil-in-pictures (accessed 20 August 2020).

67. James Kirkup and Robert Winnet, 'Theresa May Interview: "We're

Going to Give Illegal Migrants a Really Hostile Reception"', *Daily Telegraph*, 25 May 2020, https://www.telegraph.co.uk/news/0/theresa-may-interview-going-give-illegal-migrants-really-hostile/ (accessed 30 July 2020).

68. Office for National Statistics, 'International Migration and the Healthcare Workforce', https://www.ons.gov.uk/peoplepopulationandcommunity/populationandmigration/internationalmigration/articles/internationalmigrationandthehealthcareworkforce/2019-08-15#:~:text=There%20were%20over%201%20million,excludes%20NHS%20infrastructure%20support%-20staff (accessed 12 November 2020).

69. Benjamin Muller, 'Eight UK Doctors Died from Coronavirus: All Were Immigrants', *New York Times*, 8 April 2020, https://www.nytimes.com/2020/04/08/world/europe/coronavirus-doctors-immigrants.html (accessed 9 August 2020); Nigel Farage, 'EXCLUSIVE FOOTAGE OF BEACH LANDING BY MIGRANTS Shocking invasion on the Kent Coast taken this morning', *Twitter*, 6 August 2020, 9.54 a.m., https://twitter.com/Nigel_Farage/status/1291296574992257025 (accessed 9 August 2020).

70. David Goodhart, 'Too Diverse?', *Prospect Magazine*, 20 February 2004, https://www.prospectmagazine.co.uk/magazine/too-diverse-david-goodhart-multiculturalism-britain-immigration-globalisation (accessed 10 August 2020).

71. See Steve Doughty, 'Sickly Immigrants Add £1bn to NHS Bill', *Daily Mail*, 23 June 2003, https://www.dailymail.co.uk/health/article-185768/Sickly-immigrants-add-1bn-NHS-bill.html; 'Crackdown on Free Access to NHS Services for Migrants', *Daily Telegraph*, 8 May 2016, https://www.telegraph.co.uk/news/2016/05/08/crackdown-on-free-access-to-nhs-services-for-migrants/ (both accessed 25 July 2020).

72. Jessica Murray, 'A Timeline of PM's U-Turn on NHS Surcharge for Migrant Health Workers', *Guardian*, 21 May 2020, https://www.theguardian.com/society/2020/may/21/a-timeline-of-the-pms-u-turn-on-the-nhs-surcharge-a-timeline-of-pms-u-turn-nhs-surcharge-for-migrant-health-workers (accessed 28 July 2020).

73. See Guy Standing, *The Precariat: The New Dangerous Class* (London: Bloomsbury, 2011).

74. Nathan Brooker, 'Uncovering London's Hidden Property Wealth',

Financial Times, 20 March 2020, https://www.ft.com/content/bd548b0c-6762-11ea-800d-da70cff6e4d3 (accessed 18 August 2020).

75. Standing, *The Precariat*; Ronaldo Munck, 'The Precariat: A View from the South', *Third World Quarterly*, vol. 34, no. 5 (2013), pp. 747–62.

76. Jon Stone, 'Britain Could Slash Environmental and Safety Standards "a Very Long Way" after Brexit, Tory MP Jacob Rees-Mogg Says', *Independent*, 6 December 2016, https://www.independent.co.uk/news/uk/politics/brexit-safety-standards-workers-rights-jacob-rees-mogg-a7459336.html (accessed 19 November 2020).

77. Raghav Taylor, 'What Are the Chances of a UK/India Trade Deal?', Institute of Economic Affairs, 10 October 2018, https://iea.org.uk/what-are-the-chances-of-a-uk-india-trade-deal/ (accessed 18 August 2020).

78. Amelia Gentleman, 'Mother of Windrush Citizen Blames Passport Problems for His Death', *Guardian*, 18 April 2018, https://www.theguardian.com/uk-news/2018/apr/18/mother-of-windrush-citizen-blames-passport-problems-for-his-death (accessed 30 July 2020).

79. 'Windrush: Migrant Dexter Bristol Died from Natural Causes', *BBC News*, 7 October 2019, https://www.bbc.co.uk/news/uk-england-london-49966380 (accessed 30 July 2020).

Chapter 4: The Debt

1. The account of the attempted assassination of Bob Marley and the subsequent Smile Jamaica concert presented here is taken from Vivien Goldman, *The Book of Exodus: The Meaning and Making of Bob Marley's Album of the Century* (New York: Three Rivers Press, 2006), and Roger Steffens, *So Much Things to Say: The Oral History of Bob Marley* (New York: W. W. Norton & Company, 2017). For a fictionalised retelling of the shooting see Marlon James, *A Brief History of Seven Killings* (London: Oneworld, 2015).

2. Trystan Jones and Genevieve Tudor, 'World War One: Bob Marley's Father "Neurotic and Incontinent"', *BBC News*, 4 August 2014, https://www.bbc.co.uk/news/uk-england-27426329 (accessed 8 May 2020).

3. Steffens, *So Much Things to Say*, pp. 245–60.

4. For a recording of Bob Marley, 'Live at Smile Jamaica, 1976' see YouTube, 1 December 2016, https://www.youtube.com/watch?v=M658BMD_LOE&t=464s (accessed 2 May 2021).

5. Stephen Davis, 'Fear in Paradise', *New York Times*, 25 July 1976, https://www.nytimes.com/1976/07/25/archives/fear-in-paradise-the-real-jamaica-is-an-angry-state-locked-in-a.html (accessed 9 September 2020).

6. Statistic available at https://www.gov.uk/foreign-travel-advice/jamaica.

7. T. G. Burnard, '"Prodigious Riches": The Wealth of Jamaica before the American Revolution', *Economic History Review*, vol. 54, no. 3 (2001), pp. 506–24.

8. See the *Oxford English Dictionary*.

9. Alfred Sauvy, 'Three Worlds, One Planet', *L'Observateur*, no. 118, 14 August 1952, p. 14.

10. Anthony Payne, 'Obituary: Michael Manley', *Independent*, 8 March 1997, https://www.independent.co.uk/news/people/obituary-michael-manley-1271652.html (accessed 16 September 2020).

11. For Edna Manley's biography see Rachel Manley (ed.), *Edna Manley: The Diaries* (New York: HarperCollins, 1989).

12. Godfrey Smith, *Michael Manley: The Biography* (Kingston: Ian Randle Publishers, 2016).

13. Stephen A. King, 'International Reggae, Democratic Socialism, and the Secularization of the Rastafarian Movement, 1972–1980', *Popular Music and Society*, vol. 22, no. 3 (1998), pp. 39–60.

14. Davis, 'Fear in Paradise'.

15. Ibid; Michael Burke, 'PNP Strategies in the 1972 Campaign', *Jamaica Observer*, 1 March 2017, http://www.jamaicaobserver.com/columns/pnp-strategies-in-the-1972-campaign_91077 (accessed 9 September 2020).

16. Garfield Higgins, '"Political Songs" and Michael Manley's Message', *Jamaica Observer*, 1 June 2014, http://www.jamaicaobserver.com/columns/-Politics-songs--and-Michael-Manley-s-message-_16766505?fbclid=IwAR20AARvFQF2D7OAaBoXAgYZZwOigastkjolPQChg6SUN25PTNIIBwlh2Gc (accessed 9 September 2020).

17. Michael Manley, 'Overcoming Insularity in Jamaica', *Foreign Affairs*, vol. 49, no. 1 (October 1970).

18. Adom Getachew, 'When Jamaica Led the Postcolonial Fight against Exploitation', *Boston Review*, 5 February 2019, http://bostonreview.net/race/adom-getachew-when-jamaica-led-postcolonial-fight-against-exploitation (accessed 1 August 2020).

19. For the significance of the Bandung conference, see Luis Eslava,

Vasuki Nesiah and Michael Fakhri (eds), *Bandung, Global History, and International Law: Critical Pasts and Pending Futures* (Cambridge: Cambridge University Press, 2017).

20. For the significance of the Tricontinental Conference, see Anne Garland Mahler, *From the Tricontinental to the Global South* (Durham, NC: Duke University Press, 2018).

21. UN General Assembly, Twenty-Seventh Session, 2049th plenary meeting, Monday, 2 October 1972, https://undocs.org/en/A/PV.2049 (accessed 9 August 2020).

22. UN General Assembly, 3201 (S-VI), *Declaration on the Establishment of a New International Economic Order* (1974), https://digitallibrary.un.org/record/218450?ln=en (accessed 9 August 2020).

23. Theodore H. Moran, 'The United Nations and Transnational Corporations: A Review and a Perspective', *Transnational Corporations*, vol. 18, no. 2, pp. 91–112, https://www.un-ilibrary.org/content/journals/2076099x/18/2/4 (accessed 8 August 2020).

24. United Nations General Assembly, A/10302, Seventh Special Session, 'Resolution 1, Resolution Adopted on the Report of the Ad Hoc Committee of the Seventh Special Session', 1–16 September 1975, https://documents-dds-ny.un.org/doc/UNDOC/GEN/NR0/752/00/IMG/NR075200.pdf?OpenElement (accessed 8 August 2020).

25. Margaret Thatcher, note to Ralph Harris, 18 May 1979 (message of thanks to IEA), Margaret Thatcher Archives, https://c59574e9047e61130f13-3f71d0fe2b653c4f00f32175760e96e7.ssl.cf1.rackcdn.com/F7040D8846B9439E9E641A2AB6651F0B.pdf (accessed 21 August 2020).

26. 'Obituary: Lord Harris of High Cross', *Daily Telegraph*, 20 October 2006, https://www.telegraph.co.uk/news/obituaries/1531862/Lord-Harris-of-High-Cross.html (accessed 19 December 2020).

27. Marie Laure Djelic, 'Building an Architecture for Political Influence: Atlas and the Transnational Institutionalization of the Neoliberal Think Tank', in Christina Garsten and Adrienne Sörbom (eds.), *Power, Policy and Profit: Corporate Engagement in Politics and Governance* (Cheltenham: Edward Elgar, 2017), pp. 25–45.

28. Frost, *Antony Fisher*, p. 37.

29. Marie Laure Djelic, 'Spreading Ideas to Govern the World: Inventing and Institutionalizing the Neoliberal Think Tank', *Academy of*

Management Proceedings, no. 1 (2015), https://journals.aom.org/
doi/10.5465/ambpp.2015.11300abstract (accessed 16 February 2021).

30. Ibid.

31. Alejandro A. Chafuen, 'Atlas Workshop in Jamaica', in *Atlas Economic
Research Foundation (Atlas Network) Early History*, at https://sites.google.
com/a/chafuen.com/www/atlas-economic-research-foundation-
atlas-network-early-history/atlas-workshop-in-jamaica (accessed 10
July 2020).

32. Atlas Network, Global Director, https://www.atlasnetwork.org/
partners/global-directory (accessed 8 August 2020).

33. Margaret Thatcher, letter to Antony Fisher, 20 February 1980,
Margaret Thatcher Foundation, large-scale document archive,
https://c59574e9047e61130f13-3f71d0fe2b653c4f00f32175760e96e7.
ssl.cf1.rackcdn.com/91A5263F9F624C9396DB481BAFFAB768.pdf
(accessed 2 August 2020).

34. Guia Migani, 'The Road to Cancun: The Life and Death of a
North–South Summit', in Emmanuel Mourlon-Druol and Federico
Romero, *International Summitry and Global Governance* (London:
Routledge, 2014), p. 174.

35. 'The Bloody General Election that Changed Jamaica', *Jamaica
Observer*, 30 October 2012, http://www.jamaicaobserver.com/
news/The-bloody-general-election-that-changed-Jamaica (accessed
9 August 2020).

36. Christopher Dickey, 'Violence Feared in Jamaica's Election', *Washington
Post*, 29 October 1980, https://www.washingtonpost.com/archive/
politics/1980/10/29/violence-feared-in-jamaicas-election/d9d561b4-
d941-4420-b1eb-708bd13d0ce1/ (accessed 28 September 2020).

37. UKDEL Cancun to Foreign and Commonwealth Office
(FCO), 'Cancun Summit: First Day', 23 October 1981, https://
cb786b42ab2de72f5694-c7a3803abof7212d059698df03ade453.ssl.cf1.
rackcdn.com/811023%200550%20UKDEL%20Cancun%20to%20
FCO%20%28699-103%29.pdf.

38. Department of Trade, letter to Overseas Development Administration
('Cancun Briefing'), 'Cancun Summit: Trade Related "Nuggets"',
20 October 1981, https://cb786b42ab2de72f5694-c7a3803abof7212
d059698df03ade453.ssl.cf1.rackcdn.com/811020%20Trade%20to%20
No.10%20%28699-129%29.pdf (accessed 19 August 2020).

39. John Toye, *UNCTAD at 50: A Short History*, United Nations, 2014,

https://unctad.org/en/PublicationsLibrary/osg2014d1_en.pdf, p. 63 (accessed 16 August 2020).

40. Margaret Thatcher, 'House of Commons Statement: Mexico Summit Meeting', 26 October 1981, Margaret Thatcher Foundation, https://www.margaretthatcher.org/document/104725 (accessed 18 October 2020).

41. Ibid.

42. Margaret Thatcher, press conference after Cancun Summit, 24 October 1985, Margaret Thatcher Foundation, https://www.margaretthatcher.org/document/104724 (accessed 19 August 2020).

43. Karl P. Sauvant, 'The Negotiations of the United Nations Code of Conduct on Transnational Corporations: Experience and Lessons learned', *Journal of World Investment and Trade*, vol. 16 (2016), pp. 11–87; see also the draft of the United Nations Code of Conduct on Transnational Corporation, and its inclusion of a second part outlining the treatment to which corporations should be entitled in the countries in which they operate, https://investmentpolicy.unctad.org/international-investment-agreements/treaty-files/2891/download (accessed 20 August 2020).

44. See the UN Commission on Investment, Technology and Related Financial Issues, organisation profile, https://uia.org/s/or/en/1100030437 (accessed 19 March 2021).

45. Anthony Payne, 'The "New" Manley and the New Political Economy of Jamaica', *Third World Quarterly*, vol. 13, no. 3 (1992), pp. 463–74.

46. Howard W. French, 'Jamaican Premier Hailed by Old Foes', *New York Times*, 28 March 1992, https://www.nytimes.com/1992/03/28/world/jamaican-premier-hailed-by-old-foes.html (accessed 28 August 2020).

47. Michael Manley as quoted in Nathan Gardles, *At Century's End: Great Minds Reflect on Our Times*, vol. 1 (San Diego, CA: Atli Publishing, 1995), p. 78.

48. Michael Manley, 'North–South Dialogue', *Third World Quarterly*, vol. 1, no. 4 (1979), pp. 20–34.

49. Ibid.

50. David Mcloughlin, 'The Third World Debt Crisis and the International Financial System', *Student Economic Review*, 1989, pp. 96–102, p. 96, https://www.tcd.ie/Economics/assets/pdf/

SER/1989/The%20Third%20World%20Debt%20Crisis%20&%20
the%20International%20Financial%20System%20By%20David%20
McLoughlin.pdf.

51. See John Maynard Keynes, *The Economic Consequences of the Peace* (1919) (London: Palgrave, 2019).

52. 'Bloody General Election that Changed Jamaica'.

53. Davis, 'Fear in Paradise'.

54. 'Bloody General Election that Changed Jamaica'.

55. IMF Lending case study: Jamaica, May 2019, https://www.imf.org/en/ Countries/JAM/jamaica-lending-case-study (accessed 10 August 2020).

56. Nigel Clarke, 'Lessons from Jamaica for Small Countries with Big Debts', *Financial Times*, 19 February 2019, https://www.ft.com/content/ 04870fa8-2e12-11e9-80d2-7b637a9e1ba1 (accessed 9 August 2020).

57. Andrew Roth, 'Obituary: Lord Bauer', *Guardian*, 6 May 2002, https:// www.theguardian.com/news/2002/may/06/guardianobituaries (accessed 9 August 2020).

58. Peter Bauer, 'Ethics and Etiquette of Third World Debt', *Ethics & International Affairs*, vol. 1, no. 1 (1987), pp. 73–84, p. 73.

59. Ibid.

60. Ibid., p. 78.

61. Ibid., p. 84.

62. For Peter Bauer's writings against birth control see his *Population Growth: Curse or Blessing?* (Sydney: Centre for Independent Studies, 1990) and 'Foreign Aid: Abiding Issues', in Peter Bauer, *From Subsistence to Exchange and Other Essays* (Princeton, NJ: Princeton University Press, 2000), pp. 41–52.

63. Margaret Thatcher, TV interview for *Weekend World*, London Weekend Television, 6 January 1980, Margaret Thatcher Foundation, https://www.margaretthatcher.org/document/104210 (accessed 4 August 2020).

64. See Ann Pettifor, *The Coming First World Debt Crisis* (London: Palgrave Macmillan, 2006).

65. For a comprehensive history of the 2008 financial crash, see Adam Tooze, *Crashed: How a Decade of Financial Crises Changed the World* (London: Allen Lane, 2018).

66. David Cameron, 'Living within Our Means', speech given on 19 May 2008, https://conservativehome.blogs.com/torydiary/files/ living_within_our_means.pdf (accessed 4 August 2020).

67. George Parker, 'There is No Alternative, Says Cameron', *Financial Times*, 7 March 2013, https://www.ft.com/content/3a39ea0e-8723-11e2-bde6-00144feabdc0 (accessed 4 August 2020).

68. The best study of the political power of debt is David Graeber, *Debt: The First 5,000 Years* (New York: Melville House Publishing, 2011).

69. Stefan Schwarzkopf and Jessica Inez Backsell, 'The Nomos of the Freeport', *Environment and Planning D: Society and Space* (September 2020), pp. 328–46, p. 330.

70. Ibid., p. 332; Grant Kleiser, 'An Empire of Freeports', Clements Library, guest post, 22 July 2019, https://clements.umich.edu/an-empire-of-free-ports/ (accessed 7 August 2020).

71. Jean-Pierre Singa Boyenge, 'ILO Database on Export Processing Zones' (Geneva: International Labour Office, 2007), p. 1.

72. World Bank, 'Export Processing Zones, Policy and Research', Series no. 20 (New York: World Bank, 1992), http://documents1. worldbank.org/curated/en/400411468766543358/pdf/multi-page. pdf (accessed 9 August 2020); IMF, 'Export Processing Zone Growth and Development: Mauritanian Example', IMF Working Paper; vol. 1990, no. 122; 1 January 1990, https:// www.elibrary.imf.org/view/IMF001/15345-9781451938869/ 15345-9781451938869/15345-9781451938869_A001.xml?language= en&redirect=true (accessed 8 August 2020).

73. Walden Bello, *Dark Victory: The United States, Structural Adjustment and Global Poverty* (Oakland, CA: Institute for Food and Development Policy, 1994), p. 144. Out of eighty-nine Third World countries signing structural adjustment agreements with the IMF or the World Bank between 1980 and 1991, only Mexico and Pakistan signed more than Jamaica's seventeen agreements.

74. Thomas Klak, 'Distributional Impacts of the "Free Zone" Component of Structural Adjustment: The Jamaican Experience', *Growth and Change*, vol. 27, no. 3 (1998), pp. 352–87, p. 372.

75. Ibid., p. 368.

76. Andre Poyser and Jovan Johnson, 'Inside Call Centres: "No More Jobs for Life"', *Gleaner*, 17 April 2016, http://jamaica-gleaner.com/ article/lead-stories/20160418/inside-call-centres-no-more-jobs-life-jampro-president-comfortable (accessed 9 August 2020).

77. Rishi Sunak, *The Free Ports Opportunity: How Brexit Could Boost Trade, Manufacturing and the North*, Centre for Policy Studies, November

2016, https://www.cps.org.uk/files/reports/original/161114094336-TheFreePortsOpportunity.pdf (accessed 22 May 2021).

78. Ibid., p. 28.

79. Ibid.

80. Ibid., p. 31.

81. Peter Walker, 'UK Launches Freeports Consultation with Aim to Open First Next Year', *Guardian*, 9 February 2020, https://www.theguardian.com/politics/2020/feb/09/uk-launches-freeports-consultation-with-aim-to-open-first-next-year (accessed 12 July 2020).

82. Asare Adeji, 'Life in Sodom and Gomorrah: The World's Largest Digital Dump', *Guardian*, 29 April 2014, https://www.theguardian.com/global-development-professionals-network/2014/apr/29/agbogbloshie-accra-ghana-largest-ewaste-dump (accessed 11 August 2020).

83. 'Better or Worse Off?', *Gleaner*, 8 July 2011, http://jamaica-gleaner.com/gleaner/20110708/cleisure/cleisure2.html (accessed 1 September 2020).

84. Mary Williams Walsh and Matt Phillips, 'Poor Countries Face a Debt Crisis "Unlike Anything We Have Seen"', *New York Times*, 1 June 2020, https://www.nytimes.com/2020/06/01/business/coronavirus-poor-countries-debt.html (accessed 8 September 2020).

85. Clare Jones, 'The Calls for Sovereign Debt Relief Are Mounting', *Financial Times*, 14 April 2020, https://www.ft.com/content/42a69de6-0b67-4c53-b9e4-e94ae4f7142b (accessed 7 September 2020).

86. Jim Pickard, 'Business and Politicians Wary of UK Plan for Low-Tax Trade Zones', *Financial Times*, 12 July 2020, https://www.ft.com/content/122cdc16-7435-4c7b-85e1-09cd10c1ab7a (accessed 13 July 2020).

87. 'Better or Worse Off?'

Chapter 5: The Tax

1. 'The Bahamas: Bad News for the Boys', *Time*, 20 January 1967, http://content.time.com/time/subscriber/article/0,33009,843308,00.html (accessed 8 October 2020).

2. Tony Thorndike, 'Sir Lynden Pindling Obituary', *Guardian*, 28 August 2000, https://www.theguardian.com/news/2000/aug/28/guardianobituaries1 (accessed 5 October 2020); 'Sir Lynden Pindling Obituary', *Daily Telegraph*, 28 August 2000, https://www.telegraph.

co.uk/news/obituaries/1367909/Sir-Lynden-Pindling.html (accessed 9 October 2020).

3. For a full account of this incident, known as 'Black Tuesday', and Pindling's transformation of the Bahamas, see Doris Johnson, *The Quiet Revolution in the Bahamas* (Nassau: Family Islands Press, 1972).

4. Tony Freyer and Andrew P. Morris, 'Creating Cayman as an Offshore Financial Center: Structure & Strategy since 1960', *Arizona Student Law Journal*, vol. 45, no. 1297 (2013), pp. 1297–1396, p. 1329.

5. Nicholas Shaxson, 'Tax Havens: Britain's Second Empire, Tax Justice Network', a reproduction of interview with academic Ronen Palan, 29 September 2019, https://www.taxjustice.net/2019/09/29/tax-havens-britains-second-empire/ (accessed 18 December 2020).

6. Jon Stone, 'David Cameron Says it is "Unfair" to Criticise British-Controlled Tax Havens', *Independent*, 13 April 2016, https://www.independent.co.uk/news/uk/politics/david-cameron-says-it-unfair-criticise-british-controlled-tax-havens-a6982186.html (accessed 6 September 2020).

7. Ibid.

8. Rowena Mason, 'Panama Papers: A Special Investigation', *Guardian*, 8 April 2016, https://www.theguardian.com/news/2016/apr/08/david-cameron-panama-papers-offshore-fund-resignation-calls (accessed 18 September 2020).

9. Juliette Garside, 'Fund Run by David Cameron's Father Avoided Paying Tax in Britain', *Guardian*, 4 April 2016, https://www.theguardian.com/news/2016/apr/04/panama-papers-david-cameron-father-tax-bahamas (accessed 2 August 2020).

10. Ibid.

11. Lijun Li and Chris Wellisz, 'Gimme Shelter: Counting Wealth in Offshore Tax Havens Boosts Estimates of Inequality', *International Monetary Finance and Development*, vol. 53, no. 3 (2019), pp. 46–7.

12. George Parker, Chris Giles, Emma Agyemang and Jim Pickard, 'UK Withholds Backing for Biden's Global Business Tax Plan', *Financial Times*, 16 May 2021, https://www.ft.com/content/a249285a-796f-40e3-a00a-f1398e249ef9; Russell Lynch, 'UK Refuses to Back Biden Push for Minimum Corporation Tax', *Daily Telegraph*, 24 May 2021, https://www.telegraph.co.uk/business/2021/05/24/treasury-refuses-back-biden-push-minimum-corporation-tax/ (both accessed 12 June 2021).

13. Gordon Brown, 'Boris Johnson Wrecking G7 Proposals on Corporate Tax Abuse is the Last Thing We Need', *Independent*, 25 May 2021, https://www.independent.co.uk/voices/tax-abuse-g7-boris-johnson-b1853526.html (accessed 10 June 2021).

14. Emma Agyemang, George Parker and Chris Giles, 'UK Presses for City of London Carve-Out from G7 Global Tax Plan', *Financial Times*, 8 June 2021, https://www.ft.com/content/4ed18830-f561-4291-8db5-c3c1fa86c1b8 (accessed 13 June 2021).

15. Mark Bou Masor, 'New Ranking Reveals Corporate Tax Havens Behind Breakdown of Global Corporate Tax System: Toll of UK's Tax War Exposed', Tax Justice Network, 28 May 2019, https://www.taxjustice.net/2019/05/28/new-ranking-reveals-corporate-tax-havens-behind-breakdown-of-global-corporate-tax-system-toll-of-uks-tax-war-exposed/ (accessed 5 October 2020).

16. Hansard, House of Commons debates, Panama Papers, vol. 608, 11 April 2016, https://hansard.parliament.uk/commons/2016-04-11/debates/1604111000001/PanamaPapers (accessed 9 September 2020).

17. Vanessa Ogle, 'Archipelago Capitalism: Tax Havens, Offshore Money, and the State, 1950s–1970s', *American Historical Review*, vol. 122, no. 5 (December 2017), pp. 1431–58, p. 1432.

18. *Egyptian Delta Land and Investment Co. Ltd* v. *Todd (Inspector of Taxes)*, HL, 23 July 1928; UKHL 14 TC 119.

19. Ogle, 'Archipelago Capitalism'.

20. For a study of the personal aspects of decolonisation see either Jordanna Bailkin, *The Afterlife of Empire* (Los Angeles: University of California Press, 2012) or Elizabeth Buettner, *Empire Families: Britons and Late Imperial India* (Oxford: Oxford University Press, 2004).

21. Freyer and Morris, 'Creating Cayman as an Offshore Financial Center', p. 1304.

22. World Bank data on the Cayman Islands, https://data.worldbank.org/country/KY (accessed 9 September 2020), and *Medway Census Report 2011*, https://www.medway.gov.uk/downloads/file/2353/2011_census_report (accessed 7 October 2020).

23. Edward Luce and Tom Braithwaite, 'Obama Takes Aim at Multinational', *Financial Times*, 4 May 2009, https://www.ft.com/content/412f2784-38b7-11de-8cfe-00144feabdc0 (accessed 18 September 2020).

24. Freyer and Morris, 'Creating Cayman as an Offshore Financial Center', p. 1335.

25. Ibid., pp. 1333–49.

26. 'The Cayman Islands (Constitution) Order in Council 1962, Made 30th July 1962, Coming into Operation 6th August 1962', http://www.constitutionalcommission.ky/upimages/educationdoc/SI1962No1646CaymanIslandsConstitutionOrderin-Council1962_1494958748_1494958748.pdf (accessed 19 October 2020).

27. Ibid., section 5(1).

28. Ibid., section 18.

29. Freyer and Morris, 'Creating Cayman as an Offshore Financial Center', p. 1324.

30. Gary Burn, *The Re-emergence of Global Finance* (London: Palgrave, 2006), pp. 25–7; Nicholas Shaxson, *Treasure Islands: Tax Havens and the Men Who Stole the World* (London: Penguin, 2011), pp. 53–4.

31. Catherine R. Schenk, 'The Origins of the Eurodollar Market in London: 1955–1963', *Explorations in Economic History*, vol. 35 (1998), pp. 221–38, p. 228.

32. Burn, *The Re-emergence of Global Finance*, p. 6.

33. Schenk, 'Origins of the Eurodollar Market', p. 223.

34. Dean Acheson, former United States Secretary of State, quoted in 'Britain's Role in the World', *Guardian*, 6 December 1962, https://www.theguardian.com/century/1960-1969/Story/0,105633,00.html (accessed 8 October 2020).

35. John M. Lee, 'The Villain of the Crisis: Eurodollars', *New York Times*, 10 May 1971, https://www.nytimes.com/1971/05/10/archives/the-villain-of-the-crisis-eurodollars-villain-of-the-monetary.html (accessed 7 October 2020).

36. For more on the distinctive role of the City of London within the history of British capitalism, see either Geoffrey Ingham, *Capitalism Divided? The City and Industry in British Social Development* (London: Palgrave Macmillan, 1984) or Philip Augar, *The Death of Gentlemanly Capitalism: The Rise and Fall of London's Investment Banks* (London: Penguin, 2000).

37. Freyer and Morris, 'Creating Cayman as an Offshore Financial Center', p. 1335.

38. Ibid., p. 1330.

39. 'The Imperial Court of Appeal', *The Spectator*, 13 December 1890, http://archive.spectator.co.uk/article/13th-december-1890/8/the-imperial-court-of-appeal (accessed 24 July 2020).

40. Derek O'Brien, 'The Post-Colonial Constitutional Order of the Commonwealth Caribbean: The Endurance of the Crown and the Judicial Committee of the Privy Council', *Journal of Imperial and Commonwealth History*, vol. 46, no. 5 (2018), pp. 958–83, p. 959.

41. Damien McElroy, 'Britain to Impose Direct Rule on Turks and Caicos Islands', *Daily Telegraph*, 16 June 2009, https://www.telegraph.co.uk/news/worldnews/centralamericaandthecaribbean/turksandcaicosislands/5543623/Britain-to-impose-direct-rule-on-Turks-and-Caicos.html (accessed 19 October 2020).

42. Helia Ebrahimi, 'Cayman Islands Hits Back at Brown over Tax Havens Attack', *Daily Telegraph*, 28 May 2009, https://www.telegraph.co.uk/finance/newsbysector/banksandfinance/5401684/Cayman-Islands-hits-back-at-Brown-over-tax-haven-attacks.html (accessed 19 October 2020).

43. UN Special Committee on Decolonization, 4 June 2003, https://www.un.org/press/en/2003/gacol3084.doc.htm (accessed 26 August 2020).

44. Ibid.

45. Reshma Ragoonath, 'Premier Hails UK Talks as "Successful"', *Cayman Compass*, 4 March 2020, https://www.caymancompass.com/2020/03/04/premier-hails-uk-talks-as-successful/ (accessed 21 November 2020).

46. Benjamin Fox, 'Cayman Islands Removal from EU Blacklist Prompts Backlash', *Euractiv*, 7 October 2020, https://www.euractiv.com/section/economy-jobs/news/cayman-islands-removal-from-eu-blacklist-prompts-backlash/ (accessed 19 December 2020).

47. Tax Justice Network, 'Country Profile 2020: The Cayman Islands', https://iff.taxjustice.net/#/profile/CYM (accessed 31 December 2020).

48. *R. (on the application of UK Uncut Legal Action Ltd) v. Revenue and Customs Commissioners* [2013] EWHC 1283.

49. Ibid., p. 20.

50. Rowena Mason, 'Taxman Accused of Letting Vodafone Off £8 Billion', *Daily Telegraph*, 7 November 2011, https://www.telegraph.co.uk/news/politics/8875360/Taxman-accused-of-letting-Vodafone-off-8-billion.html (accessed 31 January 2021).

51. Philip Inman, 'Rich Countries Accused of Foiling Effort to Give Poorer Nations a Voice on Tax', *Guardian*, 14 July 2015, https://www.theguardian.com/global-development/2015/jul/14/

financing-for-development-conference-addis-ababa-rich-countries-accused-poorer-nations-voice-tax (accessed 16 January 2021).

52. James Whittaker, 'Leaders Unite against "Modern Colonialism"', *Cayman Compass*, 27 June 2019, https://www.caymancompass.com/2019/06/27/leaders-unite-against-modern-colonialism/ (accessed 15 January 2021).

53. Grant Tucker and Rosamund Urwin, 'Rule Britannia Faces Axe in BBC's "Black Lives Matter Proms"', *Sunday Times*, 23 August 2020, https://www.thetimes.co.uk/article/rule-britannia-faces-axe-in-bbcs-black-lives-matter-proms-0fvhwmwlm (accessed 18 June 2021).

54. Jacob Rees-Mogg, House of Commons, Register of Members' Financial Interests, 2 May 2017, 'Unremunerated director of Somerset Capital Management Ltd.', which is the parent company of Somerset Capital Management (Cayman) Ltd and Somerset Capital Management (Singapore) PTE Ltd.', https://publications.parliament.uk/pa/cm/cmregmem/170502/rees-mogg_jacob.htm (accessed 21 October 2019).

55. Juliette Garside, Hilary Osborne and Ewen MacAskill, 'The Brexiteers Who Put Their Money Offshore', *Guardian*, 9 November 2017, https://www.theguardian.com/news/2017/nov/09/brexiters-put-money-offshore-tax-haven (accessed 14 August 2019).

56. Richard Brooks, 'A Relic of Empire That Created a Tax Colony', *Financial Times*, 20 February 2015, https://www.ft.com/content/6b83be28-b863-11e4-b6a5-00144feab7de (accessed 11 March 2021).

Chapter 6: The City

1. Jamie Robertson, 'How the Big Bang Changed the City of London For Ever', *BBC News*, 26 October 2016, https://www.bbc.co.uk/news/business-37751599 (accessed 21 October 2020).

2. Paul Rodgers, 'Tour Guide Broke the Bank', *Independent*, 17 September 1995, https://www.independent.co.uk/news/business/tour-guide-broke-the-bank-1601438.html (accessed 6 November 2020).

3. Jason Rodrigues, 'Barings Collapse at 20: How Rogue Trader Nick Leeson Broke the Bank', *Guardian*, 24 February 2015, https://www.

theguardian.com/business/from-the-archive-blog/2015/feb/24/nick-leeson-barings-bank-1995-20-archive (accessed 21 October 2020).

4. Chwee Huat Tan, *Financial Markets and Institutions in Singapore* (Singapore: National University of Singapore Press, 2005), pp. 13–14.

5. Paul Farrelly, 'Rogue's Return' Haunts Barings', *Observer*, 27 June 1999, https://www.theguardian.com/business/1999/jun/27/observerbusiness.theobserver7 (accessed 8 November 2020).

6. Kenneth Clarke, Hansard, House of Commons debates, vol. 255, col. 693 27 February 1995, vol. 255, c. 693 https://publications.parliament.uk/pa/cm199495/cmhansrd/1995-02-27/Debate-1.html (accessed 22 October 2020).

7. Edward A. Gargan, 'Singapore Defends Itself over Barings', *New York Times*, 2 March 1995, https://www.nytimes.com/1995/03/02/business/singapore-defends-itself-over-barings.html (accessed 30 October 2020).

8. Hannan, *Inventing Freedom*, p. 88.

9. Lee Kuan Yew, *From Third World to First: The Singapore Story, 1965–2000* (Singapore: Marshall Cavendish, 2000).

10. Daniel Hannan, 'Britain in the World: Past, Present and Future', speech given at the 'Why Commemorate 1819?' event hosted by the Adam Smith Centre, 31 August 2019, YouTube, 2 September 2019, https://www.youtube.com/watch?v=sSzLDrYxUa8 (accessed 2 March 2021).

11. Ibid.

12. Howard Davies, 'Will the UK Really Turn into "Singapore-on-Thames" after Brexit?', *Guardian*, 17 December 2019, https://www.theguardian.com/business/2019/dec/17/uk-singapore-on-thames-brexit-france (accessed 8 September 2020).

13. Owen Paterson, 'Don't Listen to the Terrified Europeans: The *Singapore* Model is Our Brexit Opportunity', *Daily Telegraph*, 21 November 2017, https://www.telegraph.co.uk/news/2017/11/20/dont-listen-terrified-europeans-singapore-model-brexit-opportunity/ (accessed 9 September 2020); John Cope, 'Is the UK Ready to be Singapore-on-Thames? It's Going to be an Upskill Battle', *Conservative Home*, 6 February 2019, https://www.conservativehome.com/platform/2020/02/john-cope-is-the-uk-ready-to-be-singapore-on-thames-its-going-to-be-an-upskill-battle.html (accessed 9 September 2020); Luftey Siddiqi, 'Singapore is a Great Brexit Model, but is

Britain up to the Job?', *Sunday Telegraph*, 1 October 2017, https://www.telegraph.co.uk/news/2017/10/01/singapore-great-brexit-model-britain-job/ (accessed 12 September 2020).

14. Owen Paterson, 'Don't Listen to the Terrified Europeans'; Jeremy Hunt, 'Why I Am Looking East for Post-Brexit Prosperity', *Daily Mail*, 30 December 2018, https://www.dailymail.co.uk/debate/article-6539165/Why-Im-looking-east-vision-post-Brexit-prosperity-writes-JEREMY-HUNT.html (accessed 9 September 2020).

15. James Warrington, 'Sir Martin Sorrell: Post-Brexit Economy Should be "Singapore on Steroids"', *City A.M.*, 12 November 2019, https://www.cityam.com/sir-martin-sorrell-post-brexit-economy-should-be-singapore-on-steroids/ (accessed 9 July 2020).

16. John Longworth, 'Singapore Offers Shining Vision of How Britain Will Thrive on Its Own', *The Times*, 7 January 2020, https://www.thetimes.co.uk/article/singapore-offers-shining-vision-of-how-britain-will-thrive-on-its-own-svjop9tbp (accessed 6 September 2020).

17. '"Like Dunkirk": Brexit Donor Trumpets "Fantastic Insecurity" of Leaving EU', *Guardian*, 12 May 2016, https://www.theguardian.com/politics/2016/may/12/billionaire-brexit-donor-leaving-eu-like-dunkirk (accessed 8 December 2020).

18. Ibid.

19. For a full depiction of colonial society in Singapore, see Carl Trocki, *Singapore: Wealth, Power and the Culture of Control* (London: Routledge, 2006), pp. 34–95.

20. Yew, *From Third World to First*, pp. 548–52.

21. Trocki, *Singapore*, pp. 106–7.

22. Ibid., p. 105.

23. Ibid., pp. 111–15.

24. Sinnathamby Rajaratnam and Irene Ng, *The Short Stories and Radio Plays of S. Rajaratnam* (Singapore: Epigram Books, 2011).

25. 'Statement of Mr S. Rajaratnam, Foreign Minister of Singapore, at the General Assembly of the United Nations on September 21, 1965 on the Occasion of Singapore's Admission to the United Nations', National Archives of Singapore, PressR19650921, https://www.nas.gov.sg/archivesonline/speeches/.

26. Ibid.
27. Ibid.
28. Sinnathamby Rajaratnam, 'Singapore: Global City', text of address to the Singapore Press Club, 6 February 1972, National Archives of Singapore, PressR19720206a, https://www.nas.gov.sg/archivesonline/speeches/record-details/fd2918de-3270-11e4-859c-0050568939ad (accessed 12 July 2020).
29. Ibid., p. 10.
30. Lee Kuan Yew, 'Speech at the 26th World Congress of the International Chamber of Commerce, October 5, 1978', reproduced in Han Fook Kwang, *Lee Kuan Yew: The Man and His Ideas* (Singapore: Marshall Cavendish, 1998).
31. Sinnathamby Rajaratnam, speech at the Seventh Non-Aligned Summit Meeting in New Delhi, National Archives of Singapore, SR19830309s, https://www.nas.gov.sg/archivesonline/speeches/record-details/71e0d724-115d-11e3-83d5-0050568939ad (accessed 3 November 2020).
32. Kenneth Bercuson (ed.), 'Introduction', in *Singapore: A Case Study in Rapid Development* (Washington, DC: International Monetary Fund, 1995), p. 1.
33. Zhaki Abdullah, 'Singapore Tops List of Leading Maritime Capitals for Fourth Time', *Strait Times*, 11 Apri 2019, https://www.straitstimes.com/singapore/transport/singapore-tops-list-of-leading-maritime-capitals-for-fourth-time (accessed 12 July 2020).
34. Heritage Foundation, '2020 Index of Economic Freedom: Global Economic Freedom Hits All-Time High', https://www.heritage.org/press/2020-index-economic-freedom-global-economic-freedom-hits-all-time-high (accessed 19 October 2020).
35. See N. M. K. Lam, 'Government Intervention in the Economy: A Comparative Analysis of Singapore and Hong Kong', *Public Administration and Development*, vol. 20 (2000), pp. 397–421.
36. Amanda Clift-Matthews and Parvais Jabbar, 'Singapore Should be Ashamed of Its Lashings', *The Times*, 3 September 2020, https://www.thetimes.co.uk/article/singapore-should-be-ashamed-of-lashings-kxndjlcfs (accessed 30 September 2020).
37. Rick Lines, 'Singapore's Claim That the Death Penalty Deters Drug Use is Wrong, Here's Why', International Drug Policy Consortium, 17 January 2020, https://idpc.net/alerts/2020/01/singapore-s-claim-

that-the-death-penalty-deters-drug-use-is-wrong-here-s-why (accessed 25 October 2020).

38. Knight Frank Research, *The Wealth Report 2021*, 15th edition (London: Knight Frank, 2021), p. 20, https://content.knightfrank. com/research/83/documents/en/the-wealth-report-2021-7865.pdf (accessed 24 March 2021).

39. Alex Daniel, 'London is the Busiest City in Europe for Private Jets, According to research', *City A.M.*, 28 November 2019, https://www. cityam.com/london-is-the-busiest-city-in-europe-for-private-jets-according-to-research/ (accessed 21 February 2021).

40. Danny Dorling, *Injustice: Why Social Inequality Still Persists* (London: Policy Press, 2010).

41. Nathan Brooker, 'Uncovering London's Hidden Property Wealth', *Financial Times*, 20 March 2020, https://www.ft.com/content/ bd548b0c-6762-11ea-800d-da70cff6e4d3 (accessed 18 August 2020).

42. Child Poverty Action Group, 'Child Poverty in London Facts', https://cpag.org.uk/child-poverty-london-facts (accessed 22 March 2021).

43. Margaret Thatcher, 'Speech to the College of Europe' (the Bruges speech), 20 September 1988, Margaret Thatcher Foundation, https:// www.margaretthatcher.org/document/107332 (accessed 21 March 2021).

44. Michael Pooler, Peter Campbell and Stefania Palma, 'Why Dyson is shifting its HQ to Singapore', *Financial Times*, 23 January 2019, https://www.ft.com/content/02a636d8-1f2f-11e9-b2f7-97e4dbd3580d (accessed 22 June 2020).

45. 'Dyson to Move Head Office to Singapore', *BBC News*, 22 January 2019, https://www.bbc.co.uk/news/business-46962093 (accessed 9 September 2020).

46. Pooler, Campbell and Palma, 'Why Dyson is Shifting HQ to Singapore'.

47. Kwame Nkrumah, *Dark Days in Ghana and the New States of West Africa* (London: Lawrence & Wishart, 1968).

48. Deputy Prime Minister Mr Wong Kan, keynote address at the Singapore Perspectives 2011 Conference, *Singapore Perspectives 2011: Our Inclusive Society: Going Forward* (Singapore: World Scientific Publishing Company, 2011), pp. 6–7.

Conclusion: There is an Alternative

1. Martin Luther King, 'The Birth of a New Nation', sermon delivered at Dexter Avenue Baptist Church, Montgomery, Alabama, 7 April 1957, Martin Luther King Jr Research and Education Institute, Stanford University, California, https://kinginstitute.stanford.edu/king-papers/documents/birth-new-nation-sermon-delivered-dexter-avenue-baptist-church (accessed 15 December 2020).

2. Jacob Rees-Mogg, Hansard, House of Commons debates vol. 666, 17 October 2019, https://hansard.parliament.uk/Commons/2019-10-17/debates/C7D5E220-3549-4DF1-AF9E-07079573464C/BusinessOfTheHouse(Saturday19October) (accessed 11 December 2020); Deana Heath, 'Why the Curriculum Must Stop Whitewashing the British Empire – According to a Historian', *Independent*, 7 November 2018, https://www.independent.co.uk/life-style/history/jeremy-corbyn-british-empire-whitewashing-national-curriculum-slave-trade-colonialism-a8618006.html (accessed 22 December 2020).

3. Prime Minister Johnson's Brexit address, 31 January 2020, Reuters, https://www.reuters.com/article/uk-britain-eu-johnson-address/british-prime-minister-johnsons-brexit-address-idUSKBN1ZU31M (accessed 25 June 2021).

4. Theresa May's keynote speech at the 2016 Conservative Party conference, 2 October 2016, https://www.independent.co.uk/news/uk/politics/theresa-may-speech-tory-conference-2016-in-full-transcript-a7346171.html; https://www.bbc.co.uk/news/av/uk-politics-37563510 (accessed 6 October 2021).

5. Jacob Rees-Mogg, 'My Vision for a Global-facing, Outward-looking Post-Brexit Britain', speech in Speaker's House in the Houses of Parliament, 18 June 2020, in the Speaker's Series on 'Brexit and Beyond: Britain's Place in the World in the 2020s', https://brexitcentral.com/vision-global-facing-outward-looking-post-brexit-britain/ (accessed 21 October 2020).

6. 'Boris Johnson Resignation Letter in Full', *BBC News*, 9 July 2018, https://www.bbc.co.uk/news/uk-politics-44772804 (accessed 21 October 2020); James Blitz, 'Boris Johnson Raises EU Colony Question', *Financial Times*, 10 July 2018, https://www.ft.com/content/3a8059ca-8435-11e8-a29d-73e3d454535d (accessed 21 October 2020).

7. Césaire, *Discourse on Colonialism*.

8. Kemi Badenoch, Hansard, House of Commons, Black History Month debate, 20 October 2020, https://hansard.parliament.uk/commons/2020-10-20/debates/5B0E393E-8778-4973-B318-C17797DFBB22/BlackHistoryMonth (accessed 12 May 2021).

9. Ibid.

10. Dr Michael Ryan, Covid-19 virtual press conference, 27 March 2020, https://www.who.int/docs/default-source/coronaviruse/transcripts/who-audio-emergencies-coronavirus-press-conference-full-27mar2020.pdf?sfvrsn=4b72eab2_2 (accessed 1 July 2020).

11. Denis Staunton, 'Unflappable Confidence of UK's Health Establishment about to be Tested', *Irish Times*, 27 March 2020, https://www.irishtimes.com/news/world/uk/unflappable-confidence-of-uk-s-health-establishment-about-to-be-tested-1.4214245 (accessed 1 July 2020).

12. 'How the Coronavirus Advice from Boris Johnson Has Changed', *Guardian*, 23 March 2020, https://www.theguardian.com/world/2020/mar/23/how-coronavirus-advice-from-boris-johnson-has-changed (accessed 1 July 2020).

13. Boris Johnson, 'Britain Must Become the Superman of Global Trade', *The Spectator*, 3 February 2020, https://www.spectator.co.uk/article/boris-johnson-britain-must-become-the-superman-of-global-free-trade (accessed 13 December 2020).

14. Aubrey Allegretti, 'Coronavirus: "World-Beating" Track and Trace System Ready for Schools to Reopen, PM Promises', *Sky News*, 21 May 2020, https://news.sky.com/story/coronavirus-world-beating-track-and-trace-system-ready-for-schools-to-reopen-pm-promises-11991606 (accessed 10 June 2021).

15. Boris Johnson, statement at the coronavirus press conference, 3 June 2020, WiredGov, https://www.wired-gov.net/wg/news.nsf/articles/PM+statement+at+the+coronavirus+press+conference+3+June+2020+04062020123300?open (accessed 22 April 2021).

16. John Burn-Murdoch and Chris Giles, 'UK Suffers Second Highest Death Rate from Coronavirus', *Financial Times*, 28 May 2020, https://www.ft.com/content/6b4c784e-c259-4ca4-9a82-648ffde71bf0 (accessed 1 July 2020).

17. See 'Statement by President Cyril Ramaphosa on South Africa's Response to the Coronavirus Pandemic', Union Buildings, Tshwane, 13 May 2020. Government of South Africa,

Department of Health, https://sacoronavirus.co.za/2020/05/13/statement-by-president-cyril-ramaphosa-on-south-africas-response-to-the-coronavirus-pandemic-13-may-2020/; Patrick Wintour, 'UK Takes a Pasting from World's Press over Coronavirus Crisis', *Guardian*, 12 May 2020, https://www.theguardian.com/world/2020/may/12/uk-takes-a-pasting-from-worlds-press-over-coronavirus (both accessed 2 and 8 August 2020).

18. Roland White, 'John Major Says Britain Is No Longer No. 1. So Where Do We Rank?', *The Times*, 15 November 2020, https://www.thetimes.co.uk/article/john-major-says-britain-is-no-longer-no-1-so-where-do-we-rank-3358n5wtk; Joe Middleton, 'John Major Says UK No Longer "Great Power"', *Independent*, 10 November 2020, https://www.independent.co.uk/news/john-major-brexit-referendum-uk-b1720180.html (both accessed 29 February 2021).

19. Stanley Johnson, 'Why I'm Delighted My Holiday Let Loophole Has Been Given Legal Backing', *Daily Telegraph*, 26 March 2021, https://www.telegraph.co.uk/travel/news/stanley-johnson-delighted-holiday-let-loophole-has-given-legal/ (accessed 17 June 2021).

20. Graeme Wearden, 'UK National Debt Highest since 1960s after Record October Borrowing – As It Happened', *Guardian*, 20 November 2020, https://www.theguardian.com/business/live/2020/nov/20/uk-national-debt-october-borrowing-covid-19-retail-sales-ftse-business-live; Chris Giles and Jim Pickard, 'UK Government Deficit Soars to Record High on Pandemic Borrowing', *Financial Times*, 20 November 2020, https://www.ft.com/content/13d3c0bf-449b-4a28-916b-3c3ec9033267 (both accessed 2 December 2020).

21. Chris Giles and Adam Samson, 'UK Public Debt Exceeds 100% of GDP for First Time since 1963', *Financial Times*, 19 June 2020, https://www.ft.com/content/57974640-8bea-448c-9d0b-32f34825f13e (both accessed 30 January 2021).

22. Gabriel Pogrund and Tom Claver, 'Chumocracy First in Line as Ministers Splash Covid Cash', *The Times*, 15 November 2020, https://www.thetimes.co.uk/article/chumocracy-first-in-line-as-ministers-splash-covid-cash-7wb5b8qow (accessed 3 December 2020); David Conn, David Pegg, Rob Evans, Juliette Garside and Felicity Lawrence, '"Chumocracy": How Covid Revealed the New Shape of the Tory Establishment', *Guardian*, 15 November 2020,

https://www.theguardian.com/world/2020/nov/15/chumocracy-covid-revealed-shape-tory-establishment (both accessed 3 December 2020).

23. 'David Cameron Calls Nigeria and Afghanistan "Fantastically Corrupt"', *BBC News*, 10 May 2016, https://www.bbc.co.uk/news/uk-politics-36260193 (accessed 15 March 2021).

24. House of Commons Education Committee, *The Forgotten: How White Working-Class Pupils Have Been Let Down and How to Change It*, report published 22 June 2021, p. 8, https://publications.parliament.uk/pa/cm5802/cmselect/cmeduc/85/8502.htm.

25. Gabriel Pogrund, 'Dido Harding: Make NHS Less Reliant on Foreigners', *Sunday Times*, 20 June 2021, https://www.thetimes.co.uk/article/dido-harding-make-nhs-less-reliant-on-foreigners-ot6mq9w2b (both accessed 22 June 2021).

26. Office for National Statistics, 'Household Income Inequality, UK: Financial Year Ending 2019', https://www.ons.gov.uk/peoplepopulationandcommunity/personalandhouseholdfinances/incomeandwealth/bulletins/householdincomeinequalityfinancial/financialyearending2019 (accessed 22 March 2021).

27. For an analysis of this moment, see Gargi Bhattacharya, Adam Elliott-Cooper, Sita Balani, Kerem Nişancıoğlu, Kojo Koram, Dalia Gebrial, Nadine El-Enany and Luke de Noronha, *Empire's Endgame: Racism and the British State* (London: Pluto Press, 2021).

28. Anna Mohdin and Glenn Swann, 'How George Floyd's Death Sparked a Wave of UK Anti-Racism Protests', *Guardian*, 29 July 2020, https://www.theguardian.com/uk-news/2020/jul/29/george-floyd-death-fuelled-anti-racism-protests-britain (accessed 18 November 2020).

29. Ipsos Mori, 'Half of Britons Support the Aims of the Black Lives Matter Movement', poll published 1 October 2020, https://www.ipsos.com/ipsos-mori/en-uk/half-britons-support-aims-black-lives-matter-movement (accessed 25 December 2020).

30. See Andrew Doyle, 'Now That BLM Has Gone Mainstream Our Children Are Being Brainwashed by a Divisive New Dogma That I Fear Will Stoke, Not Heal, Racial Tensions', *Daily Mail*, 12 September 2020, https://www.dailymail.co.uk/debate/article-8726235/ANDREW-DOYLE-children-brainwashed-divisive-new-dogma.html (accessed 25 December 2020).

31. YouGov survey results, 11 March 2020, British Empire Attitudes, https://docs.cdn.yougov.com/z7uxxko71z/YouGov%20-%20 British%20empire%20attitudes.pdf (accessed 11 November 2020).

32. Neil O'Brien, 'Johnson Should Instruct a Team of Ministers to Wage War on Woke', *Conservative Home*, 21 September 2020, https:// www.conservativehome.com/thecolumnists/2020/09/neil-obrien-johnson-should-empower-a-ministet-to-wage-war-on-woke.html (accessed 9 May 2021); Badenoch, Black History Month debate (accessed 31 October 2020).

33. YouGov/NEON survey results, 11 May 2020, https://docs.cdn. yougov.com/p54plxogh9/NEON_PostCovidPolicy_200508_ w4.pdf (accessed 9 November 2020).

34. We Own It, 'Public Services and Outsourcing Issues Poll', 6 May 2014, https://survation.com/wp-content/uploads/2014/05/Public-Sector-and-Outsourcing-We-Own-It.pdf (accessed 18 December 2020).

35. Nancy Kelley, *British Social Attitudes 36* (London: National Centre for Social Research, 2019), p. 152.

Index

healthcare
  Accra 14
  outsourcing 37–8, 40
  see also NHS
Heath, Ted 96
hedge funds 186
Heritage Foundation 204
history, linear theory 3–5, 45–6, 116,
  219
holiday money 105
home rule 29, 47
Hong Kong 7–8, 146
honours, names of 187
House of Lords 45, 178–9
housing
  insecurity 115
  Jamaica 126
  London costs 209
  mortgages 142–3
  racism 93
Hu, Richard 193
Hudson Bay Compnay 57–8
Hungary 226
hydroelectric schemes 72
hyper-financialisation 170

identity politics 11, 229, 237
IMF *see* International Monetary Fund
immigration *see* migration
Immigration Act 97
immigration centres 38
Imperial Conference 1937 49
Imperial Federation (Defence)
  Committee 30
Imperial Federation League 30, 31
imperialism *see* empire
independence
  1920s 26
  Bahamas 156
  economic 126–9
  Ghana 26, 52, 66, 67–8, 174, 216–17
  India 20, 32, 66, 85–6
  Ireland 26, 48
  Jamaica 121, 122, 169, 171
  Scottish referendum 46–7
  Singapore 195–6, 199–201
  United Nations involvement 64–5
India
  Britannia Unchained vision 87, 116
  Centre for Public Policy Research
    132
  freeports 146

independence 20, 32, 66, 85–6
  legal system 116
  nationalism in 1920s 26
  Powell on sovereignty 90
  trade deals 116–17
Indian Rebellion 57
Indonesia 198
industrialisation 72, 74
inequality
  austerity measures 184
  blame redirection 226
  Britain 4–6, 16, 141, 208–9, 228,
    233
  in cities 13–14, 211
  Covid-19 pandemic 161, 224
  current public opinion 237–8
  education 227
  embedded in global history 124
  empire legacy 234
  'end of history' era 2–3
  financialisation 228
  Ghana 217–18
  global increase 4, 13, 141–2, 158,
    161, 185–6, 213
  Jamaica 150
  precariat class 115–16, 211–12
insecurity 115, 147, 197, 211–12, 228, 238
Institute of Economic Affairs (IEA) 99,
  100–2, 103, 107, 116, 130
insularity 16, 34
intellectual property 83
International Centre for the Settlement
  of Investment Disputes (ICSID)
  83
International Court of Justice 61
international law 60–1, 64–5, 83
International Monetary Fund (IMF)
  73, 104, 135, 138–9, 151, 237
internationalism, Third World 126–9
interventionism 197, 203, 205–7, 210,
  213, 236
investment funds 158–9, 188
Iran
  Abadan oil crisis 59–62, 63, 78
  nationalisation programme 58–9, 78
  theocracy 45
Ireland
  18th-century rebellions 47
  borders 9
  colonialism 121
  financial crisis 143
  home rule 29

USA *(cont.)*
   exchange rates 104, 107, 173
   growth in 19th century 29
   Korean War 60
   racism 98
   role in capitalist globalism 18–19
   Suez crisis 67

violence, domination 229–30
Virginia Company 57
Vodafone 184
Volta River Dam 72
von Mises, Ludwig 78, 103

wages
   Jamaican national minimum wage 126
   minimum wage campaigns 237
   Singapore regulations 203
Wales 48
Wall Street Crash 105, 173
Walter Eucken Institute 107
water access 82
wealth
   extractivon 18
   globalisation 13–14, 114
   inequality global increase 4, 13, 141–2, 158, 161, 185–6
   inequality in Britain 4–5
   in London 208
   'non-dom' taxpayers 188–9
   offshoring 19, 157, 158–61
   'old' versus 'young' countries 2, 3
welfare state
   criticism of 87, 88, 99
   cuts to 115, 152, 184
   formation 88–90
   impact of immigration 114
   levelling up 228–9
   as part of British culture 100–1

West Africa, National Congress of British West Africa (NCBWA) 23–5
West African Students Union 50
West Indies 146, 153, 163, 169
Westphalian Peace 64
white supremacy 30
Wilson, Harold 168
Windrush generation 1, 91–3, 94–5, 117–18
'Winds of Change' speech 69–70
women's organisations 68, 73
women's rights 88–9, 234
Wong Kan Seng 212
work
   'essential' 112–13
   Indian ambition 87
   insecurity 115, 147, 211–12, 228
   post-WWII labour shortages 92
   racism 93, 95
   see also wages
World Bank
   formation 104
   International Centre for the Settlement of Investment Disputes (ICSID) 83, 151
   Third World debt 135, 137, 138
World Health Organisation (WHO) 221
World Trade Organisation 140
World War I *see* First World War
World War II *see* Second World War

Yarl's Wood Immigration Removal Centre 38
youth of Britain, changing attitudes and expectations 231–2

Zahedi, Fazlollah 61